Vampires, Burial, and Death

Vampires, Burial,
and Death

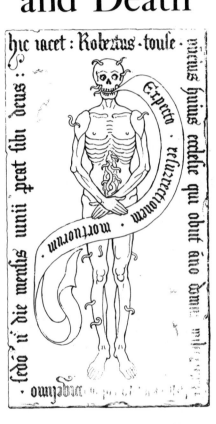

Folklore and Reality

PAUL BARBER

Yale University Press
New Haven and London

Published with assistance from the Louis Stern Memorial Fund.

Printed in the United States of America by Vail-Ballou Press, Binghamton, N.Y.

Library of Congress Cataloging-in-Publication Data

Barber, Paul, 1941–
Vampires, burial, and death: folklore and reality.
Bibliography: p.
Includes index.
1. Vampires. 2. Postmortem changes—Folklore. 3. Dead—Folklore. I. Title.
GR830.V3B35   1988   398'.45   88–143
ISBN 0–300–04126–8 (cloth)
0–300–04859–8 (pbk.)

The paper in this book meets the guidelines for permanence and durability of the Committee on Production Guidelines for Book Longevity of the Council on Library Resources.

10   9   8   7   6   5

Title page art: Tombstone, Rouen Cathedral (13th–16th c.) From E. H. Langlois, *Essai historique, philosophique et pittoresque sur les danses des morts* (Rouen, 1872), plate 37.

Contents

Preface

Some years ago I set out to answer a single, seemingly limited question—
what was the relationship, if any, between the bog bodies of Northern
Europe and the vampires of the Slavs—and blundered into an ambush
of far more complicated and hostile questions. Were the phenomena
common to the bogs and to vampires—the stakes, rocks, the position of
the body—related to the exigencies of burial? What are the most efficient
ways of getting rid of an unwanted body? How do people perceive death
in preliterate societies? The questions gradually became more general; at
the beginning, for example, I could not have suspected that I would be
obliged to investigate early conceptions of how our bodies are animated
or the relationship of water to such conceptions. I began with vampires,
progressed to an investigation of burial practices, and ended by considering death itself, or, to stay within the mythopoeic context, Death himself. My title, in other words, reflects the course of my research.

Fortunately I had much support from a large number of people who
sacrificed their time to help me. Several pathologists answered my questions with exceptional patience and thoughtfulness: Dr. John Blanchard
of Santa Barbara, California, Dr. Terence Allen of the Los Angeles
Medical Examiner's Office, and Dr. Thomas Noguchi, former Chief Medical Examiner of Los Angeles County. Dr. Guido Majno of the University
of Massachusetts Medical School read an earlier treatment of my thesis
and offered suggestions that have been incorporated into this book.

A number of folklorists have shown great generosity in making resources available: Marija Gimbutas, Wayland Hand, and Frances Tally of UCLA; Alan Dundes of UC Berkeley; and Felix Oinas of Indiana University. Dr. Oinas, with inexhaustible patience, has offered much helpful and exacting criticism of my thesis. I would also like to offer special thanks to Professor Scott Littleton of Occidental College, who invited me, some years ago, to come to his class in folklore and lecture about a little idea that I had and then persuaded me to write an article about that idea. I would like to thank Edward Tripp, Editor-at-large of Yale University Press, for his exacting and valuable critical reading of the manuscript, and Laura Dooley, the manuscript editor, for her great patience and helpfulness in dealing with the manuscript. And I would like to thank Dr. Annabelle Rea, also of Occidental College, who engaged in a heroic effort to correct my translations from French.

A number of libraries have given their all, and I would like to thank in particular the very helpful and long-suffering staffs of the UCLA Research Library, Doe Research Library at Berkeley, Sterling Library and Beinecke Rare Manuscripts Collection at Yale, Firestone at Princeton, Widener and Houghton at Harvard, the Bodleian at Oxford, and the Vienna Staatsbibliothek.

Finally, I would like to thank my wife, Betchen, both for her help and for her patience. Over the past years she has not only read and criticized the manuscript but has also listened, without complaint, to enthusiastic recitals of a great deal of dank and distressing material on forensic pathology. As an archaeologist, she has been a uniquely valuable resource in my course of study. And while I would not want her to share the blame for my mistakes, it is safe to say that I could not have written this book without her.

Vampires, Burial, and Death

Introduction

If a reader were to glance through the first chapters of this book, he might reasonably conclude that he had come upon a book on the folklore of the European vampire. The vampire, however, is only a local manifestation—albeit a particularly dramatic one—of a worldwide phenomenon, and I have chosen him as an example merely because it is convenient to do so: not only do we have a great deal of data on the folklore of the European vampire, but that data is published in languages familiar to a Western scholar.

What this book is really about is how people in preindustrial cultures look at the processes and phenomena associated with death and the dissolution of the body. As it happens, their interpretations of such phenomena, from our perspective, are generally quite wrong. What makes them interesting, however, is that they are also usually coherent, cover all the data, and provide the rationale for some common practices that seem, at first glance, to be inexplicable.

As we shall see, it is not enough merely to study their reports—what they say about the dead and the undead. If we just stand back and look at the folklore, without putting ourselves in the position of the people creating it, we will get a very distorted view. What we must do is look at what they are looking at. Like Copernicus, we will find that when we change our vantage point, our data shift around and form an elegantly simple pattern.

Before proceeding, however, we must rid ourselves of a burden of false data from the fiction industry. If a typical vampire of folklore, not fiction, were to come to your house this Halloween, you might open the door to encounter a plump Slavic fellow with long fingernails and a stubbly beard, his mouth and left eye open, his face ruddy and swollen. He wears informal attire—in fact, a linen shroud—and he looks for all the world like a disheveled peasant.

If you did not recognize him, it is because you expected—as would most people today—a tall, elegant gentleman in a black cloak. But that would be the vampire of fiction, a figure *derived* from the vampires of folklore but now bearing precious little resemblance to them. His classic examplar is Count Dracula, who in this century has had unparalleled success in the movies. The count, the villain of Bram Stoker's novel *Dracula*, was not Slavic: he lived in Transylvania and was based, more or less, on Vlad Tepes, a figure in Romanian history who was a prince, not a count, ruled in Walachia, not Transylvania, and was never viewed by the local populace as a vampire.*

If the origin of Stoker's character is confusing, folklore is scarcely less so, for there we find many kinds of "vampires." We might limit the discussion to a particular type of Slavic revenant—the one actually called *vampir*, or *upir*, or some other etymological equivalent of the word. But there are similar creatures in Europe that are referred to within their cultures by different names entirely. With a persistent sense of the fitting (and a deplorable sense of taxonomy), European scholars have commonly referred to these, and to the undead in far-off cultures—for example, China, Indonesia, the Philippines—as "vampires" as well.[1] There are such creatures everywhere in the world, it seems, in a variety of disparate cultures: dead people who, having died before their time, not only refuse to remain dead but return to bring death to their friends and neighbors. As we shall see, they bear a surprising resemblance to the European vampire, for reasons that should become clear.

This tendency to use the term *vampire* rather loosely will be evident in my discussion. One encounters insuperable difficulties in discussing the genus "vampire/revenant" without violating the integrity of the terms for the various species. If I am discussing the "revenant" as a class, any term I use will in a strict sense be inappropriate for most members of that class. As a rule, therefore, I refer to the "undead" by the generic term *revenant*, and

---

*Harry Senn and Grigore Nandris have given complete and lucid accounts of the figure of Dracula (see Bibliography). It is not clear that Stoker based his character on just one of the various Vlads in Romanian history.

where the process of transformation is at issue, I use the word *vampirism* (it is probably asking too much of the language to expect it to put up with *revenantism*). Finally, following a venerable scholarly tradition I shall refer to the Slavic revenants as vampires, even though this solution too is a compromise: many have other names entirely.

Besides the cultural distinctions among vampires, there are also distinctions based on the form in which the vampire's story is told. In European tradition, for example, vampires occur occasionally in fairy tales, where they are subject to the usual requirements of such stories and have a rather different character from those that are the subject of this book. I shall concentrate mostly on the vampire as he is described by those who knew him best: the people who dug up bodies in European graveyards and, having declared them to be vampires, "killed" them by a variety of means. We have, as it happens, a number of eyewitness accounts dealing with such vampires, written by outsiders. When we read these reports carefully and compare their findings to what is now known about forensic pathology, we can see why people believed that bodies came to life and wreaked havoc on the local population. The vampire lore proves to be in large part an elaborate folk-hypothesis designed to account for seemingly inexplicable events associated with death and decomposition. In order to understand it, let us pursue the following course:

1. We shall look at the fullest accounts of vampires and other supposed revenants that were exhumed.
2. We shall look at what we are told about their appearance, their origins, and how to ward them off and kill them.
3. We shall compare this information to what is now known about the events of death and decomposition, while considering how these events have influenced body-disposal practices in general, as well as those associated specifically with supposed vampires and revenants.

As we do this we will discover that we are not considering a local phenomenon at all, but a problem that arises naturally in any preliterate culture. Lacking a proper grounding in physiology, pathology, and immunology, how are people to account for disease and death? The common course, as we shall see, is to blame death on the dead, who are apt to be observed closely for clues as to how they accomplish their mischief. Our sources, in Europe as elsewhere, show a remarkable unanimity on this point: the dead may bring us death. To prevent this we must lay them to rest properly, propitiate them, and, when all else fails, kill them a second time. And the staking of the vampire, while it has become virtually a symbol for this procedure, is just one of many methods of ending the threat from the dead.

Finally, it should be noted that, in addition to the many types of vampires, there are also different kinds of books on vampires. Some of these are written by people with full, vital imaginations and the courage and will to believe (these are on the shelf labeled "Occult"). Often such books do not make fine distinctions between fiction and folklore. Consequently, a great deal has been written about the folklore that is simply not true, and I have found it necessary to distinguish repeatedly between the fictional and the folkloric vampire.[†] The former sucks blood from the neck of the victim, for example, while the other—when he sucks blood at all—attacks the chest area of the victim, in the vicinity of the heart, with only rare exceptions (see chapter 6). The fictional vampire tends to be tall, thin, and sallow, the folkloric vampire is plump and ruddy, or dark in color (see chapter 5). The two would be unlikely to meet socially, for the fictional vampire tends to spring from the nobility and to live in a castle, while the folkloric vampire is of peasant stock and resides (during the day at least) in the graveyard in which he was buried.

As we shall see, fictional and folkloric vampires are confused in many ways. We must proceed carefully through the data: it is a minefield of misinformation and half-truths. In the first half of this book, therefore, I will try to give an accurate and detailed account of the folklore of the vampire/revenant. We shall begin by looking closely at some of the best-attested vampires of past centuries. Our first example is a Serbian peasant named Peter Plogojowitz, whose lot it was, after his death, to be blamed for the deaths of some of his fellow citizens.

---

†If experience had not taught me otherwise, I would think it superfluous to remark that I use simple declarative sentences ("the vampire sucks blood") for convenience's sake, in order to avoid appending "people believe that" to each such sentence. I point this out only because so many people have concluded—bafflingly—that if I am writing a book on vampires, then I must believe in them. Apparently many people entertain the possibility that such a creature might exist: a scholar of my acquaintance found, by doing a survey, that about 27% of her respondents answered affirmatively to the question, "Do you believe it is possible that vampires exist as real entities?" (Personal communication with Norene Dresser, folklorist, California State University, Los Angeles.)

Peter Plogojowitz

Europeans of the early 1700s showed a great deal of interest in the subject of the vampire. Indeed, the word itself entered English in 1734, according to the *Oxford English Dictionary*, at a time when, in Germany especially, many books were being written on the subject.

In retrospect it seems clear that one reason for all the excitement was the Peace of Passarowitz (1718), by which parts of Serbia and Walachia were turned over to Austria. Thereupon the occupying forces, which remained there until 1739, began to notice, and file reports on, a peculiar local practice: that of exhuming bodies and "killing" them.[1] Literate outsiders began to attend such exhumations. The vampire craze, in other words, was an early "media event," in which educated Europeans became aware of practices that were by no means of recent origin, but had simply been provided, for the first time, with effective public-relations representatives. The story of Peter Plogojowitz (1725) illustrates this, in an involuted style characteristic of the bureaucratic German of the eighteenth century. This account is usually paraphrased, not translated, perhaps because its stylized expressions of deference create, in English, a misleading impression of mawkish obsequiousness. (The German, because of its formalistic character, does not give quite the same effect.) I translate it here nonetheless, because efforts to paraphrase the story usually omit important details. As we shall see, it is important to know *exactly* what was being said about vampires. Here, then, is the story of Peter Plogojowitz:

After a subject by the name of Peter Plogojowitz had died, ten weeks past—he lived in the village of Kisilova, in the Rahm District—and had been buried according to the Raetzian custom, it was revealed that in this same village of Kisilova, within a week, nine people, both old and young, died also, after suffering a twenty-four-hour illness. And they said publicly, while they were yet alive, but on their death-bed, that the above-mentioned Plogojowitz, who had died ten weeks earlier, had come to them in their sleep, laid himself on them, and throttled them, so that they would have to give up the ghost. The other subjects were very distressed and strengthened even more in such [beliefs] by the fact that the dead Peter Plogojowitz's wife, after saying that her husband had come to her and demanded his opanki, or shoes, had left the village of Kisilova and gone to another. And since with such people (which they call vampires) various signs are to be seen—that is, the body undecomposed, the skin, hair, beard and nails growing—the subjects resolved unanimously to open the grave of Peter Plogojowitz and to see if such above-mentioned signs were really to be found on him. To this end they came here to me and, telling of these events, asked me and the local pope, or parish priest, to be present at the viewing. And although I at first disapproved, telling them that the praiseworthy administration should first be dutifully and humbly informed, and its exalted opinion about this should be heard, they did not want to accommodate themselves to this at all, but rather gave this short answer: I could do what I wanted, but if I did not accord them the viewing and the legal recognition to deal with the body according to their custom, they would have to leave house and home, because by the time a gracious resolution was received from Belgrade, perhaps the entire village—and this was already supposed to have happened in Turkish times—could be destroyed by such an evil spirit, and they did not want to wait for this. Since I could not hold such people from the resolution they had made, either with good words or with threats, I went to the village of Kisilova, taking along the Gradisk pope, and viewed the body of Peter Plogojowitz, just exhumed, finding, in accordance with thorough truthfulness, that first of all I did not detect the slightest odor that is otherwise characteristic of the dead, and the body, except for the nose, which was somewhat fallen away, was completely fresh. The hair and beard—even the nails, of which the old ones had fallen away— had grown on him; the old skin, which was somewhat whitish, had peeled away, and a new fresh one had emerged under it. The face, hands, and feet, and the whole body were so constituted, that they could not have been more complete in his lifetime. Not without astonishment, I saw some fresh blood in his mouth, which, according to the common observation, he had sucked from the people killed by him. In short, all the indications were present that such people (as remarked above) are said to have. After both the pope and I had seen this spectacle, while the people grew more outraged than distressed, all the subjects, with great speed, sharpened a stake—in order to pierce the corpse of the deceased with it—and put this at his heart, whereupon, as he was pierced, not only did much blood, completely fresh, flow also through his ears and mouth, but still other wild signs (which I pass by out of high respect) took place. Finally, according to their usual practice, they burned the often-mentioned body, *in hoc casu*, to ashes, of which I inform the most laudable Administration, and at the same time would like to request, obediently and humbly, that if a mistake was made in this matter, such is to be attributed not to me but to the rabble, who were beside themselves with fear.

Imperial Provisor, Gradisk District.[2]

Thanks be to God, we are by no means
credulous. We avow that all the light which
science can throw on this fact discovers
none of the causes of it. Nevertheless, we
cannot refuse to believe that to be true
which is juridically attested, and by persons
of probity.
—Dom Calmet, 1746

Plogojowitz has a place of honor in any book on vampires, since his case is remarkably complete and shows most of the classic motifs—and some of the misconceptions—of vampirism. Since I shall be discussing these in detail later, I shall merely mention them at this point:

1. Plogojowitz's village is usually identified as Hungarian ("Niederungarn," according to Zedler's *Universal-Lexikon* of 1745), but this is because of the confused political situation of the time. Actually, Kisilova was in Serbia.[3]

2. Characteristically, vampirism occurs as an epidemic, as it does here, and it is typical that Plogojowitz, as the first person who died, is held responsible for the deaths that followed: *post hoc, ergo propter hoc.*

3. Vampirism may cause a lingering death (especially in fictional treatments of the subject), but in folklore we are often told that the victim's death was viewed as sudden and unexpected. Plogojowitz's "victims," for example, died after a one-day illness.

4. Typically, where the vampire is of the ambulatory type—for example, the Yugoslavian vampire—he appears before the victim in the night and either strangles him or sucks blood. In any case, the victim often complains of a feeling of suffocation before death.

5. The body is said to be "completely fresh," but it is not unchanged: the nose has fallen in somewhat, the hair, beard, and nails have grown, and new skin has formed under the old. Our witness does not make nice

distinctions as to what he himself saw and what he was told: presumably he could not know whether Plogojowitz's hair and beard had grown. Incidentally, accounts differ as to how long Plogojowitz was in the grave: Horst cites one that has him there for three weeks, rather than ten.[4]

6. It is not necessarily typical that the body has no unpleasant odor. Indeed, Dom Calmet, the eighteenth-century French ecclesiastic, observed that "when they [vampires] have been taken out of the ground, they have appeared red, with their limbs supple and pliable, without worms or decay; but not without great stench."[5] And de Tournefort, the French botanist who observed a supposed Greek revenant (see chapter 4), was so graphic in his description of its stench that later editions of his book, in both French and English, thoroughly bowdlerized that part of his text dealing with the subject.

The stench of the vampire, by the way, is one aspect of the nexus between vampirism and the plague. In European folklore, vampires "cause" epidemics (even in the movies, vampirism is catching).

Now, foul smells were commonly associated with disease, also as a cause,[6] perhaps because people reasoned that, since corpses smelled bad, bad smells must be a cause of disease and death. Typically, by way of combating such smells, people introduced good-smelling (or strong-smelling) substances: "Pleasant smells were important, for they drove away noxious plague fumes. Those threatened by plague were urged to burn aromatic softwoods such as juniper and ash. Oak, pine, rosemary, aloe, amber and musk were other good smells."[7] This account is from a description of fourteenth-century beliefs, but such views have been common over many centuries.*

7. It is clear from the description that Plogojowitz, if our sources are to be believed, was all but caught in flagrante delicto, since he actually had fresh blood in his mouth when he was dug up. Moreover—and this is characteristic of such stories—his own blood was fresh, not coagulated, as one might expect.

8. The staking of the vampire, so familiar from the movies, is, in south Slavic territory, perhaps the most common method of disposing of him, and when this is done the vampire is usually reported to have bled profusely. It is also typical for the vampire to be burned as well, especially

---

*In New Orleans, e.g., during the yellow fever epidemics of the nineteenth century, people commonly burned barrels of tar at street corners during the night to purify the air (Duffy, 74). See Ariès, 482, for similar accounts from Paris.

if piercing him with a stake does not end his depredations. I shall discuss such methods in greater detail in chapter 16.

Also, while Plogojowitz is not reported to have protested his fate, some vampires were said to scream or groan when pierced by the stake. This was true, for example, of Arnold Paole, the subject of chapter 3.

9. It is generally assumed that the "wild signs" (*wilde Zeichen*) imply that the corpse was believed to have an erection.[†] The vampire of folklore is a sexual creature, and his sexuality is obsessive—indeed, in Yugoslavia, when he is not sucking blood, he is apt to wear out his widow with his attentions, so that she too pines away, much like his other victims.[8]

There are a few characteristic things that we are *not* told about Plogojowitz as well. Often people who became vampires were difficult, contentious people while alive (see, for example, de Tournefort's account in chapter 4). When they died, if anything untoward happened in their vicinity, the suspicion arose that they had something to do with it. Nothing of this sort is reported about Peter Plogojowitz: he seems merely to have been the first person in his village to have caught a good case of vampirism and, by infecting others, to have made a place for himself in the history of folklore. And all this after his own death.

[†]Such "erections," according to coroners I have spoken to, actually result from the bloating, with decomposition, of the sexual organs (Svensson, 411). They may have contributed to the common belief that, as Wiedemann ([1917], 29) remarks, the dead are generally regarded as particularly sensual beings. Spitz, 349, discusses physiological aspects of the matter in greater detail.

The Shoemaker of
Silesia

Even before Peter Plogojowitz's death there were detailed accounts of exhumations, and not just from Slavic territory. And if you look at just the exhumation, rather than the folklore associated with the revenant, many of these accounts are very much like the Slavic ones: vampire and *Nachzehrer* (from *nach* [after] and *zehren* [consume, prey upon]: a northern German variety of revenant) seem to be identical in the grave.

We see this in the following account. This particular revenant is referred to in the text simply as a "ghost" (*Gespenst*) and is found in Grässe's collection of Prussian folklore.[1]

The Shoemaker of Breslau

In the year 1591, on the twentieth of September, a Friday, early in the morning in the garden behind his house, a well-to-do shoemaker in the city of Breslau cut his throat—for what reason, no one knew. He had cut the veins of his throat with his knife, and was obliged to die from the wound. When his wife had seen this and told her sisters, they were all most distraught about this sudden misfortune, but sought to conceal it however they could, considering it a great disgrace. She, therefore, told everyone who asked her about her husband's death, that a stroke had taken him. She also had the doors locked, so that no one could see what had happened. But when her neighbors and acquaintances came to speak with her and to console her, the sisters of the widow did not allow it and said that she recognized their love and well-meaning very well, but the dead man had no need of their services and the widow, in her first distress, did not want to accept visitors. They should, therefore, if they liked, come some time later. Then they sent to the church fathers and ordered the burial, the grave site, and the ringing of the bells, which they achieved without hindrance, since the dead man had been considered a rich man. But so that everything would remain secret and no one would learn anything about the murder [that is, suicide], they hired an old woman who had to wash the corpse, which had lost its blood, and tie up the wound so tightly that one could not see anything of it. When she had done that, together they laid him into the coffin. The widow herself, who was recovering from childbirth—she had been lying in for just ten days—had the priest come, so that he could comfort her in this grievous instance. And he did come and comfort the widow, but when he wanted to leave, the sisters of the widow suggested—and he knew nothing of the matter—that he should at least look at the body once. This he did, without any thought that there was anything behind this. For the body was so well wrapped up on all sides with linen, that even someone who was paying close attention would not have noticed anything, and they had placed it so high that the folded and twisted wraps could not arouse suspicion. The third day thereafter—it was on a Sunday—he was buried with great ceremony, in the manner of those who are pious and distinguished. And such a send-off and funeral speech were held, as though he had led a holy and guilt-free life and had been a splendid Christian.

If the relatives of the deceased believed that the murder would remain concealed, since they had arranged things so carefully, nonetheless a rumor came about among the people, to the effect that the man had killed himself and had not been killed by a stroke. At first people did not want to believe it, but nonetheless the rumor got stronger and stronger, so that the council saw itself obliged precisely to question those who had been with the deceased, and to demand that they admit, in accordance with the truth, what they had seen or heard and what each of them was aware of. Perhaps because all these people tried to talk their way out of it, and did not stay with one answer, they could soon see that not everything was right. Finally they conceded that he had fallen and had hit a sharp rock and had injured himself in this way. They said also that an awl had been found in his clothing, but they had removed it so that it could never again injure anyone else. The council, since the evidence continued to increase, now considered what was to be done. This too did not remain quiet, and some friends of the widow persuaded her under no circumstances to allow the body of her husband to be dug out or put at a dishonorable location or viewed as a sorcerer or suicide, if they could not come up with stronger proofs. In the meantime a ghost appeared now and again, in just such a form as the shoemaker had in his lifetime, and during the day as well as at night. It scared many people through its very form, awakened others with noises, oppressed others, and others it vexed in other ways, so that early in the morning one heard talk everywhere about the ghost. But the more the ghost appeared, the less the relatives wanted to celebrate. They went to the president of the court and said that too much credence was being placed in the people's unfounded rumors, the honorable man was being abused in his grave, and they found themselves obliged to take the matter to the Kaiser. But now that the matter actually brought about a prohibition, the state of haunting became even worse. For the ghost was there right after sundown, and since no one was free of it, everyone looked around constantly for it. The ones most bothered were those who wanted to rest after heavy work; often it came to their bed, often it actually lay down in it and was like to smother the people. Indeed, it squeezed them so hard that—not without astonishment—people could see the marks left by its fingers, so that one could easily judge the so-called stroke [that the shoemaker was alleged to have died from]. In this manner the people, who were fearful in any case, became yet more fearful, so that they did not remain longer in their houses, but sought for more secure places. Most of them, not secure in their bedchamber, stayed in the rooms, after bringing many others in, so that their fear was dispersed by the crowd. Nonetheless, although they all waked with burning lights, the ghost came anyway. Often everyone saw it, but often just a few, of whom it always harassed some.

As the clamor grew worse from day to day, with the whole city confirming the being, the council decided to do something so that the ghost would stay away. The corpse had lain in the grave now into the eighth month, from September 22, 1591, to April 18, 1592, when the grave was opened, by high command. Present were the entire council, the innkeepers, and other functionaries. In the opened grave they found the body complete and undamaged by decay, but blown up like a drum, except that nothing was changed and the limbs all still hung together. They were—which was remarkable—not stiffened, like those of other dead people, but one could move them easily. On his feet the skin had peeled away, and another had grown, much purer and stronger than the first, and as almost all sorcerers are marked in an out-of-the-way place, so that one does not notice it easily, so did he have on his big toe a mole like a rose. No one knew the meaning of this. There was also no stench to be noticed, except that the cloths in which he was wrapped had a repulsive smell. The wound in his throat gaped open and was reddish and not changed in the slightest. The body was guarded day and night on its bier, from the fourth to the twenty-fourth of April, except that in the day he was put out in the air, whereas in the evening he was put in a house there. Everyone could see him up close, and every day many citizens, and many people from the neighboring areas, went there. Nonetheless the exhumation did not help: the ghost, which they had hoped to banish by this means, caused still more unrest. The corpse was laid under the gallows, but this didn't help either, for the ghost then raged so cruelly that one cannot describe it.

But now, as the ghost was raging so terribly and thereby causing great inconvenience to many citizens as well as his good friends, the widow went to the council and said that she would admit everything, they could deal with her former husband with all strictness. But in the short time from April 24 to May 7, the body had grown much fuller of flesh, which everyone could see who remembered how it had looked before. Whereupon, on the seventh, the council had the hangman take the corpse out of the other grave. Then its head was cut off, its hands and feet dismembered, after which the back was cut open and the heart taken out, which looked as good as that of a freshly slaughtered calf. Everything together was burned on a pyre built up of seven klafters* of wood and of many pitch rings. But so that no one would gather the ashes or the bones and keep them for sorcery, as tends to happen otherwise, the guards were not allowed to let anyone near. Early in the morning, when the stack of wood had burned up, the ashes, in a sack, were thrown into the flowing water, whereupon, through God's help, the ghost stayed away and was never seen again.

Much in this story, clearly, is implausible, but, as we shall see later, many details—notably in the description of the dead body—are accurately depicted, leaving us with no choice but to conclude that we are dealing here with an account based on real events, however badly those events have been misinterpreted. The bloated body, for example, and the "new skin" (a phenomenon known to pathologists as "skin slippage") are normal events associated with decomposition and provide convincing proof that an exhumation took place. In general we will find that such accounts are accurate as to their data, inaccurate as to their interpretations. And this particular account conveys much that is typical:

1. The revenant dies as a suicide, murder victim, drowning victim— indeed, in almost any way that causes him to end his days somewhat earlier than expected: he "dies before his time." We do not know, of course, how this particular revenant died—he may have been murdered— but it is clear that his death was out of the ordinary and was therefore viewed as a possible source of disturbance within his community.

2. Such bodies are dealt with differently from "honorable" ones— buried in a different place, often with a very different set of funerary rites—and the resulting disgrace to the survivors of the deceased is such that they typically go to great lengths to prevent such treatment of the body. Klapper gives an account, for example, from Upper Silesia, of a woman who demanded (successfully) that her mother's body be exhumed so that it could be turned right-side-up and various other apotropaic measures could be undone.[2]

3. The body, when exhumed, looks rather different than expected (it is bloated, does not show rigor mortis, has a mole on the big toe, does not have a sufficiently rank odor).

*An old measure: one *Klafter* was about three cubic meters of wood.

4. The body is "killed" in a variety of ways, one after another—dismembered, excoriated, and cremated, then thrown into a river: nothing is left to chance. An accelerant (pitch) is used to encourage the fire: such bodies burn only reluctantly.

5. The account ends, typically, when the ghost is finally laid. The ghost, incidentally, appears to be independent of the corpse in one sense—nothing is said of the *corpse* leaving the grave—yet dependent on it in another, for to kill the ghost, you only need to kill the body in the right way. I stress "in the right way" because sometimes several methods must be tried and the right one selected, finally, by trial and error. In this instance, apparently, the methods were used all at once, to dispense with the nuisance of waiting to see which one worked.

Even this account, however, as detailed as it is, does not present us with such a dramatic juxtaposition of physiological anomalies and compelling testimony as our next account, *Visum et Repertum*, which was written by a doctor who presided over the exhumation and dissection of a graveyard full of Serbian vampires.

Visum et Repertum

Perhaps the most notable instance of "vampirism" is that associated with the name of Arnod Paole, who fell off a haywagon and into history in the first quarter of the eighteenth century. Paole, an ex-soldier from Serbia, was the first of a series of vampires that finally attracted the attention of the authorities and led to the investigative report known as *Visum et Repertum* (*Seen and Discovered*). Paole himself, as it happens, was not studied closely: the investigators arrived on the scene several years after he had been exhumed, staked, and burned.

The report itself is a curious document. Hardly a literary masterpiece, it has seldom made its way in complete form into English-language books on the vampire, and this may be because it is difficult to translate: the language is stilted, the author is indifferent to questions of grammatical parallelism, and several versions are extant, each of which, incidentally, gives a different spelling of the author's name, the most innovative of which (Clickstenger) is to be found in the English translation of Calmet (see Bibliography). For my translation I have used a text published in Nuremberg in 1732 and reprinted in Sturm and Völker's excellent anthology, *Von denen Vampiren oder Menschensaugern*. And since I was more concerned with accuracy than with elegance, I make no apologies for the style:

Visum et Repertum

After it had been reported that in the village of Medvegia the so-called vampires had killed some people by sucking their blood, I was, by high decree of a local Honorable Supreme Command, sent there to investigate the matter thoroughly, along with officers detailed for that purpose and two subordinate medical officers, and therefore carried out and heard the present inquiry in the company of the captain of the Stallath Company of haiduks [a type of soldier], Gorschiz Hadnack, the bariactar [literally: "standard-bearer"] and the oldest haiduk of the village, as follows: who unanimously recount that about five years ago a local haiduk by the name of Arnod Paole broke his neck in a fall from a hay wagon. This man had, during his lifetime, often revealed that, near Gossowa in Turkish Serbia, he had been troubled by a vampire, wherefore he had eaten from the earth of the vampire's grave and had smeared himself with the vampire's blood, in order to be free of the vexation he had suffered. In twenty or thirty days after his death some people complained that they were being bothered by this same Arnod Paole; and in fact four people were killed by him. In order to end this evil, they dug up this Arnod Paole forty days after his death—this on the advice of their Hadnack, who had been present at such events before; and they found that he was quite complete and undecayed, and that fresh blood had flowed from his eyes, nose, mouth, and ears; that the shirt, the covering, and the coffin were completely bloody; that the old nails on his hands and feet, along with the skin, had fallen off, and that new ones had grown; and since they saw from this that he was a true vampire, they drove a stake through his heart, according to their custom, whereby he gave an audible groan and bled copiously. Thereupon they burned the body the same day to ashes and threw these into the grave. These same people say further that all those who were tormented and killed by the vampires must themselves become vampires. Therefore they disinterred the above-mentioned four people in the same way. Then they also add that this Arnod Paole attacked not only the people but also the cattle, and sucked out their blood. And since the people used the flesh of such cattle, it appears that some vampires are again present here, inasmuch as, in a period of three months, seventeen young and old people died, among them some who, with no previous illness, died in two or at the most three days. In addition, the haiduk Jowiza reports that his stepdaughter, by name of Stanacka, lay down to sleep fifteen days ago, fresh and healthy, but at midnight she started up out of her sleep with a terrible cry, fearful and trembling, and complained that she had been throttled by the son of a haiduk by the name of Milloe, who had died nine weeks earlier, whereupon she had experienced a great pain in the chest and became worse hour by hour, until finally she died on the third day. At this we went the same afternoon to the graveyard, along with the often-mentioned oldest haiduks of the village, in order to cause the suspicious graves to be opened and to examine the bodies in them, whereby, after all of them had been dissected, there was found:

    1. A woman by the name of Stana, twenty years old, who had died in childbirth two months ago [three in Horst's account], after a three-day illness, and who had herself said, before her death, that she had painted herself with the blood of a vampire, wherefore both she and her child—which had died right after birth and because of a careless burial had been half eaten by dogs—must

also become vampires. She was quite complete and undecayed. After the opening of the body there was found in the *cavitate pectoris* a quantity of fresh extravascular blood. The *vasa* [vessels] of the *arteriae* and *venae*, like the *ventriculis cordis*, were not, as is usual, filled with coagulated blood, and the whole *viscera*, that is, the *pulmo* [lung], *hepar* [liver], *stomachus*, *lien* [spleen], *et intestina* were quite fresh as they would be in a healthy person. The uterus was however quite enlarged and very inflamed externally, for the placenta and lochia had remained in place, wherefore the same was in complete *putredine*. The skin on her hands and feet, along with the old nails, fell away on their own, but on the other hand completely new nails were evident, along with a fresh and vivid skin.

2. There was a woman by the name of Miliza (sixty years old, incidentally), who had died after a three-month sickness and had been buried ninety-some days earlier. In the chest much liquid blood was found, and the other viscera were, like those mentioned before, in a good condition. During her dissection, all the haiduks who were standing around marveled greatly at her plumpness and perfect body, uniformly stating that they had known the woman well, from her youth, and she had, throughout her life, looked and been very lean and dried up, and they emphasized that she had come to this surprising plumpness in the grave. They also said that it was she who had started the vampires this time, because she had eaten of the flesh of those sheep that had been killed by the previous vampires.

3. There was an eight-day-old child which had lain in the grave for ninety days and was similarly in a condition of vampirism.

4. The son of a haiduk, sixteen years old, was dug up, having lain in the earth for nine weeks, after he had died from a three-day illness, and was found like the other vampires.*

5. Joachim, also the son of a haiduk, seventeen years old, had died after a three-day illness. He had been buried eight weeks and four days and, on being dissected, was found in a similar condition.

6. A woman by the name of Ruscha who had died after a ten-day illness and had been buried six weeks previous, in whom there was much fresh blood not only in the chest but also *in fundo ventriculi*. The same showed itself in her child, which was eighteen days old and had died five weeks previously.

7. No less did a girl of ten years of age, who had died two months previously, find herself in the above-mentioned condition, quite complete and undecayed, and had much fresh blood in her chest.

8. They caused the wife of the Hadnack to be dug up, along with her child. She had died seven weeks previously, her child—who was eight weeks old—twenty-one days previously, and it was found that both mother and child were completely decomposed, although earth and graves were like those of the vampires lying nearby.

9. A servant of the local corporal of the haiduks, by the name of Rhade,

---

*In Mackensen's version of *Visum et Repertum*, which is taken from a book published in 1751, the name of this youth is given as Milloe (p. 20). It is apparently he, and not the Milloe of #12, who tormented Stanacka in the night.

twenty-three years old, died after a three-month-long illness, and after a five-week burial was found completely decomposed.

10. The wife of the local bariactar, along with her child, having died five weeks previously, were also completely decomposed.

11. With Stanche, a haiduk, sixty years old, who had died six weeks previously, I noticed a profuse liquid blood, like the others, in the chest and stomach. The entire body was in the oft-named condition of vampirism.

12. Milloe, a haiduk, twenty-five years old, who had lain for six weeks in the earth, also was found in the condition of vampirism mentioned.

13. Stanoicka [*sic*], the wife of a haiduk, twenty years old, died after a three-day illness and had been buried eighteen days previously. In the dissection I found that she was in her countenance quite red and of a vivid color, and, as was mentioned above, she had been throttled, at midnight, by Milloe, the son of the haiduk, and there was also to be seen, on the right side under the ear, a bloodshot blue mark, the length of a finger.[†] As she was being taken out of the grave, a quantity of fresh blood flowed from her nose. With the dissection I found, as mentioned often already, a regular fragrant fresh bleeding, not only in the chest cavity but also *in ventriculo cordis*. All the viscera found themselves in a completely good and healthy condition. The hypodermis of the entire body, along with the fresh nails on hands and feet, was as though completely fresh. After the examination had taken place, the heads of the vampires were cut off by the local gypsies and then burned along with the bodies, and then the ashes were thrown into the river Morava. The decomposed bodies, however, were laid back into their own graves. Which I attest along with those assistant medical officers provided for me. *Actum ut supra:*

(L.S.)[‡] Johannes Fluchinger, Regiment Medical Officer of the Foot Regiment of the Honorable B. Fürstenbusch.

(L.S.) J. H. Sigel, Medical Officer of the Honorable Morall Regiment.

(L.S.) Johann Friedrich Baumgarten, Medical Officer of the Foot Regiment of the Honorable B. Fürstenbusch.

The undersigned attest herewith that all that which the Regiment Medical officer of the Honorable Fürstenbusch Regiment had observed in the matter of vampires—along with both of the medical officers who have signed with him—is in every way truthful and has been undertaken, observed, and examined in our own presence. In confirmation thereof is our signature in our own hand, of our own making. Belgrade, January 26, 1732.

(L.S.) Büttener, Lieutenant Colonel of the Honorable Alexandrian Regiment.

(L.S.) J. H. von Lindenfels, Officer of the Honorable Alexandrian Regiment.

A number of motifs here are typical of instances of "vampirism":

1. The authorities step in to deal with a situation that is clearly causing a major disruption in the lives of the local people.

[†]That is, the blue mark is taken for evidence that she was throttled.
[‡]*Locus sigilli* ("the place of the seal").

2. In two instances (Arnod Paole and Stana) people are said to have used the blood of the vampire as an antidote to vampirism. In both cases, the remedy appears to have failed.
3. People complain that the (dead) Arnod Paole is terrorizing them.
4. The disinterment takes place forty days after his death. In Slavic tradition, Paole had no business being intact at this point.
5. Paole's body has not decayed, his blood is fresh, and his hair and nails have continued to grow after death.
6. Paole's body is staked, then cremated. Note that the corpse groans and bleeds. Note also that—unfortunately for us—Flückinger does not observe this: Paole's disinterment antedated Flückinger's arrival on the scene by five years.
7. The victims of the vampire must themselves become vampires.
8. The vampire also attacks cattle. Those who eat the flesh of the cattle must also become vampires.
9. Stana's child, which is buried carelessly, is dug up by dogs. This incident suggests that—as one would expect of the time and place— the child, at least, was not in a coffin. The bodies were probably buried in linen shrouds. Coffins, as a medical examiner pointed out to me, are intended to prevent events of this sort.
10. In one instance (Miliza) a vampire has not remained unchanged but is described as plump, even though she was lean when alive. Here it must be stressed that quite different, even contradictory, conditions are believed to indicate vampirism.
11. To demonstrate that the undecayed bodies are unusual, it is noted that other nearby bodies have decayed properly.
12. The woman named Stanoicka is "in her countenance quite red and of a vivid color."

All these are typical observations in the history of vampirism. It would also be useful, however, since Flückinger was an outsider and a medical officer, to separate out what he himself observed that is unusual. Here we must leave Arnod Paole out of consideration: his famous groan is hearsay, and Flückinger mentions no similar event occurring as he dissected the vampires. Here, then, is a list of unusual phenomena observed by Flückinger:

1. Corpses which, after having been buried for lengths of time ranging from eighteen days to three months had not decomposed or showed only slight changes in their appearance.
2. Fresh or liquid blood in these corpses.

3. Two bodies that had fresh skin and nails.
4. Bodies that, under conditions similar to those of the "vampires," had decomposed completely. These bodies, four in number, were similar to those of the vampires, except that one (#9: Rhade) had undergone a lengthy illness, unlike all but one of the vampires (Miliza, who had also changed somewhat, having become plump in the grave). Since this suggests that the duration of the illness might have something to do with the distinction between vampires and nonvampires, it is unfortunate that Flückinger does not mention the length of illness of three of the four decomposed bodies. In fact, according to Glaister and Rentoul, "Bodies of persons dying suddenly in apparent health decompose less quickly than those of persons dying from acute or chronic diseases, especially infective diseases."[1] Presumably this is one reason some of the bodies had not decomposed (another reason is suggested by the date of the report: the exhumations took place in the winter!).
5. One body (#13: Stanoicka) that had the distinctive ruddy face of the typical vampire.
6. One vampire (Stanoicka) who had a mark under the ear. Flückinger apparently takes this for evidence of the "throttling," but since it was customary to look for such a mark on the skin of a witch or vampire, this would in any case have confirmed the belief that something spooky was going on.[§]

One may see from this list that, however persuaded Flückinger was that something very strange was going on, he confirms little of what we have been told, in folklore, about vampirism. In fact, if we were to attempt a definition of a vampire, based on Flückinger's reported observations, we would come up with something like the following: "A vampire is a body that in all respects appears to be dead except that it does not decay as we expect, its blood does not coagulate, and it may show changes in dimension and in color." Indeed, as we shall see in the next chapter, one of our observers watched the dissection of a revenant and concluded that it was, in fact, merely a dead body.

[§]Vampires and witches are not always viewed as distinct species (see chap. 15). Grässe (2:199) quotes an early description of the exhumation and "killing" of a witch (*Hexe*) who was causing trouble after her death. The body is treated, in other words, like a vampire. And Burkhart, 237, points out that one defends one's self against witches with the same apotropaics as one uses against vampires.

De Tournefort's *Vrykolakas*

At the beginning of the eighteenth century, the French botanist Pitton de Tournefort had the opportunity to observe, firsthand, the dissection of a Greek vrykolakas on the island of Mykonos. His account follows:

We saw a rather different and quite tragic scene on the same island occasioned by one of those corpses that are believed to return after their burial. The one of whom I shall give an account was a peasant of Mykonos, naturally sullen and quarrelsome—a circumstance to be noted concerning such matters. He had been killed in the fields, no one knew by whom nor how. Two days after he had been buried in a chapel in the town, it was bruited about that he had been seen walking during the night, taking long strides; that he came into houses and turned over furniture, extinguished lamps, embraced people from behind, and played a thousand little roguish tricks. At first people only laughed, but the matter became serious when the most respectable people began to complain. Even the popes acknowledged the fact, and doubtless they had their reasons. People did not fail to have masses said, but the peasant continued his little escapades without mending his ways. After a number of meetings of the town leaders and of the priests and monks, they concluded that it would be necessary—in accord with I don't know what ancient ceremony—to wait till nine days after the burial.

On the tenth day they said a mass in the chapel where the body lay, in order to drive out the demon that they believed to be concealed in it. The body was disinterred after the mass, and they set about the task of tearing out its heart.

The butcher of the town, quite old and very maladroit, began by opening the belly rather than the chest. He rummaged about for a long time in the entrails, without finding what he sought, and finally someone informed him that it was necessary to cut into the diaphragm. The heart was torn out to the admiration of all the bystanders. But the body stank so terribly that incense had to be burned, but the smoke, mixed with the exhalations of this carrion, did nothing but increase the stench, and it began to inflame the minds of these poor people. Their imagination, struck by the spectacle, filled with visions. They took it into their heads to say that a thick smoke was coming from the body, and we did not dare say that it was the incense. People kept calling out nothing but "Vrykolakas!" in the chapel and in the square before it, this being the name they give to these supposed revenants. The noise spread through the streets as if it were being roared, and this name seemed to be invented to shake the vault of the chapel. Several of the bystanders claimed that the blood of this unfortunate man was quite red, and the butcher swore that the body was still warm, from which they concluded that the deceased had the severe defect of not being quite dead, or, to state it better, of letting himself be reanimated by the devil, for that is exactly the idea they have of a vrykolakas. They caused this name to resound in an astonishing manner. And then there arrived a crowd of people who professed loudly that they had plainly seen that the corpse had not become stiff, when they carried it from the fields to the church to bury it, and that as a result it was a true vrykolakas. That was the refrain.

I do not doubt that they would have maintained that the body did not stink, if we had not been present, so stunned were these poor people from the business, and so persuaded of the return of the dead. As for us, who had placed ourselves near the cadaver to make our observations as precisely as possible, we almost perished from the great stench that emerged from it. When they asked us what we thought of the deceased, we answered that we thought him quite adequately dead. But because we wanted to cure—or at the least not to irritate their stricken imaginations—we represented to them that it was not surprising if the butcher had perceived some warmth in rummaging about in the entrails, which were putrefying; that it was not extraordinary if fumes were emitted, just as such emerge from a dung heap when one stirs it up; and as for the pretended red blood, it was still evident on the hands of the butcher that this was nothing but a stinking mess.

After all our reasoning, they were of a mind to go to the seashore and burn the heart of the deceased, who in spite of this execution became less docile and made more noise than ever. They accused him of beating people at night, of breaking in doors, and even roofs; of breaking windows, tearing up clothes, and emptying pitchers and bottles. He was a very thirsty dead man: I believe that he did not spare any house but that of the consul, with whom we lodged. However, I have never viewed anything so pitiable as the state of this island. Everyone's head was turned: the wisest people were struck like the others. It was a regular illness of the brain, as dangerous as madness or rage. One saw entire families abandon their houses and come from the outlying areas of the town into the square, carrying their pallets, to pass the night there. Everyone complained of some new insult, and there were nothing but groans at the coming of night. The most intelligent ones withdrew to the country.

In so general a prepossession, we chose not to say anything. They would have treated us not just as fools but as infidels. How is one to bring an entire population back to its senses? Those who believed in their soul that we doubted the truth of the matter, came to us to reproach us for our incredulity and claimed to prove—by authoritive passages taken from the *Shield of Faith* of Père Richard, a Jesuit missionary—that there was such a thing as a vrykolakas. He was a Latin, they said, and therefore you should believe him. Nor should we have got anywhere by denying the conclusion. They made a scene every morning, by a faithful recitation of the new jests committed by this nightbird, who was even accused of having committed the most abominable sins.

Those citizens who were most zealous for the public good believed that the most essential part of the ceremony had been deficient. The mass should not have been said, according to them, until after the heart of this unfortunate man had been torn out. They maintained that, with this precaution, the devil could not have failed to have been surprised, and that without a doubt he would not have returned. Whereas in starting with the mass, they said, he had had all the time necessary to flee and to come back afterward at his convenience.

After all these reasonings, they found themselves in the same difficulty as the first day. They meet night and day, debate, and organize processions for three days and three nights. They oblige the popes to fast, and one sees them running among the houses, the aspergillum in their hand, sprinkling holy water and washing the doors with it. With it they even filled the mouth of this poor vrykolakas.

We said so often to the administrators of the town, that in a similar situation, in Christendom, one would not fail to establish a watch at night, to observe what would happen in the town, that finally they arrested a few vagabonds who certainly had had a hand in these disorders. But apparently they were either not the principal agents, or else they were released too soon, for two days later, to make up for the fast that they had undergone in prison, they began again to empty the jugs of wine of those who were so foolish as to leave their houses during the night. Whereupon people were obliged to take recourse again to prayer.

One day, as they recited certain prayers, after having planted I don't know how many naked swords in the grave of the corpse—which they disinterred three or four times a day, according to the caprice of whoever came by—an Albanian, who happened to find himself in Mykonos, took it upon himself to say, in a professorial tone, that it was extremely ridiculous to use the swords of Christians in such a case as this. Can you not see, you poor blind people, he said, that the guard of these swords, forming a cross with the handle, prevents the devil from leaving this corpse! Instead, why don't you rather use Turkish sabres?* The opinion of this clever man was of no use: the vrykolakas did not

*Folklore tends to look more coherent in a book than in the field, because informants lack adequate data-retrieval systems—they must rely on their memories—and are often obliged to reason from few data. Perhaps the inhabitants of Mykonos had not dealt with a revenant for

appear to be any more tractable, and everyone was in a strange dismay. They didn't know which saint to call upon, but with one voice, as though they had given one another the word, they began to cry out, throughout the village, that they had waited too long—it was necessary to burn up the vrykolakas entirely. After that they defied the devil to return to set up quarters there. It was better to resort to such an extreme than to have the island deserted. And in fact there were already whole families who were packing up, with the intention of retiring to Syra or Tinos. So then they carried the vrykolakas, by the order of the administrators, to the tip of Saint George's Island, where a great funeral pyre had been prepared, with tar, out of fear that the wood, as dry as it was, would not burn fast enough for them on its own. The remains of this unfortunate cadaver were thrown on and consumed in a short time (this was the first of January, 1701). We saw the fire as we returned from Delos. You could call it a true fire of rejoicing, for one no longer heard the complaints against the vrykolakas. They were content to observe that the devil had certainly been caught this time, and they composed a few songs to ridicule him.

In the whole archipelago people are persuaded that it is only the Greeks of the Orthodox Church whose corpses are reanimated by the devil. The inhabitants of the island of Santorini are terribly afraid of such types of werewolves, and the people of Mykonos, after their visions had dissipated, were equally afraid of prosecution by the Turks and by the bishop of Tinos. Not a single pope wanted to be present at Saint George, when they burned the body, out of fear that the bishop would exact a sum of money for their having exhumed and burned the deceased without his permission. As for the Turks, it is certain that, at their first visit, they did not fail to make the community of Mykonos pay for the blood of this poor devil, who became in every way an abomination and horror to his country. And after that, is it not necessary to point out that the Greeks of today are not the great Greeks, and that there is among them only ignorance and superstition!

Again, let us look at what is typical in such cases:

1. The revenant is an ill-natured, quarrelsome person while alive.
2. He is a murder victim.
3. After his death, he makes a great nuisance of himself. Note that, unlike the South Slavic vampires we have looked at, de Tournefort's vrykolakas does not suck blood or even kill anyone. A modern article on the vrykolakas, in fact, quotes an informant who says that he never heard of one drinking blood.[1] It must be said that in considering the nocturnal activity of vampires and revenants, even of the Slavic variety, it is difficult to find a clear pattern. Vampires and revenants, it would appear, are not

---

many years, which would explain their having only an approximate notion of the procedure. It is common for such procedures to be a matter for debate.

specialists at all in their chosen profession of tormenting human beings but are more in the way of general practitioners. Elwood Trigg, for example, in his discussion of the vampires of the Gypsies, gives the following summary of their activity:

> Appearing most often to those whom he considers his enemies, he may seek to kill them by sucking their blood, eating parts of their bodies, doing other violence to them, or simply causing them such terror that they die.
> Short of this, they have been known to cause the living physical harm by beating them and destroying their property. They have been known also to disturb families by causing loud noises, setting fires, turning over caravans, breaking dishes, and killing domestic animals by choking them to death.[2]

4. The decision not to deal with the vrykolakas until nine days after the burial is based on ancient preconceptions. The number nine is simply a standard number, endowed with significance, much the way forty is in the Bible (where it designates the duration of such diverse events as the Flood and Jesus' stay in the wilderness).

5. The mass is evidently considered a necessary but not a sufficient condition for the destruction of the vampire. There are instances in which the religious ceremony is itself said to have been sufficient to deal with the vampire,[3] but the methods of laying vampires and revenants clearly antedate Christianity even though they have obviously been influenced by it. In folklore the religious authorities were sometimes brought in when a vampire was to be killed, but this was more likely to happen in those areas of Europe in which the Orthodox church was dominant, since it did not attempt to stamp out pre-Christian beliefs, or at least not with the tenacity of the Catholic church.

6. The heart of the vrykolakas is cut out. The popular view of the matter is that it is difficult, at best, for a vampire to function without either (1) his head or (2) his heart. But while it is seldom mentioned explicitly, it is clear that, like the starfish, vampires and revenants have some potential for regeneration, and in Northern Europe, where the body of the Nachzehrer was likely to be decapitated—often with a sexton's spade—the head was then buried behind the body, with a wall of dirt between them, so that the two could not find their way together again. Such decapitations have been reported even in this century.[4] The heart, too, would sometimes be burned, as happened in New England in the nineteenth century,[5] or boiled in wine,[6] by way of ensuring that it would be of no further use to its owner.

7. Incense is burned because of the odor of the corpse. De Tournefort

may be assuming that the incense was intended to mask the smell, but there is evidence that, as I shall argue in chapter 13, the smell of the corpse was believed to be destructive and was therefore opposed with similarly strong smells, according to the notion *similia similibus curantur* (similar things are cured by similar things).

8. The blood of the revenant is said to be fresh (note that de Tournefort disputes this, however).

9. It is worth noting that, according to de Tournefort, the vrykolakas is believed to have been reanimated by the Devil. This is one of several common views of the matter: sometimes it is the body's own soul that reanimates it, usually after having wandered about in an extracorporeal condition for a specified period of time. And often, as we shall see, a person is viewed as living on after death in some limited aspect (for example, as dream image or shadow).

10. The body shows no signs of rigor mortis and is warm to the touch. Neither de Tournefort nor Flückinger was in a position to tell us just how warm it was, for while the thermometer had been invented,[7] it was not put to use in determining body temperature until later in the eighteenth century. The lack of rigor mortis, incidentally, however spooky it seemed to de Tournefort's informants, is a normal event, for rigor mortis is a temporary condition. Presumably the body had not been discovered for a day or two.

11. As often happens with revenants, de Tournefort's vrykolakas was not deterred by a mere cardioëctomy and had to be stabbed repeatedly and then burned to end his doings. And the choice of site—an island— is a further measure to prevent the dead man from returning: spirits cannot cross water.

12. It is noteworthy that de Tournefort refers to revenants as "werewolves" (*loups-garous*).[†] The relationship between the two is well established and might prompt us—if, as seems evident, de Tournefort's vrykolakas was actually a dead man—to look for an ecological nexus between wolves and dead bodies. We shall consider this problem in chapter 10.

As we see from the incident with the Albanian visitor, folkloric traditions may interfere with one another, requiring a resolution. Everyone

---

[†]This might also have been translated as *bug-bears*, a curious word that has to do with neither bugs nor with bears, but is related to the word *bogey*, as in *bogeyman*, and means either a spirit, spook, hobgoblin, and so forth or merely something that causes needless fear. *Bear* presumably got into this expression because, like the name of the animal, it meant the color brown.

knows that spirits have a pronounced aversion to sharp steel, but the Albanian observes that the particular swords being used form a kind of cross, by the design of their guard. Out of this (if his argument carries the day) might come a new formulation: only Turkish swords may be used in the killing of revenants. Such a statement, once it had lost its rationale, would appear to us to be bafflingly opaque and hence quite collectible. From this point of view, it might seem reasonable to define folklore as "common beliefs that I [the folklorist] don't share." If the folklorist shared them, after all, they would presumably be moved into a different category entirely, perhaps something like "well-known facts." And sometimes folklore is merely fact that seems too implausible for belief. In European and American tradition, for example, it is commonly believed that cats must be kept away from corpses, because they will attack them.[8] In fact, according to medical examiners I have spoken to, this is occasionally observed—cats are carnivorous, after all. If the folklorist had believed it, however, he would probably not have collected it: it is not his job, after all, to collect "well-known facts."

But this analysis is inadequate, for once a startling event takes place and is told of, it may acquire a life of its own and be retold endlessly, over many years, and always as though it had happened recently, to a "friend of a friend" of the narrator. In the process the narration usually acquires a set of standard (if variable) motifs that lend it verisimilitude. In other words, even though cats do sometimes mutilate corpses, most of the people who say so have had no direct experience of the matter and may be telling a version of the event that never happened.

If we ask ourselves, as we did with *Visum et Repertum*, what de Tournefort actually saw of a supernatural nature in his encounter with a vrykolakas, we must conclude that he will be of little help to us in our quest. The blood, he suggests, was not fresh; the smoke did not come from the body but from the incense; the warmth of the body was a natural phenomenon; and the mischief reported was the responsibility of people, not revenants. Structurally, his account is quite similar to that in chapter 2, with the difference that de Tournefort—unlike the narrator of that account—was not persuaded that anything spooky was going on.

We have proceeded from a rather gory revenant (Plogojowitz) through a whole graveyard full of placidly lethargic ones, and finally to one that, if the observer is to be believed, was not a revenant at all, but merely a dead body *posing* as one. At this point, if we consider that we have been looking at what are, by all accounts, some of the best-attested vampires and revenants in history, we might feel that our credulity has been sadly abused. The closer one gets to the vampire, it appears, the more reluctant he is to display himself.

But if we were now to demand an end to the matter, on the grounds that the vampire is a poor creature indeed, if he does not even protest as his attackers cut off his head, rip out his heart, and make a bonfire of him, then we would still be left with the problem of answering the following question: How is it that the people of Europe came to believe in the vampire at all? To discover the answer to this question, we will first want to consider, in detail, just what they did believe.

How Revenants Come into Existence

From the point of view of our informants, the factors that bring revenants into existence fall into the following broad categories: (1) predisposition; (2) predestination; (3) events: things that are done to people, things that they do, things that happen to them; and (4) nonevents: things that are left undone.

PREDISPOSITION

We have already looked at one example of a revenant—de Tournefort's vrykolakas—who apparently achieved this status merely by being a difficult and troublesome person. This is quite common: people who are different, unpopular, or great sinners are apt to return from the dead. It may be merely a corollary of this rule that in Eastern Europe alcoholics are regarded as prime candidates for revenants. Löwenstimm gives accounts from Russia of people who were unearthed merely because while alive they were alcoholic: "In the year 1889 the peasants of the village Jelis-chanki, in the Saratow District, opened the grave of a man who had died of alcoholism and had been buried in the general churchyard, and they threw his body into the nearest river."[1]

A more universal category is the suicide. It is partly because of their potential for returning from the dead or for drawing their nearest and dearest into the grave after them that suicides were refused burial in churchyards. The force of this prohibition can be seen in those cases where the authorities attempted to thwart the will of the populace and require that the body of the deceased be properly buried in the usual place:

> In Roschitz a weaver hanged himself in 1771, because of all-too-great poverty, and the court ordered that he be buried in the churchyard. The community, however, opposed itself to this order for so long that Henry XXX sent off a strong military detachment, and the deceased had to be buried under their authority and protection, in the Roschitz churchyard. A similar incident took place in the same year in Roben. There a regular revolt took place, and only the military was able to restore peace.[2]

There are also numerous reports that sorcerers tend to become revenants, and in Romania it is said that a sorcerer can cause a corpse to become a revenant.[3]

In general, lists of potential revenants tend to contain people who are distinguished primarily by being different from the people who make the lists. Burkhart, for example, gives the following categories of revenants-by-predisposition: "the godless (people of a different faith are included here, too!), evildoers, suicides, in addition sorcerers, witches, and werewolves; among the Bulgarians the group is expanded by robbers, highwaymen, arsonists, prostitutes, deceitful and treacherous barmaids and other dishonorable people."[4]

PREDESTINATION

Frequently people become revenants through no fault of their own, as when they are conceived during a holy period, according to the church calendar, or when they are the illegitimate offspring of illegitimate parents.[5] Indeed, in Romania it is reported that merely being the seventh child in a family is apt to cause one to become a revenant.[6]

Often potential revenants can be identified at birth, usually by some abnormality, some defect, as when (among the Poles of Upper Silesia and the Kashubes) a child is born with teeth.[7] Similarly suspicious are children born with an extra nipple (Romania);[8] with a lack of cartilage in the nose, or a split lower lip (Russia);[9] or with features that are viewed as bestial, such as fur down the front or back or a tail-like extension of the spine, especially if it is covered with hair (Romania).[10] (This can actually occur, according to Mackenzie.)[11] And Wilhelm Hertz makes mention of a belief that a revenant is born with two hearts, one of which is dedicated to the destruction of humanity. Burkhart also mentions this and adds that this belief is most common in the Ukraine, that it applies also to witches, and that it is sometimes souls, rather than hearts, that are superabundant.[12] One recognizes such vampires, according to Jaworskij, by the fact that they talk to themselves![13] In the case of the Romanian *strigoï*, which is also sometimes reported to have two hearts, the second is apparently credited with providing the mechanism whereby the creature remains alive. If pierced (by way of preventing the corpse from returning), it will cause blood to spurt high into the air.[14]

When a child is born with a red caul, or amniotic membrane, covering its head, this is regarded throughout much of Europe as presumptive evidence that it is destined to return from the dead.[15] The normal caul is a clear or grayish-white membrane, but in the event of hemorrhage it has a reddish tinge. Among the Kashubes the caul itself has an apotropaic quality, like the blood of a vampire, and must be dried, stored up, and crumbled into the child's food after a fixed period of time, because when the child consumes it, the threat of vampirism is ended.[16] Among the Kashubes in Canada, the caul may also be burned.[17]

Adrien Cremene gives the following mythological account of how a child comes to be born with a caul: "Such an infant is born to a woman who has drunk of impure water mixed with the saliva of a demon, or to a woman who, having gone out in the night, her head bare, met a demon which gave her a red cap (*coiffe*) like his own, which cap causes the child to be born with a caul."[18]

Incidentally, the caul is mentioned frequently in the literature, but its red color is mentioned only occasionally. My suspicion that those which cause vampirism must be red actually antedated my finding the evidence that this was so. The mechanisms whereby vampires come into being have a kind of internal logic. The caul, by itself, suggested no relationship to other indications of the origins of the vampire, but if it was red, it would fit in nicely. By a curious and far-reaching analogy, since bloodiness is a principal characteristic of the vampire or revenant, and blood is red, it follows that anything red in color tends to predispose toward vampirism. In the nineteenth century, a red birthmark suggested to the Kashubes that a child was destined to return from the dead and that when he died, his corpse would have a red face.[19] This was regarded as an ominous sign: "In the middle of the last [eighteenth] century, a member of the Wollschläger family died, in western Prussia, and a number of his relatives followed him shortly thereafter, unexpectedly, without any particular reason for death. People thought that they remembered that the visage of the dead person had never lost the red color, and there arose the general conjecture that he was a revenant (*Blutsauger*)."[20]

I have found one account, from East Prussia, that recommends that the face of the corpse be covered with spirit-soaked cloths to keep it fresh: "That keeps the dead person as fresh as if he were alive; and he has such red cheeks for the burial—that just has to be that way."[21] In general, however, red cheeks are held to be evidence of the potential for vampirism. In addition, people with red hair and blue eyes are said to be viewed (in Romania) as potential strigoï.[22]

In short, a revenant is bloody and blood is red; redness, therefore, must predispose toward vampirism. As we shall see, it is quite common for a decomposing corpse to acquire a ruddy color.* The belief that red = blood = life may also be supported by the idea that, as Cremene and Haase report, blood is sometimes viewed as the vehicle of the soul.[23]

EVENTS

In most fiction about vampires, only one means of achieving the state of vampirism is ever shown: people become vampires by being bitten by one. Typically, the vampire looms over his victim dramatically, then bites into her neck to suck her blood. When vampires and revenants in folklore suck blood—and many do not—they instead bite their victim somewhere on the thorax. Among the Kashubes, it is reported that they choose the area of the left breast;[24] among the Russians, they leave a small wound in the area of the heart;[25] and in Danzig (now Gdansk), they bite on the nipple.[26] Mannhardt reports that in Krain (an area of Walachia) vampires both suck blood and create new vampires by doing so.[27] Cremene adds that (again in Romania) the bite is never at the jugular but usually over the heart, the blood of which is in demand. More rarely, the victim is bitten between the eyes.[28] It is true, however, that, in folklore as well as in fiction, the vampire's bite tends to cause the victim to become a vampire as well.

*At the Los Angeles Medical Examiner's Office I was shown such a corpse.

The relationship of fictional vampires to mirrors also seems to be quite different than in folklore. In fiction, vampires tend to avoid mirrors because they fear that someone may notice that they cast no reflection. In the folklore I have found only two allusions to this tradition,[29] neither with any reference to a primary source. At the very least, the belief must be uncommon.

Mirrors do have a place in the folklore of death, however: in Bulgaria it is considered best to cover mirrors or turn them to the wall in the presence of a corpse, lest the face of the corpse be reflected and thereby bring about another death.[30] In his account of the funerary customs of Mecklenburg, Bartsch says that the mirror should be covered so that the corpse "is not doubled by reflection, for if this is the case, the deceased will fetch someone in the house after him."[31] Breaking a mirror is commonly regarded as unlucky, and the Blums cite a Greek informant who suggests that this is because "[the mirror] can have your soul and then, when it breaks, you will die."[32] According to the same informant, in northern Greece a camera is believed to have this ability to capture one's soul.

A very common belief, reported not only from much of Slavic territory but from China as well,[33] holds that a body may become a revenant when an animal jumps over it. Usually the animal is a dog or a cat, but seemingly anything animate—including people—may, by leaping over the body, or even reaching across it, cause it to become a vampire. Among the Aromunes of Romania, for example, a black hen was said to have this effect.[34] It may seem as if the danger could be averted by throwing out the cat, closing the doors and windows, and issuing a stern warning to anyone with a habit of leaping over corpses, but among the Slavs, where this idea is particularly prevalent, it is considered necessary to keep the doors and windows open so that the soul may escape.

In Romania it is reported that by flying over a corpse a bat can create a vampire.[35] This circumstance deserves remark if only because of its rarity, for as important as bats are in the fiction of vampires, they are generally unimportant in the folklore. The Blums cite the following account: "I learned from my grandmother that nothing, specifically nothing animal, bird, insect, or candle [presumably alight?—that is, *animated*], should be allowed to fly over, jump over, or be carried over the corpse because it will become a vorkalakas (a vrikolax)."[36] Indeed, Ralston reported that in Russia vampirism could come about because the wind from the steppe had blown over the body.[37]

Cremene mentions two less common ways in which a body can become a revenant: if the brother of a deceased person is a sleepwalker, and if, during his lifetime, a person's shadow is stolen.[38] The stealing of the shadow takes place at a construction site, when the victim's shadow is measured against a wall and then secured by driving a nail through its head. The purpose of this practice is to ensure that the building will be durable (Romania is subject to earthquakes). This is apparently a remnant of an ancient practice of sacrifice, by immurement, for the same purpose.[†]

In Russia, suicides, murder victims, people who drowned, and even victims of stroke were particularly at risk, and their bodies were usually disposed of differently from those of other people. Haase cites the following account from the year 1506:

> We do not dignify with burial the bodies of those who are drowned, or murdered and thrown out: instead we drag them into the fields and fence in the place with stakes, and—what is completely unlawful and Godless—when a cold wind blows in the spring, so that what we have planted and sown does not prosper, we stop praying to the creator and founder of everything . . . we learn of some person who was drowned or killed and was buried not long ago, . . . we dig up the condemned person and throw him somewhere in an out-of-the-way place and leave him unburied . . . because we believe, as a result of our great foolishness, that his burial is the cause of the cold.[39]

The bodies could not be buried because Mother Earth would object—sometimes even spewing them out—and they could not be left unburied because the authorities would object. The Russians solved this dilemma by putting such bodies together, in a kind of charnel house dug into the ground and roofed, and waiting until spring had safely arrived before conducting an appropriate service for them.[40] Not just in Russia, however, are the dead believed to influence the weather, for Cajkanovic gives an account of a prophetess from Slavonia who, in a curious syncretism of pagan and Christian beliefs, went to a cemetery to beg God for rain.[41]

As we saw in the case of Peter Plogojowitz, a person may become a vampire simply by being the first person to die of an epidemic, and the epidemic is interpreted as the effect of his depredations. Stated thus, this interpretation seems more bizarre than it really is: after all, that first person

---

[†]In Iasi, in 1979, not long after a major earthquake, my wife and I were given a tour by two archaeologists at the university, in the course of which we were shown a new mural in the rebuilt wing that depicts another form of the tradition: the architect, who is shown in despair, had been obliged to immure his wife, whose form is visible in the building.

is, in a sense, responsible for the later deaths, insofar as he carried the disease to the others. As a rule, or at least where we know more than our ancestors did, we do not have the same fears: no one, nowadays, is afraid of catching a heart attack from a sick person. But where we are similarly uninformed (our recent experience with AIDS comes to mind), we seem to react with the same methods of quarantine as the Russian peasants.

It may be that the awareness of contagion is one of the reasons for the common practice, throughout much of Europe, of breaking or disposing of objects that have come in contact with the dead person. According to Vakarelski,

> The containers used in the bathing of the deceased are smashed on the spot. They break some teeth out of the combs, hide them together with the soap and water in a remote place, or throw them into a river, if there is one in the vicinity. In some areas they put the comb and soap next to the corpse in the grave, "so that he can wash and comb himself in the beyond." They overturn the kettle in which the water was heated. The smashing and overturning of the containers is done with the intention of preventing the return of the dead person, for he could, after all, intend to wash himself again, or people say simply that it is not good for the living to use the same objects, because they would quickly follow the dead.[42]

This last statement describes a very real possibility if death occurred as the result of a communicable disease. A similar awareness seems to be suggested in the practice, also among the Bulgarians, of attempting to secure or destroy the influence of death by putting a heavy or sharp object at the place where the head of the corpse lay, or driving in a nail, or scattering burning coals where the feet of the corpse had been.[43]

The force of this belief—that the first victim of a disease is a vampire— can be seen in Löwenstimm's account, from nineteenth-century Russia, of the disinterment of a young woman:

> On the seventeenth of August, 1848, the pastor of the Veliko-Shukhovits church informed the local district judge that the peasants, against his will, had disinterred the deceased peasant girl Justina Yuschkov, had taken her out of the coffin, and had performed on her a 'bestial operation'; and they had done this in order to end the reign of cholera among them. When an investigation was opened in this matter, the peasants admitted everything and recounted the following: Juschkow had been the first to die of cholera, but in August, when the epidemic grew in strength, the medical officer Rubtsov, who lived among them, had assured all the peasants that a dissolute girl who had died in a condition of pregnancy was the cause of the sickness. In order to drive away the cholera, it was necessary to open the grave and see what was the situation of the unborn child and whether

or not the girl Yuschkov's mouth was open. If the mouth was open, then a stake must be driven into it. At first the peasants had not listened to the medical officer, but when the cholera continued to increase, they had decided to take refuge in the suggested method. They had opened the grave, taken out the corpse, and cut it open. But an unborn child was not to be found in the mother's body, and so they had looked through the coffin and had found the body of a baby. Then they had thrown Yushkov back into the grave, but had first driven an ashen stake into her, since they had found her with her mouth open. After the peasants had done all this, they had covered up the grave and gone home in the complete expectation that the cholera had been disposed of.[44]

In all but a few details, this account is quite standard, if a bit more gruesome than most. Although vampires are far more often male than female, the exceptions to the rule are commonly mothers who have died in childbirth, as the peasant girl in this account seems to have. Among the Slavs, it is commonly reported that a corpse with an open mouth is likely to be a vampire, and in *War and Peace* the mouth of the elder Bolkonsky is tied shut after his death, presumably to avert this possibility. Similarly, the Greeks are reported to tie the hands and feet of the corpse together and to tie the mouth shut, but the bonds are later untied, since it is believed that otherwise the corpse will not decompose.[45] The cutting into the body is not unusual, as we have seen with de Tournefort's and Flückinger's vampires, nor is the staking, although the staking through the mouth seems to occur mostly in Slavic accounts.[46] And finally, the reburial is just one of a number of possibilities for disposing of a body that has been cut open, staked, and, presumably, killed once and for all. Sometimes such bodies are cremated, sometimes they are thrown away in an isolated spot; sometimes—as was frequently reported from Russia, for example—they are thrown into the nearest body of water, whether river or lake. Such a reinterment as is mentioned above, while reported often enough in other countries, seems to have been uncommon among the Russians because of the belief that the earth could not tolerate the presence of the actual or potential revenant, at least under its surface.

In Greece, a priest's anathema was regarded as sufficient to cause a body to become a vrykolakas, or a curse, and both Lawson and the Blums cite such curses.[47] One account from Romania states that an open wound, if not covered, will cause a corpse to become a revenant;[48] and Cremene says that, also in Romania, if one were to cut oneself in a churchyard at night and let blood get on a tomb, the corpse inside could become a revenant.[49] In the Kosovo District of Yugoslavia it is said that the condition of vampirism is present when a corpse swells before burial.[50]

If we consider the evidence from the history of burial practices, it becomes clear that the belief in revenants antedates Christianity. Christianity did, however, add to the lore of the revenant, augmenting the supply of practices that brought about the condition. In Romania, for example, it is reported that Christians who convert to Islam become revenants, as do priests who say Mass in a state of mortal sin and children whose godparents stumbled while reciting the Apostles' Creed at their baptism.[51]

As we see from this last item, even babies may be doomed to a condition of vampirism, through the action, or inaction, of others. Commonly this is reported of children who die without being baptized, or who, having been weaned, suckle a second time (the North German *Doppelsauger*).[52]

THINGS LEFT UNDONE

The great majority of things that, if left undone, may cause a body to become a revenant are, not surprisingly, funerary and burial practices. These are so diverse that it is scarcely practical to attempt a survey of them, though we shall discuss many of them in the chapters on apotropaics.

Generally, it is considered dangerous for a corpse to be left unattended. Indeed, the Blums cite an informant who actually defines the Greek revenants as "dead people who had died alone and had no one there to take care of them."[53] Lee quotes an informant who says, "When people die of a contagious disease, and no one will go near them and they bury them without a priest, without anything, they become vrykolakes."[54] Here we see again that the fear of the revenant was not entirely irrational: often people were afraid of contagion, without having defined its limits so closely as we have nowadays.

Burkhart cites similar conditions for a Bulgarian revenant, saying that "vurkolaks" come from "heydukes, robbers, highwaymen, and arsonists who lead their asocial life in a nurturing wild and also die there, decompose unburied, or are eaten by wild animals; this condition is not stressed—which is striking—with the term 'vampire.' "[55]

Such observations are quite common. Vukanovic, for example, says that, among the Gypsies, "if somebody dies unseen" he becomes a vampire, and among the Finns it is enough that a corpse is neglected for it to return to harm the living.[56] In Oldenburg, in the last century, it was believed that a body could become a revenant merely by not being buried deep enough.[57] And when Dömötör observes that Hungarian revenants are found on battlefields, we may suspect that that here again we are actually looking at an absence of funerary or burial rites: during war, as in times of plague, bodies are likely to be dealt with in a less complete and methodical manner.[58]

Still other causes of vampirism include the following: Among the Wends, a mother may return from the dead if her child is not cared for or needs her, as may someone who dies with something on his conscience or dies unrepentant and without the last unction.[59] In northern Germany a person may become a Nachzehrer if his name is not removed from his clothing when he is buried.[60] And in Romania, according to Cremene, it is common for the legs of a corpse to be tied in the interests of keeping them straight. When the body is put in the coffin, the ropes, having been cut away, should be put near it, and if this is not done (because the ropes are valuable as magical charms), the body will become a strigoï.[61]

It is important to note here that some of our categories overlap. Murder victims, suicides, and victims of plague, who are commonly regarded as especially subject to vampirism, also fulfill two other important conditions: they die quickly (as victims of stroke may, for example), and they tend not to be accorded proper burial rites. A murderer will sometimes bury his victim by way of hiding the crime, but he will seldom do the job well, as he is likely to consider the possibility that, should he be caught with shovel in hand, this might be viewed as circumstantial evidence of the most persuasive sort. A suicide cannot bury himself, and in times of war or plague many bodies are buried hurriedly, often in a communal pit, or not at all.

Lack of burial is itself, then, a sufficient reason for murder victims and suicides to become revenants, but another common explanation for their transformation is that they have not lived out their allotted span of life.[62] Ernst Bargheer has made the interesting suggestion, in an interpretation of a remark by a medieval preacher named Geiler von Keisersberg, that the promise of a seventy-year life (from Psalm 90) has led to the conclusion that a person killed too soon is apt to spook around until the time of natural death.[63] As we shall see later, however, other factors seem to be involved here as well. But for now, having determined what brings revenants into the world, we shall consider them from another point of view, asking the question, what do revenants typically look like? The answer to that question is likely to surprise the habitué of the horror films.

The Appearance of
the Vampire

Of the various vampires from folklore and fiction, perhaps the most easily described is that of the cartoons, since there the artist's object is to create, as quickly and efficiently as possible, something that will be recognized instantly, by anyone, as a blood-sucking monster rather than, say, a tall, brooding fellow in old-fashioned clothing. I suspect that a cartoonist allowed to use only two vampire-markers would demand a black cloak and long canine teeth. With these the artist could transform any figure into something vampirelike.

What is curious about this is that neither the cloak nor the canines finds a place in the folklore of the vampire: here again, fiction has little to do with folklore.

The vampires of the cartoons are usually rather lanky, have long, sometimes crooked fingernails, and affect, as a characteristic stance, a kind of hunched loom, except when they are lying in their coffins. Then—again unlike the vampires of folklore, who usually lie prone—they are represented in a supine position. Sometimes the hoods of their black cloaks will be seen to have a kind of fringe that suggests, in its shape, the wing of a bat.

The vampires of the movies, too, are usually tall and thin, with pale, usually narrow faces, which sprout a pair of very prominent canine teeth. These, however, are by no means a constant quality in their appearance, for they are most prominent—indeed, unconcealable—only at the time of the full moon. Quite often such vampires are shown with a trickle of blood at the corner of the mouth.

The coffin was observed carefully on all sides, and they found it as undamaged as they themselves had made it. We opened the coffin, and, to be sure, with most of the dead, one saw that a foaming, evil-smelling, brown-black ichor welled out of their mouths and noses, with the one more, with the other less. And what kind of joy did this cause among the people? They all cried, "Those are vampires, those are vampires!" . . .
. . . But with those [deceased] that had died of lengthy diseases, and had lain buried for a while, the epidermis lifted away, but the thick skin underneath was not red but yellow-white. When one pushed on their chests, blood flowed out of the mouth, but by far not so much as the others [in the previous paragraph]. They had not all decomposed. I asked the bystanders if these were not also vampires, but they declined to answer.
—Eighteenth-century account from Walachia'

On the top of the bones of other men there was found lying a corpse perfectly whole; it was unusually tall of stature; clothes it had none, time or moisture having caused them to perish; the skin was distended, hard, and livid, and so swollen everywhere that the body had no flat surfaces but was round like a full sack. The face was covered with hair dark and curly; on the head there was little hair, as also on the rest of the body, which appeared smooth all over; the arms by reason of the swelling of the corpse were

> stretched out on each side like the arms
> of a cross; the hands were open, the
> eyelids closed, the mouth gaping, and
> the teeth white.
> —Seventeenth-century Greek account[2]

In folklore, as may be seen from the above quotations, the vampire is very different from his counterpart in the movies. His color is never pale, as one would expect of a corpse: his face commonly is described as florid, or of a healthy color, or dark, and this may be attributed to his habit of drinking blood. Burkart says, "The limbs remain flexible, the body is undamaged and swollen up and can give forth fresh blood, the face [is] red from blood he has drunk . . . the eyes [are] open."[3]

While many accounts mention the ruddy face of the revenant, some suggest a darker color. In the Kosovo-Metohija Province in Yugoslavia,[4] for example, the Gypsies are reported to believe that a body that will become a vampire turns black before burial.* The revenant Glam, in *Grettir's Saga*, is said to be "dark-blue in colour and swollen up to the size of an ox."[5] And we may be seeing a version of this idea when we are told that Greek villagers, on exhuming the remains of the dead, are said to believe that if these are yellowish-brown, the person lived a good life, whereas if they are black, he lived badly.[6]

As we have seen with de Tournefort's vrykolakas and the shoemaker of Breslau, the absence of rigor mortis is considered strong evidence of vampirism. So too are open eyes, an open mouth, and the presence of blood at the lips or nose, sometimes even at the eyes and ears.[7] Indeed, heavy drinkers, who often acquire a ruddy complexion from the distension of their capillaries by alcohol, may be compared to the vampire: "The Serbians, referring to a red-faced hard-drinking man, assert that he is 'blood-red as a vampire'; and both the Serbians and Slovaks denote a hard drinker as a vlkodlak."[8]

The liquid blood is considered presumptive evidence of the vampire's habit of blood-sucking. It is especially persuasive when, as with Flückinger's Miliza, it is observed in conjunction with a tendency to be plump

---

*I have found a report from Missouri (early 1900s) saying, "A mixture of soda and cold water is put hourly on corpses to keep the skin from turning dark before the burial. This is done where embalming doesn't take place" (UCLA folklore encyclopedia collection). This is also reported from Ohio: "You can't keep them for more than three days that way in the summer. They get a bluish or black tone to the face" (Puckett [1981], 2:1222).

or swollen (note the description of Glam, above), quite unlike the vampires of fiction.[9] Richard Andree, for example, in describing the Greek vrykolakas, says, "It is an infallible sign of a vampire when the body does not decompose in the grave, but instead swells up, while the skin becomes taut like the skin of a drum."[10] A Serbian immigrant has described the vampire as follows: "When he is dug up he will be bloated with blood and uncorrupted."[11] Norbert Reiter cites the South Slavic view that the vampire "has no bones, but is a blood-filled sack that comes into being when the devil pulls the skin off a particular body and blows it up."[12]

Here we see how, in the makeup of the revenant, two characteristics stand out: the presence of a great deal of blood (he is in fact full to bursting with fresh blood) and the swollen body. Indeed, the Silesian shoemaker was reported to have gained in girth between his first and second interments: "the body had grown much fuller of flesh." Sometimes the vampire's face, rather than his body, is swollen: a Kashube vampire was described by a Canadian informant as having a "bloated, blood-red face."[13]

The Nachzehrer of Northern Europe shares many qualities with the Slavic vampires, but because of his habit of chewing on his extremities, his hands and feet may be rather tattered. Often the coffin or gravesite is described as "swimming in blood," which is viewed as spillage resulting from his excessive appetite for the stuff. In Prussia, "they claim to have dug up such corpses after a year, where the face showed itself to be very ruddy, but the body was mostly lacerated and swimming in blood."[14]

It might be noted that the presence of blood, especially at the lips, may be one of the circumstances that associated the vampire with the plague. The pneumonic form of the plague causes the victim to expell blood from the mouth,[15] and the combination of visible blood with unexpected and quite sudden deaths may have contributed to the belief that vampirism was responsible for this disease. The observer does not realize that the blood comes from the lungs but instead sees it as evidence that the body has been sucking blood from the living.

Blood is the most distinctive characteristic of the revenant, but it is by no means the only unusual one. The hair and nails have grown since death, or there are no fingernails at all.[16] Often, as with Plogojowitz, Flückinger's vampires, and the shoemaker of Silesia, the skin has been sloughed off and replaced by new, healthy skin. And often the left eye or both eyes are said to be open and staring. In Romania this latter condition is reported to be evidence that the corpse is trying to warn the living that it is in the process of becoming a strigoï.[17] As we have seen, the revenant's mouth is apt to be open. And when the vampire or revenant is located in his grave, he is often found sitting up, or at least in a different position from that in which he was buried.[18]

One of the more curious reports has to do not with the outer appearance of the revenant but with that of his liver, which is said to be white in color. This is reported not only for the Slavic vampire but also for the German Nachzehrer, witches, and women whose husbands die one after another.[19] In English *white-livered* (or *lily-livered*) means *cowardly*, in accordance with an old belief that a coward's liver is of a lighter color than a normal one, owing to a deficiency of bile, or *choler*.[20] Interestingly, these various types of white-livered people match fairly well those who were sometimes dissected, as we have seen with some of our "vampires." Now it is clear that our sources would have known something about the color of the human liver, considering how many vampires and witches have been disassembled over the centuries. But because it appeared obvious to me that a liver cannot turn white, I did not consider the matter further. One day, however, I found myself in the company of a physiologist and a biologist and asked them if they could think of any reason for a liver to change color in this way. The physiologist pointed out that cirrhosis lightens the color of the liver because the veins become clogged, preventing the circulation of blood.[†] Indeed, it changes color at an early stage of disintegration, during what is called "fatty metamorphosis." This is the condition induced in geese, by force-feeding, to create pâté de foie gras, or "pasty of fat liver." The biologist added that if the liver were exposed to fresh water, it would turn white because the red blood cells take in water until they burst, the water having a lower salt content than the cell. The biologist also pointed out that, if one were to cut into a body, the liver would be one of the more noticeable organs because of its position and size, especially where cirrhosis has caused the liver to distend greatly.

Either interpretation seems to present problems. While the cirrhotic interpretation is supported by the folk belief that alcoholics become vampires, the liver actually turns more of a yellow color than white. To allow for this divergence, we would have to assume either (1) that *white* is a broader term for our informants than for us or (2) that in the course of oral transmission, the subtleties of shade are lost.

[†]Dr. Thomas Noguchi also suggested cirrhosis as a means of accounting for the change in color, and he is the source for the following remarks about fatty metamorphosis.

The other interpretation corresponds nicely with the Eastern Slavic practice of throwing bodies into lakes and streams when it is feared that they may become revenants. But the liver would have to be exposed somehow to the water. This would seem to require that the corpse be cut open near the liver before being thrown into water. Although we have endless accounts of mutilations of revenants, both at their initial disposal and on their later retrieval, I have seen no pattern that would suggest this.

Finally, there is no reason to argue that only one of these theories can be correct: both may be. As is true of so much of the vampire lore, the matter of the white liver suggests that our real problem may be with our own perspective or with the limits of our own information or imagination. We shall see some more striking—and far more conclusive—examples of this later.

In describing the appearance of the vampire, Montague Summers says that "the lips which will be markedly full and red are drawn back from the teeth which gleam long, sharp, as razors, and ivory white."[21] Here the scholar seems to have switched into a fictional mode, for not only does scarcely anything in the folklore provide a description of a vampire's lips, precious little is said about his teeth.

Although in fiction the vampire's teeth are an essential characteristic, distinguishing him from some other monsters, in folklore the teeth are not especially prominent. Only occasionally is it remarked that his teeth had grown while he was a vampire.[22] Some vampires do not even use their teeth to draw blood. Zelenin, for example, reports the belief that the Russian vampire has a pointed tongue, which he uses to puncture the skin of his victims.[23] When a vampire's teeth are remarked on at all, it is usually as the observation that children born with teeth are destined to become vampires.

For all the differences between vampires of fiction and folklore in appearance, there is one notable correspondence: when found in their graves, both lie quietly, in a kind of trance, awaiting their fate. They are not dangerous in this condition, at least until attacked. Even here, however, the two differ noticeably: the fictional vampire sleeps away the daylight hours in a supine position. In folklore, if a dead person was expected to become a vampire, then he would have been buried face down, for reasons explained in the next chapter.

Some reports leave it unclear as to whether the vampire lies prone because he was buried that way or because he chooses to. But it was said of a Walachian vampire that "he can be destroyed only if one digs up his body, which can be recognized by its inverted position, with the face down, and by its bloated appearance, and forces a nail through its forehead or a wooden stake through its heart, or also burns it."[24] We see here that the vampire is actually recognized by his prone position rather than having been placed thus for apotropaic reasons.

The differences between fictional and folkloric vampires do not seem difficult to account for: the former are designed solely to create a sinister, frightening aura. Qualities that are not thought to imply such an aura, such as the chubbiness and florid complexion of the vampires of folklore, are usually omitted, even by authors who are quite familiar with the folklore, as Bram Stoker seems to have been.

As one might expect, where the exigencies of drama can be aligned with the facts of folklore, the writers of fiction tend to stick with the facts: their vampires, too, are apt to let out a scream when a stake is driven into them, and blood may flow from their mouths as they die. Also, fictional vampires age with astonishing speed at their death, turning into mummified corpses within moments, or even disappearing—a happy circumstance for the living, who would otherwise be obliged to dispose of the body. In folklore the body does not self-destruct after its second death, but must be got rid of by a variety of methods that we shall discuss later.

But first we must investigate the methods of preventing the corpse from becoming a vampire. An ounce of prevention, after all, is worth a pound of cure.

Apotropaics I

Apotropaics, or methods of turning evil away, are diverse: they include mutilation of the corpse, physical restraints, various funerary rites, and even deception intended to trick the spirit world. Witness the following account from Bukowno, Poland:

> The wife of the peasant who had met the revenant, told about it in the whole village, but people did not want to believe her. Only when a number of people had convinced themselves that the revenant was actually coming into this village, did they tell the priest. He then had the revenant taken out of the grave, had a slip of paper put under his tongue with his name on it, had him laid face down and struck with a shovel on the hind end. Since then he never came into the village again.'

Strictly speaking, this account shows methods of dealing with the actualized revenant, rather than methods of preventing the transformation from taking place. As we shall see, however, the two sets of methods overlap a great deal: to prevent a corpse from becoming a revenant, you may bury it face down; but to cause it to rest in peace—you may bury it face down.

Quite common is the practice of placing objects with the corpse, and these objects are usually expected (1) to satisfy it somehow, thereby relieving it of the need to return from the dead, (2) to render it incapable of returning, or (3) to satisfy or thwart any demonic force that attempts to interfere with the corpse. Sometimes these two purposes are confused or reinterpreted. The obolus of ancient Greece—a small coin (the sixth part of a drachma) that was put in the mouth of the corpse—was held to serve the first purpose: with it, the dead person could pay Charon for passage across the River Styx. Lawson has argued plausibly that this view "was only a temporary and probably local misinterpretation of the custom, and that the coin or other object employed was really a charm designed to prevent any evil spirit from entering (or possibly the soul from re-entering) the dead body."[2] He notes that in modern times a similar practice was observed in connection with the belief in the vrykolakas: in Chios a cross of wax or cotton was placed on the lips of the corpse; and during the funeral service, the priest put a piece of pottery, bearing the legend "Jesus Christ conquers," on the lips of the body.

The use of a potsherd has also been reported for the Kashubes of western Prussia, where it was said to be put in the mouth so that the corpse would have something to chew on that would not bring about the death of relatives.[3] A coin was also used, and often the mouth would be filled with dirt or propped shut with a chunk of sod or a songbook, so that the corpse could not begin to chew. From Pomerania, in the late nineteenth century, Otto Knoop reported a reinterpretation of this use of a songbook: in Cecenow it was provided for the corpse so that it could sing![4]

The corpse was usually either given something to chew on that did not cause death (as his chewing on the shroud or his limbs would do, for example), or else his mouth was propped shut so that he could not chew at all. But Perkowski cites a Kashube informant from Canada who seems to combine these two traditions, saying, "A brick is put under [the corpse's] chin, so that he may break his teeth on it."[5] The same effect may be achieved by tying the mouth of the corpse shut—a very old practice, depicted on vases from ancient Athens[6]—although in some cultures the knots must be undone or cut before burial.

Frequently the assumption is made that if the corpse is provided with food, it will not find it necessary to feed on the living. In Romania, in the Banat, it is reported that, a few days after the burial, a relative of the deceased carries wine and bread to the grave. The wine is poured over the grave* and the bread given to passersby in remembrance of the deceased. It is believed that the presence of such food will relieve the strigoï of the need for human blood and flesh.[7] The practice of providing food for the dead is, of course, common throughout the world and throughout history, either to prevent corpses from becoming restless or, more simply, because it is assumed that the realm of the dead is analogous to that of the living and they need to eat.

In Romania, it was reported that a candle, a coin, and a towel were given to the corpse in order to prevent vampirism.[8] In Pomerania a light was provided to allow the deceased to see on his way to heaven.[9] This is also reported for Bulgaria: "They light a candle and place it either at the head of the sick person or in his hands. In many places it is considered a disgrace or a sin to neglect this. For people believe that the soul wanders on dark ways and needs a light in order not to get lost."[10]

Other objects and substances may also be provided for the grave. In Eastern Serbia, a small hawthorn peg may be driven into the grave, beside the cross, to prevent the corpse from turning into a vampire.[11] In Romania, it has been reported in recent times that incense is put in the nostrils, ears, and eyes of the corpse,[12] and in Bulgaria millet and garlic have been used thus.[13]

Worldwide, it is quite common for substances and objects to be stuffed into the orifices of corpses. In China, for example, jade objects, sometimes tubular in shape, were often put in the openings of the body.[14] In Australia soft plant fibers were used thus,[15] and some Gypsies in the Balkans are said to stuff wool in the mouth of the deceased.[16] I have seen Peruvian mummies (in the Kunsthistorisches Museum, Vienna) also with wool stuffed in the mouth and nose.[17]

Such practices appear to change only very slowly. Indeed, Schneeweis ventures the opinion that nowhere are old practices and views so resolutely preserved as in funerary rites.[18] People are most likely to alter their habits when they migrate, but Perkowski has demonstrated that the methods of the Canadian Kashubes in dealing with revenants have changed little as they have moved from Northern Europe to Canada: "The only innovation of note is the use of poplar crosses during burial instead of a rosary crucifix. All else has been retained."[19] According to Beitl,[20] such

---

*Danforth, 42, reports the pouring of wine over the body in a modern Greek burial. This is not a new concept, as readers of Homer (whose funeral pyres and offerings to the gods are typically quenched with wine) will attest.

crosses among the Germans in Kashube territory are to be made of ash, which, in the north, is generally the wood chosen to stake the vampire.

Various granular substances are put into graves or strewn along the path to the graveyard in order to hinder the revenant, and these include millet, sea sand, mustard seeds,[21] oats,[22] linen seeds,[23] carrot seeds,[24] and poppy seeds.[25]

The poppy seed is apparently chosen because of a supposed narcotic effect: it would encourage the deceased to "sleep" rather than walk.[26] In fact poppy seeds contain only traces of narcotic, but in the workings of analogy, as with horseshoes and hand grenades, close is good enough. For two things to be thought to function similarly, it is enough that they share qualities. Also, the analogy between death and sleep is well established, evident not only in the derivation of the word *cemetery* (from a Greek word meaning "to put to sleep"), but also in the mythological kinship relation between the two concepts: according to Hesiod, Sleep and Death were brothers, being children of Night.

I have found only one account[27] that says explicitly that the poppy seeds are to be eaten (at the rate of one per year). Usually what is at issue is a harnessing of the revenant's compulsions: he must collect the grains one at a time, and often just one grain per year. This so engages his attention that he is obliged to drop all other pursuits.

The revenant is similarly obsessed, in northern Germany, with untying knots. Often nets or stockings were buried with corpses, to provide them—at a rate of one knot per year—with many years of what was apparently an utterly riveting occupation.[28] The Kashubes in northern Germany, on the other hand, were said to be reluctant to provide the corpse with a net, since untying the knots was felt to be a torturous effort;[29] and the Greeks would not consider leaving knots in the coffin, as anything tied would prevent the corpse from being "loosed" (that is, would prevent decomposition, again by analogy).

In order to prevent potential vampires or revenants from finding their way to the surface, they were commonly buried face down, as in the account quoted above. The purpose, according to Reiter, was to cause them to bite their way firmly into the earth.[30] I have found another interpretation of this practice (from Silesia), according to which the gaze of the putative revenant was regarded as fatal, and his corpse was turned face down to protect those who had to deal with it at his death.[31] Prone burials of this sort are quite old (they are attested for the Celts, for example),[32] and they appear to be an example of the common folkloric phenomenon of "widdershins," the practice of reversing the direction of anything that is to gain access to the spirit world.

Sometimes the corpse is believed to turn over by itself, as in the popular saying that a dead man would "turn over in his grave" if he were to learn something disagreeable. In modern times this process may take place at a more hectic pace than in the past, for it is sometimes suggested that the corpse might "spin" in its grave. The original notion that the corpse is preparing to return from the dead, not just shifting about, appears to have been lost.

Besides nets and various grains, other grave goods are provided to prevent vampirism. Often these are sharp objects, and in Romania and Hungary the one most often mentioned is the sickle. Schulerus, in an account of Transylvanian customs, says that a sickle or a tin plate was laid on the stomach of the corpse, allegedly in order to prevent swelling, and was usually buried with it.[33] Dömötör gives a similar report for Hungary, adding that, while the practice is explained as a means of preventing the body from swelling, its *real* purpose is to prevent it from becoming a revenant.[34] A modern report from Bulgaria tells of a priest putting an icon on the midsection of the corpse, which suggests that the church has preempted a folk custom and given it a religious character.[35] And Cremene says that in Romania a sickle is left on the body if it lies alone in the house before burial.[36]

Sometimes it is made clear that the cutting edge of the sickle is significant in laying the revenant, as when Reiter cites the Yugoslavian practice of putting the sickle around the neck of the corpse, so that, should it attempt to rise up out of the grave, it would cut off its own head.[37] Similarly, Perkowski cites a Romanian informant who says, "Unmarried persons run a greater risk of becoming a strigoï at death, so measures must be taken. You have to stick a sickle into the corpse's heart in order to protect yourself and your relatives. If not, the strigoï draws his relatives to the grave."[38]

And sometimes the presence of the sickle is given another interpretation entirely, as when Vakarelski reports that in some parts of Bulgaria and Macedonia sickles are said to be buried with women so that after death they have something with which to mow.[39] Even in the Balkans, apparently, "women's work is never done."

The burial of a sickle with the corpse is, again, quite an old practice, dating at least to the ninth century, according to Balassa and Ortutay.[40] (The sickle itself dates back to the earliest Neolithic period.) This leads to an interesting hypothesis: we know that in Hungary and Romania it was a common practice to bury a sickle with a dead body, to prevent the body from "walking," and it follows that such a practice would result in bodies, or what is left of them, being found in the presence of such implements. It seems at least possible that this has contributed to our portrayal of death as a skeleton (the Grim Reaper) carrying a sickle or scythe and dressed in a shroud; among the Transylvanian Saxons, for example, "Death is . . . generally portrayed as a pale skeleton that holds a scythe or a sickle in his hand."[41] And among the Eastern Slavs, Haase has found a number of representations of death, including the following: "Death appears as . . . an old woman with a torch in the left hand and a scythe in the right; as an old woman in a white robe [Gewand] with a sickle and a rake; as a skeleton with exposed teeth and without a nose."[42] If what we are seeing is a representation of death that is based in part on characteristic grave-finds, then neither the torch nor the sickle or scythe, neither the skeleton nor the robe (shroud?), is unusual.[†]

Usually Death is represented as "mowing down" the living with his scythe or sickle. This would seem to be a reinterpretation of the instrument's function, which would not be at all obvious when a sickle was found in the grave with a skeleton. Such reinterpretations are common enough, and Robert Eisel captured a particularly charming one in 1871: a report from Saxony that stated that, in the old days, "They buried the dead just as the plague had surprised them as they harvested: with the sickle in their hand. Such corpses with so-called tooth-sickles (sickles with sawteeth) have in recent times been dug up in the Seifersdorf churchyard."[43] Here we see that the tradition has evidently died out—sickles are no longer being buried with bodies locally—and the citizens, on excavating a graveyard, conclude that people were being buried with sickles merely because that was what was in their hand at the time of their (remarkably sudden) death. Eisel gives still another interpretation of the same phenomenon: "In the year 1725 rows of graves were found above the Göschitz churchyard, and in the one row tooth-sickles were found, formed like saws, and in the other wheel-nails.[‡] The two things

---

[†]Erwin Panofsky, 77, derives this motif from Rev. 14:14–17.

[‡]*Radekoppen*: an eighteenth-century account (see Grässe, 2:222) glosses this word with *Radnagel*, which literally means "wheel nail." *Nagel*, according to Grimm, can be used for *Achsnagel*, or linchpin. My best guess is that a *Radekoppe* is an iron object that has some function in the manufacture of wheels and that—because of its association with burials—it might have a sharp point.

had been put in so that, with the opening of these graves, people would know which community the one or the other corpse belonged to."[44] It seems more likely, of course, that the objects—both of them sharp implements—had been put in the graves to prevent the dead from walking, although they may well have provided a de facto distinction between two communities.

Edward Westermarck reports such a use of sharp objects from Morocco as well: "In many places a dagger or some other object of steel or iron is put on the abdomen of the dead body (Fez, Tangier, Andjra, Bni ʿĀroṣ): among the Aiṯ Sáddĕn a ploughshare (tagursa) is used for this purpose. It is said to be done to prevent the abdomen from swelling; but I have also been told that its object is to keep away Šíṭan or the jnūn (Fez, Andjra, Bni Ăroṣ). The Amanūz prevent swelling by placing a lump of earth over the navel."[45] And Westermarck cites evidence—also from Arab territory—that a heavy object, sword, or knife is to be put on the belly of the deceased.[46]

Among the ancient Slavs, sharp objects—iron knives, hair needles, awls—have been found in urn burials containing cremated remains, and Haase views their function as preventing the return of the dead. The upside-down burial of the urn had, in his opinion, a function similar to the prone burial of corpses.[47]

And here I might mention that other practices besides the placement of sharp objects on the corpse have as their avowed purpose the prevention of swelling. Lemke, for example, mentions the practice in eastern Prussia in the late nineteenth century of placing a bowl of cold water under the board on which the body was lying and of putting quantities of tin spoons on top of the body.[48]

Besides sickles, other sharp or spiny objects are used to hinder the corpse from walking. Thorns are frequently put in the grave for this purpose. Cremene, for example, cites reports from Romania that the head and feet of the corpse may be bound with thorns or that a kind of briar may be put into the coffin after the head of the corpse has been pierced with a needle. In the latter case, the head may then be anointed with the fat of a pig killed at Christmas.[49] At the end of the nineteenth century, Wlislocki reported a similar practice among the Hungarians, saying that either thorns or a piece of a saw would be put with the corpse, so that the corpse would catch the material of its shroud in it and so be prevented from returning from the grave.[50]

Among the Slavs, the thorn may be used in a somewhat different way, being inserted under the tongue of the corpse to prevent it from sucking blood,[51] and such thorns—as well as nails and knives—have been found in skulls in a medieval burial ground.[52] Grenz, going by their position, suggests that they were probably forced through the tongue from above, presumably to prevent the corpse from chewing by pinning the tongue in place.

In addition to thorns, other sharp things may be used to prevent the corpse from returning. Among the Romanians, a needle may be inserted in the navel or in the heart, or a skewer that has been heated red hot, or a sharpened stake which is forced into the heart of the corpse.[53] Similar mutilations in Serbo-Croatia, where the corpse is also apt to have a wound inflicted on it, have, according to Schneeweis, the function of frustrating the intention of the Devil to blow up the corpse and cause it to become a vampire, inasmuch as the air is allowed to escape through the wound.[54]

Romania is also the home of what may be thought of as the "automatic vampire-piercing device," which is a sharpened stake, or group of them, driven into the grave, so that if the body seeks to rise up, it will be punctured and "killed." Cremene cites a variation of this practice: three days after the burial, relatives of the deceased go to the grave with nine spindles,[§] which they drive into the ground, again in the expectation that the strigoï, should he seek to escape the grave, will transfix himself.[‖] For Serbia, Krauss gave a similar report in the late nineteenth century: after covering the grave with flammable materials and igniting them, the people would drive "five old knives or four hawthorn spikes into the grave: the knife into the breast and two spikes into the feet, two into the hands of the deceased, so that he would impale himself on the knives and thorns if, having become a vampire, he should attempt to climb out of the grave."[55]

Sometimes, however, the object seems to be actually to drive the stake into the corpse rather than merely position it above the body so that the vampire would impale himself on attempting to leave the grave. Trigg says, "At one time it was the practice [of the Gypsies] to take poles made of such woods as ash, hawthorn or juniper and drive them into the suspected grave. In some instances the graves were first covered with hide

---

[§]The number nine—one of the Indo-European standard numbers—is a curious relic here, and its presence hints at the great continuity of such traditions. Readers of Homer are familiar with the tendency for everything to happen in nines: the Achaeans besiege Troy for nine years, and the ointment used on Patroclos's body is nine years old. The number is used similarly in Icelandic mythology: Odin hung for nine days from Yggdrasil, the world tree.

[‖]Cremene, 90. In Europe, spindles come in a variety of shapes, including pointed ones. Sleeping Beauty pricks herself on a spindle (a magical one, to be sure).

or cloth and then these stakes were hammered through the material, so as to be driven either through the stomach or the head of the corpse. Evidence that the corpse had been a vampire could be seen later when the grave was covered with a blister filled with blood."[56] Covering the grave is similar to covering the *body* of the vampire, described in chapter 9, to prevent his blood from getting on his killers when they drive a stake through him.

I have found an account from the beginning of this century from Hungary that may describe the remnants of a similar practice. In a village in the Szekler area, a graveyard was found that had meter-high poles stuck into the graves, two at the head, two at the foot. These poles had been used to carry the coffin to the graveyard, and the author of the account supposed that, to go by their name (*kopjafa*), which is derived from the word for "spear," in the past they were probably the spears of the deceased. If this is so, of course, then they would have been well adapted to fulfill the function of the stakes that are driven into Romanian graves.[57] Whatever the function of these poles, however, it is clear that the local inhabitants believed in revenants in the past, for Wlislocki cites an account saying that the people of this area used to fire rifles into the grave after the coffin had been lowered to prevent the return of the dead.[#]

The corpse was frequently prevented from returning by physical restraints, as when the Finns tied its knees together.[58] And it is possible that the fear of revenants accounts for the nineteenth-century Bulgarian practice, attested for some villages in the south and west of the country, of wrapping the deceased in a carpet.[59] This too seems to be an ancient practice, as Haase cites a Russian instance of it from a chronicle of the year 1015.[60]

In Romania the feet of the corpse may be tied so that the body remains straightened, but the ropes are later cut and are supposed to be disposed of near the body. If they are stolen, for use in black magic, the body will become a strigoï.[61] But binding the corpse, however effective a means it is of securing the corpse in its grave, tends to interfere with a common belief that the presence of knots in the grave will disturb the dead person's ability to make an easy transition to the afterlife. For this reason the

[#]Wlislocki, 134. In fiction, a vampire may be killed with a gun, but only if the bullet is silver. In folklore, guns may either kill or scare away vampires and revenants, even without silver bullets. One account by a Serbian immigrant states that a silver coin with a cross on it could, if broken into four pieces and loaded into a shotgun shell, be used to kill a vampire (Folklore Archives, UC Berkeley).

Transylvanian Saxons untied before burial both the bands with which the hands and feet of the corpse had been tied and the piece of cloth that held the mouth shut.[62]

Often the body would be wrapped in or covered with a fishing net, sometimes as a physical restraint (which seems to have been the case in Bulgaria).[63] There is also a report of a tribe of Gypsies who believed that vampires could be kept out of the home by casting fishing nets over the doors: "Before the vampire can enter the house, he must count all the knots."[64]

And here I might mention that, along with many other theories on the subject, it has been suggested that burial in a contracted position, which is so well attested for Europe and the Mediterranean, may be explained by the corpse having been tied up so that it could not return from the dead.[65] Certainly there is no doubt that bodies were often buried thus: even if the ropes have disintegrated and left no evidence of their existence, the bodies are drawn up in unnatural positions that are most easily explained as the result of binding. In the Naturhistorisches Museum in Vienna, I observed a skeleton of this sort, which the excavators had concluded had been bound. Also, the bogs of Northern Europe have preserved for us a number of bodies that were bound with ropes that, like the bodies, were preserved by the chemical composition of the bog water.[66]

Besides being treated differently, as by the use of various rites, the placement of apotropaic grave goods, and so forth, the putative revenant might also be quarantined by being buried away from other graves. Eventually the methods of quarantine were made official: the church refused to participate in the burial of suicides, which meant that they were obliged to be buried elsewhere than in consecrated ground.[67] This usually meant that a suicide was buried either at a crossroads or at a location distant from habitations. The latter led in turn to the practice of burying the dangerous dead at boundaries—that is, as far as possible from my place without trespassing on yours.[68] Boundaries, like crossroads, became places to stay away from at night, and their associations apparently brought into being one of the odder categories of revenants: those who move boundary stones.[69]

Much of the lore of revenants and vampires makes a certain kind of sense if one considers alternatives. This is true of the common practice of disposing of corpses in bodies of water. If the corpse is dangerous, one would prefer to be rid of it both quickly and in such a way as to ensure that it could not return. A deep burial achieves the second goal but not the first, and if the topsoil is shallow or rocky, it is not even always possible (Werner Geiger comments on these problems in a study of the burial practices of the Odenwald.)[70] In water, however, a body can be submerged within moments, and it is presumably for this reason that, now as in the past, people who wish to conceal a body, and to do so quickly, often weigh it down and dispose of it in a lake or throw it into a river so that it is carried away. Certainly the dangerous dead were commonly disposed of in this way.[71] In a later chapter I shall discuss the problems caused by such disposal of the body and their typical solutions as seen in both folklore and archaeology.

Many cultures have developed methods of tricking the forces involved in the reviving of dead bodies. Such forces, although they are a source of grave danger, can often be thwarted by even the simplest means. We shall consider some of these in the next chapter.

Apotropaics II

When one considers that vampires commonly infect others with their condition, it will become obvious that, if even a single vampire escapes the ministrations of the local people, vampirism may increase in geometric proportion. In a short time there may be more vampires than normal people.

This was believed to explain epidemics of plague, although it was sometimes thought necessary to find and destroy only the original vampire, not his every victim, to end the plague.* The mechanism whereby this happens is never explained, but I have seen nothing to suggest that, as in the movies, the vampire recruits a small army of vampire-minions intended to take over the world. The folkloric vampire is very much a loner; he creates more like himself without seeking to govern them or even, apparently, deriving satisfaction from their depredations. Indeed, his condition is intolerable even to him, as is illustrated by the fact that some of his kind—the Greek revenants, for example—can acquire their condition through a curse. A Serbian word (*ocajnik*) that originally meant

---

*In *Visum et Repertum*, however, all the vampires were dug up and killed, not just the one believed to be the first to be transformed.

"an undecayed corpse" has come to mean only "an unhappy, disconsolate person."[1] The vampire inhabits an in-between world, inaccessible to salvation. As we have seen, his acts are explained as the result of compulsions: we are told that he "must," not that he "likes to." He is singularly lacking in options. If it is a Saturday, and he is Serbo-Croatian, then he is obliged to remain in his grave, even though the citizens know this and will, if they suspect his existence, come looking for him with a hawthorn stake in hand.

That the revenant's condition is accursed is demonstrated by the tendency of our informants to equate "killing the vampire" with "giving him peace." This tendency is so strong that I am inclined to suspect a typographical error in the following low-German account from Mecklenburg: "Dormit en sülstmürder kein Rooh hett, stött men mit'n Pal up sin Sark."[2] ("So that a suicide would have no peace, they drive a stake onto his coffin.") As it stands, this statement is anomalous and unsupported by other evidence—indeed, it makes little sense to disturb the peace of the dead if doing so will cause them to disturb ours. But if one reads *sein* (his) for *kein* (no), then the report is one of many that equate killing the vampire with allowing him—and therefore his killers—to be at peace.

Because of the vampire's limited, rigid, and compulsive nature his numbers do not usually get out of control. As we have seen, a vampire may come into existence through the merest oversight. But if everything is done right, he will never come into existence at all, and his habits are so rigid that he can easily be thwarted.

This is most evident in the common accounts of ways to prevent him from returning to his former home. Since he must return as he left, a revenant can be kept away by the simple expedient of lifting the threshold and taking the corpse out under it; by removing the corpse through a window or a hole in the wall; by removing the corpse from the house feet first; or by pouring water behind the coffin to provide a kind of barrier that, however insubstantial it might seem, suffices to prevent the return of the dead.[3]

And the spirit world is easily tricked, even by the most seemingly transparent methods. According to Drechsler the Silesians believed that a dead person would return to fetch parts of the body that had been left behind (if he was dissected, for example). If such could not be returned to him, then one had to fetch a human bone from another graveyard and bury it at his grave.[4] And in the region of Vrancea in Romania it is said to be unwise to cry over the dead. Instead, one must dance and sing so that any evil spirits in the vicinity will imagine that they are observing a celebration, not a burial. "Sometimes, especially if it is a matter of crossing a bridge, two men who are especially strong will take hold of the deceased and dance with him."[5]

While this is the most dramatic of such accounts, others also suggest that one should not mourn excessively. The eastern Prussians were said to believe that, if one cried too much, the dead could not attain peace.[6] And the Bulgarians recommend against crying or making noise when someone is dying. "Crying, they say, tears the soul, and the sick person is tortured."[7]

As is so often the case, however, one can find an opposite interpretation of the same phenomenon, for a Romanian account suggests that paid mourners should be supplied at the funeral, so that the deceased feels that he or she has been appropriately loved and is not tempted to come back and harm the living.[8]

The rites that protect the dead, providing them with a peaceful transition to the next life, do not by any means end with the funeral. Often, especially in the Balkans, a secondary burial takes place. Loring Danforth, in a study of Greek burial customs, has given the following analysis of the procedure:

In many societies throughout the world dying is a slow process of transition from one state (life) to another (death). In these societies the burial, which occurs soon after death, is temporary and provisional, and the funeral marks only the beginning of a long and highly elaborated liminal period during which a person is neither fully alive nor fully dead. During this period of transition the corpse decomposes until all the flesh has decayed and only the bones remain. The end of the liminal period is marked by rites of secondary burial or secondary treatment during which the remains of the deceased are recovered, ritually treated, and moved to a new location where they are permanently stored.[9]

In the Balkans such exhumations usually take place some years after the funeral (in Greece usually three years). It is critical that the remains be found to have decomposed completely. The duration of decomposition seems, in fact, to be what determines the length of the period of transition. As we have seen, revenants do *not* decompose. In Romania it is said that an offering of forty-four jars of water is made to the corpse, seven weeks after burial, with the object of aiding decomposition.[10] Since moisture is necessary for decomposition (where it is lacking, the body mummifies), such a practice might provide exactly the intended aid. In any case, the Romanians leave the corpse in place longer than the Greeks (five to seven years) and then exhume it, or what is left of it, wash the bones, and rebury them.[11]

Figure 1. Ossuary at Hallstatt, Austria.

I found an engaging reinterpretation of this practice in the town of Hallstatt, Austria, where until as late as the 1960s exhumation was practiced after the body had decomposed completely, and the skull and long bones were then put on display in a charnel house that has become a tourist attraction (fig. 1). My guide said that this form of burial had come into existence as a space-saving procedure: the town had run out of available places to bury its citizens and so had taken to digging them up again, after burial, and storing their bones in a shed. He did not explain why, if this was the case, the town had abandoned the practice—perhaps more land had become available for burial sites?—and I did not point out that such exhumations had been practiced by the Celts[12] (Hallstatt is the type site for a very early Celtic culture) and continue to be practiced in the Balkans and elsewhere, not to save space but to ensure that the body has completed its decomposition and the soul has escaped to the beyond.[13]

These skulls were painted in rather cheerful colors, mostly bright red and green, often with a legend across the forehead that identified them and gave their dates. Many were painted with trailing vines; most also had a cross rather like a Maltese cross. Sometimes, according to my guide, the painting indicated the manner of death: for example, a skull with a snake portrayed on it implied that the owner had died from a snake bite. This too is probably a reinterpretation: snakes have an ancient and complex relationship to funerary procedures. One pre-Scythian (Bronze Age) burial, for example, yielded the skeletons of two large snakes.[14]

As noted, many means of preventing vampirism are identical to those used to destroy an existing vampire or revenant. Mutilation of the corpse is a common form of this preemptive strike. In Greece it has been reported that murder victims or executed criminals might have their extremities cut off and strung on a chain around the neck.[15] Such methods of preventing the return of the dead are not of recent vintage in Greece: Oedipus's ("Swollen Foot") ankles were pinned together when, just three days old, he was discarded on a mountain. At this age, he would scarcely have walked home alive. More likely he would have "walked" after death. In modern times similar mutilations have been visited on corpses to prevent them from "walking": the Serbians are said to have cut the knee ligaments of the corpse for this purpose.[16] And Wilhelm Hertz cites an Icelandic practice of driving a nail through the sole of the supposed revenant.[17]

Sometimes the head of the corpse was cut off and placed on, or at, the feet, a practice that Cremene reports as occasionally found in Romania.[18] But this is far more common in Northern Europe, and I shall discuss it in greater detail when we explore further methods of killing the vampire.

The body might have a stake driven through it for apotropaic purposes, so that it did not have a chance to become a vampire, and often the corpse was pinned in the grave by this method, as among the Finns.[19] This too was a common method of killing a revenant—virtually the only method shown in fictional treatments of the subject.

The last-resort method of dealing with a vampire or revenant throughout much of Europe is cremating the body. Cremation recurs throughout the ages in Europe—the ancient Greeks cremated about as often as they buried—and while various explanations[20] have been proposed to explain its seemingly random incidence (it clearly does not spread out from a single center),[21] the most likely explanation is that it was seen as the most efficient method of preventing the return of the dead. It is abundantly clear that most methods of killing the revenant are also viewed as methods of preventing the body from *becoming* a revenant. It seems plausible that this was equally true in the distant past. The assumption would be made that if a revenant could be "killed" by cremation, then its transformation could be prevented by the same means.

The ancient Slavs used three methods to deal with corpses: cremation, burial, and disposal in a desolate area. Though cremation is no longer practiced, clear vestiges remain in Slavic funerary procedures. In Bulgaria the corpse may be surrounded with flammable material that is then burned, the mourners may walk through fire or throw a coal behind them after a funeral, or (in Thrace) mourners may toss glowing coals down where the feet of the corpse lie.[22] In Serbia a candle is provided for the corpse to light its way in the beyond, and this may be used to singe the hair of the deceased if he or she is over twenty years old.[23] The easiest explanation of such practices, which are designed to prevent vampirism and ward off death, is to view them as traces of the practice of cremation used for the same purpose. It is clear, in any case, that whatever brings revenants into folklore is apparently nullified by cremation, for it has been observed that cultures that cremate generally do not have revenants that return in corporeal form.[24]

I should mention one notable exception to this rule: the Greek island of Thera, or Santorini, has long been considered to have a particularly thriving population of vrykolakes. The expression "vampires to Santorini" was said to be equivalent to "coals to Newcastle" or "owls to Athens."[25] In ancient times Thera was also notable for having chosen cremation over burial, even though cremation must have been an expensive procedure.[26] The inhabitants acquired a reputation for dealing efficiently with revenants, and Lawson cites two stories that "actually end with the despatch of a vampire's body to Santorini for effective treatment there."[27] It has been suggested that the presence of the vrykolakas on Thera, in such numbers, might be accounted for by the tendency of bodies not to decompose in the antiseptic soil of the island (a lack of decay being a particularly noteworthy characteristic of the Greek revenant).[28] Since Santorini is a volcano, its soil is very new. The present form of the island dates only from a volcanic eruption in the fifteenth century B.C.

Many traditional means of warding off vampires and revenants have become less common or disappeared in modern times. According to Danforth, the belief in revenants "is dismissed as outmoded superstition by most Greek villagers today."[29] In the past such beliefs were much more common. According to Vakarelski, in his study of Bulgarian folk belief, "Even at the end of the nineteenth century there were cases in which people drove a needle, a thorn, or a sharp iron into the heart, the abdomen, or the navel; laid thorns into the grave; scorched the deceased with a glowing iron; wrapped easily ignitable material (powder, tow, matches) into his sash; slit the flat of his hands and the soles of his feet with a knife; drove a nail into his foot, or even, toward the end of the eighteenth century, took his heart out—everything out of the fear that the deceased could become a vampire."[30] (Schneeweis cites such an excoriation from the nineteenth century: in Zajecar, in eastern Serbia, according to official documents dated June 1, 1839, the hearts of supposed vampires were cut out, boiled in wine, and set back into the body.)[31]

One need hardly point out the extraordinary fear that motivated practices involving the mutilation of a relative's or friend's body. In a study published in 1937, Alexander Petrovich described Serbian Gypsies returning from a burial: "This return home often looks like a real flight. They all go at a run, nobody daring to look back, because if the *coxano* sees him, he will think that the one who has looked back is calling him, and will then hurry after him."[32] But again, it must be remembered that the fear is generated by nothing less than death. They knew (as we do) that the dead person may well carry death to his nearest and dearest, but having little comprehension of the mechanisms of contagion whereby this can happen, they did not make the distinctions we do and shunned death in any guise.

A number of practices have evolved to ward off a corpse that has been transformed into a vampire. Various substances are deemed effective. One of these—and here, for a change, fiction and folklore come together— is garlic, which may not only be put in the grave but may also be hung around one's neck to keep vampires, and perhaps everyone else, at a distance. In the Folklore Archives at the University of California, Berkeley, I found several accounts of people who as children had been forced to wear garlic around their necks, and one particularly touching story of a girl who had finally quit doing so "because no one would play with her." I have found one account of an immigrant (from eastern Germany) who reported the use of wolfsbane (a plant that grows in the mountainous regions of Europe) and silver knives, placed under mattresses and cribs, to keep away both vampires and werewolves.[33]

Burkhart gives an interesting example of the principle of "hedging your bets" when she says that, as a defense against the *mora* in Yugoslavia, one may rub on strong-smelling substances: garlic, green nutshells, or cow dung that one has found on a hawthorn bush.[34] The last item combines the apotropaic forces of the strong smell—and that seems to be the significant quality of garlic—and the sharp thorns. Andree mentions another strong-smelling apotropaic: human feces spead on a cloth, which is then laid on the chest.[35] Similarly, when vampires are to be cremated, the wood recommended is often that of thorn bushes, presumably so that the apotropaic forces of thorns and fire are combined.[36]

The most remarkable example of apotropaic substances, however, gives a peculiarly morbid twist to the vampire lore. Many accounts over the past centuries suggest that the blood of the supposed revenant is an apotropaic against attacks by revenants. We have seen this in Flückinger's report, in which both the revenant's blood and dirt from his grave were said to have this function, and Perkowski cites such a belief among the modern Kashubes in Canada.[37] Indeed, Bargheer provides a recipe: in Pomerania it was recommended that one dip part of the shroud in the blood of the revenant, leach the blood out into brandy, and drink the mixture to protect oneself against revenants.[38] Whether or not vampires drank the blood of human beings, we have most persuasive evidence that human beings have drunk the blood of vampires.

Examining the uses of blood in European folklore would take us far from our original topic, but I might note that in Europe blood was considered a lucky charm. In a study of eastern Prussian customs, Lemke remarked that the blood of an executed person was considered valuable for its ability to ensure luck.[39] He does not say how it was to be used. Knoop remarked that in Pomerania if a merchant could just catch the blood of a beheaded murderer on his handkerchief, he could thereby gain clients.[40] Among the Wends, such blood, drunk fresh, was considered to be effective against a serious illness.[41]

Certain objects can also keep vampires away, most notably anything sharp, which, since vampires are about mostly at night, should be kept under one's pillow.[42] Such objects may also be put at the threshold of one's house to prevent the vampire from entering. One report suggests that in Serbia a wooden cross, placed over the door frame, served the same function.[43] When near a graveyard at night, according to the same informant, one could keep vampires at bay by making the sign of the cross, and Reiter says that tar, smeared crossways on the door of a house, is similarly effective. (Tar is also reported as an apotropaic in Morocco.)[44] In general, however, the vampires of folklore do not exhibit the violent reaction to the cross that is found in fiction, where its very touch is apt to brand the vampire with a kind of holy tattoo. Vampires, then, simply avoid crosses, anything sharp, and anything that has a strong odor—this last a curious prejudice, since they themselves are distinguished by a loathsome odor.[45]

Finally, some reports suggest that in Serbia the vampire can be directed into the forest (where he is likely to be eaten by wolves) and that in Croatia one may propitiate him with hospitality. "If his hunger is satisfied, he does not attack anyone."[46] As a general rule, however, when man meets vampire, one of them will die. While the means whereby vampires kill men are fairly limited, the means whereby men kill vampires are diverse. We shall consider them in some detail.

Search and Destroy

I saw the Count [Dracula] lying within
the box upon the earth, some of which
the rude falling from the cart had
scattered over him. He was deathly pale,
just like a waxen image, and the red eyes
glared with the horrible vindictive look
which I knew too well.
As I looked, the eyes saw the sinking
sun, and the look of hate in them turned
to triumph.
But, on the instant, came the sweep
and flash of Jonathan's great knife. I
shrieked as I saw it shear through the
throat; whilst at the same moment Mr
Morris' bowie knife plunged in the heart.
It was like a miracle; but before our
very eyes, and almost at the drawing of a
breath, the whole body crumbled into
dust and passed from our sight.
—Bram Stoker, *Dracula*

If the means of preventing vampirism—or warding off actualized vampires—are unsuccessful, then one must find the creature and kill it. This is, as it turns out, somewhat more difficult in folklore than in fiction, where the conventions are much simpler and more limited. In fiction, for example, the "native earth" theory often hampers the movements of the vampire, who is frequently under the obligation to rest, during the day, over soil

from his native land (that means Transylvania: fictional vampires are usually Romanian, even when, like Bela Lugosi's Dracula, they speak with
a Hungarian accent). Because of this, to find a vampire you need only look
for an unattended coffin with a squeaky hinge in the dreariest part of a
dreary house or castle—the basement, for example—at dawn, on a particularly dank and lifeless day, in thick fog or roiling CO_2. Once you
have found your vampire, you will of course wish to kill him, and this
is best done by pounding a stake into his chest with a mallet.

Curiously enough, the archetypal (fictional) vampire, Count Dracula,
does not fit the model well at all, for although he was resting on his native
earth, he was in a cart, not in his castle, when he died, and he was killed
not by a stake but rather by two knives. (His female vampire companions,
however, were killed by the stake.)

In folklore the problems are rather different, the situation less uniform.
The vampire or revenant might be of virtually any nationality—such
creatures occur (or have occurred) in the folklore of most (if not all)
cultures in Europe—and the coffin is seldom mentioned except with reference to its contents. He, too, like the fictional vampire, is bound by the
constraints of the world of the spirits, but they are different constraints
and different spirits. The "native earth" theory of fiction, for example,
seems to have arisen out of the (folkloric) belief that the vampire must
remain in his grave part of the time—during the day—but with few
exceptions folkloric vampires do not travel.* They are not itinerants, like
Dracula, and nothing is said of their being able to circumvent their
obligation to remain in their graves merely by taking with them a supply
of dirt.

Throughout much of Southern Europe, including Greece, the revenant
is obliged to remain in his grave only on Saturday, which thereby becomes
the usual day for his killing.[1] In Serbo-Croatia, this is because people
born on that day can see and kill the vampire on a Saturday, whereas he
can do nothing to them.[2] Knowing, then, that he will be at home on that
day, one has only the problem of finding his home.

> An old man died and they buried him.
> But a day later a healthy youngster died,

---

*Like ghosts, vampires are usually bound to a particular location, but in Kosovo-Metohija,
Yugoslavia, "the Orthodox Gypsies think that a vampire wanders far and wide around the
world, and passes through many settlements, where it is bound to meet a wolf some day and
be attacked and torn asunder" (Vukanovic [1960], 49). The principle of analogy may be operating
here: since the Gypsy people are nomadic, Gypsy vampires must be too.

> then again a young innkeeper, and so
> each day another person died in the
> village. Finally the only son of a rich
> peasant died. The peasant could not get
> over this and went to the priest and told
> him that someone was eating the people
> in the village, and that it was certainly
> the old peasant who had died first. They
> must dig him up and render him
> harmless. The priest allowed this. Now
> the peasant went with three others to the
> widow of the vampire and said, "Come
> along, little mother, because we're going
> off to dig up the old man." They took a
> large piece of cloth from her and went
> with her to the churchyard. They dug
> up the grave and behold! the vampire sat
> there, supported on his hands, with a
> blood-red face, for he had already sucked
> out a great deal of blood from the
> people. When the wife saw that, she spat
> out and said, "You are to disappear;
> don't get up again and don't move!"
> Then they pulled him out of the grave,
> cut him into pieces and tied him in the
> cloth. Then they threw him onto a thorn
> bush, set this on fire, and burned the
> vampire. Hereupon a strong wind arose
> and blew after them, howling, all the
> way to the village.
> —South Russian folktale

Sometimes, as in this account and in the case of Peter Plogojowitz, finding the vampire can be as simple as determining who died first of an epidemic. This is the one who is drawing the others after him, and when he is "killed," the dying will stop. But there is a regular technology of vampire-detection as well. Among the Slavs it is reported that one may strew ashes or salt around the graves in a cemetery to determine, by looking for footprints later, if any of the bodies are leaving their graves at night.[3]

One may also detect vampires and revenants by leading a horse through the graveyard, over the graves, because it will balk at stepping over the grave of a vampire.[†] Among the Albanians, such a horse should be white;[4]

[†]An eighteenth-century physician, Georg Tallar (p. 73), claimed to have been present at this

in some cultures it should be black.[5] Whatever the color, it is usually specified that the horse should be immaculately uniform in color,[6] sometimes that it be ridden by a virginal youth or that it never have stumbled.[7]

If these methods do not succeed in locating the vampire, then one must exhume the most recent bodies, in order of burial, and determine, by the degree of decomposition, which is the vampire.[8] Frequently, however, the grave itself will reveal the presence of a vampire, for it is likely to be fallen in,[9] or the earth will be freshly turned up.[10] Friedrich Krauss quotes from a Serbian schoolbook from the early nineteenth century that advises, "If the grave is sunk in, if the cross has taken a crooked position, and [if there are] other indications of this sort, [they] suggest that the deceased has transformed himself into a vampire."[11] Often there is said to be a hole in the grave from which the vampire emerges.[12]

Finding the vampire is complicated, as it happens, by his tendency to become invisible. Those vampires that we have considered closely—Flückinger's vampires, for example—were apparently quite visible, however, and it may be stated as a general principle that the vampire is least likely to be invisible when exhumed from his grave.

There is no consensus on how to render a vampire visible, but the methods usually involve sorcery of one sort or another, or, in one case, an accident of birth combined with a peculiarity of dress. In Yugoslavia, among one group of Moslem Gypsies, "there is a belief that a vampire can be seen by a twin brother and sister born on a Saturday, who wear their drawers and shirts inside out."[13] This would seem to be another example of widdershins, or ritualistic reversing. More commonly it is reported that the vampire can be seen by his son or by people who are born on a Saturday, the day when, in much of the Balkans, he is obliged to remain in his grave.[14]

Visible or not, a vampire may be detected by various animals, not just horses, a motif that fiction and folklore have in common. In fiction dogs are likely to howl or snarl, hackles raised, in the presence of the vampire, as in Alexis Tolstoy's "The Family of the Vourdalak."[15] In folklore this particular motif is not especially common—indeed, in one area of Yugoslavia, the Moslem Gypsies take a contrary view, believing that "there is no vampire in the village if the dogs are barking, but if they are quiet then the vampire has come."[16]

---

test on two occasions. He said that the horse hesitated—a circumstance he attributed to the piled-up earth and the smell of the corpse—but then, when goaded, went over the grave.

Sometimes the revenant is discovered because his grave is visible, usually by either a blue fire or a blue glow. In *Grettir's Saga*, for example, Grettir is attracted to the mound of Kar the Old by a fire on the moor.[17] The blue glow, in European tradition, is frequently interpreted as the soul,[18] and it is seen as an indicator of buried treasure through much of Europe, apparently because it shows where a body is buried, and bodies were frequently buried with valuable grave goods.

As with much of the lore of vampires and revenants, this motif may have a basis in fact, although the facts are not so clear-cut as one would like. According to Grace Partridge Smith, the "corpse light" "has been explained as caused by, possibly, an atmospheric condition or gaseous emanation from the ground."[19] Now since a decomposing corpse produces great quantities of flammable gas, mostly methane, there is little doubt that a "gaseous emanation" would occur at a burial site.[‡] The question remains, however, why it would be subject to combustion.

The question is complicated by another possible explanation for the glow (if not the fire) reported at the grave of the vampire. Luminous bacteria, such as *photobacterium fischeri*, can swarm over decomposing flesh and cause it to glow with a faint light—a phenomenon that seems to be reflected in the etymologies of two Greek words for "revenant."[20] Presumably the body would have to be exposed for this to occur, but pending further investigation—and I shall leave the experiments to someone else— the matter must remain in doubt.

> "About 2 1/2 years ago my mother, Eva D., died and was buried in the Catholic churchyard in Putzig (according to this it seems to be a question of Putzig in the province of Posen) in grave #1002. After the death of my mother, seven deaths took place in my family, one after the other. I do not know what the doctor determined was the cause of death of the last to die. I only heard from all sides that my dead mother had no peace in the grave, and therefore was drawing other

[‡]The flammability of the gas is not in question. Several reliable sources have told me that pathologists sometimes dramatize the presence of flammable gases in the (bloated) corpse by touching them off with a match when they make their first incision. For a more extensive discussion of the ignis fatuus, or will-o'-the-wisp, see Corliss (130–36), who has excerpted analyses of the phenomenon from scientific and meteorological journals.

members of the family along into the
grave. I was told by a number of people
. . . especially of evangelical faith, that in
order to put a stop to the cases of death
in the family, one had to help the dead
person to find peace. That could be done
only by cutting off her head and putting
it in front of her feet.' Feeling very weak
himself, and believing that he too must
now go to the grave, he carried out the
act that he had at first doubted. He
believes firmly that by doing so he saved
his life.
—Ernst Bargheer, citing an account from
a court case in 1913[§]

The classic method of killing a vampire is to drive a stake through his
heart. The scenic possibilities of this situation have been irresistible to
countless writers and directors. Count Dracula lies in a comfortably
appointed coffin, dressed formally as always. The dauntless vampire-killers
put a sharpened stake at his heart, then pound it in with a mallet. The
count's features contort into a hateful stare, he screams and shudders
convulsively. Suddenly—through the miracle of trick photography—his
age catches up with him, all at once, and he is transformed into a mummified corpse or a skeleton.

Our versions of such events in folklore contain little of this but the
tension and the stake, and sometimes even the stake is absent. This is
because staking is just one of many methods to dispose of vampires and
revenants, and it is sometimes a mere preliminary to their cremation,
since the staking does not always work, as the following account from
Wendic folklore demonstrates:

In order to free themselves from this plague, the people dug the body up, drove
a consecrated nail into its head and a stake through its heart. Nonetheless, that
did not help: the murdered man came back each night. Then they decided to

---

[§]Bargheer, 80–81. He (p. 97) made the interesting suggestion that this practice may have
brought into existence the concept of the headless ghost—a suggestion substantiated by a more
recent report from Lithuania according to which a particular kind of revenant, when beheaded,
must have his head placed at his feet so that he cannot reach it; otherwise he would wander
about with it under his arm (Balys and Biezais, in Haussig, 445).

dig up the corpse once again—it had been buried again—and they burned it at the Branitz pool and strewed the ashes into all the winds.[21]

Let us consider, in detail, the various methods of killing a revenant:

Staking might be considered under two aspects: the magical and the mechanical. While it is true that we may consider an act to be magical merely because we do not understand its mechanics (and we will see abundant evidence of this later), there are aspects of the killing of the vampire that are purely magical. We see this in the choice of wood out of which to make the stake: in the north—Russia, the Baltic—the appropriate wood for the purpose is ash.[22] I have found one account, from Silesia,[23] of an oaken stake being used, and in Serbia the stake is to be made of hawthorn, a choice that may be influenced by the fact that hawthorn is, as the name suggests, a thorny tree or shrub, and vampires have a pronounced allergy to thorns. (Among the Moslem Gypsies of Novopazarski Sandzak, a stake from a wild rose tree is used.)[24] Moreover, the word for "hawthorn stake" is *glogovac*, which is also the name for *aporia cratigi*, a type of butterfly.[25] The relation between the two things, stake and butterfly, is a close (if confusing) one, for in Serbia a vampire can transform himself into a butterfly.[26] Moreover, among the Slavs and in the Balkans generally, the human soul is believed to take on a corporeal form when it leaves the body, and one of the forms reported is that of a butterfly (compare Greek *psyche*: "soul," "butterfly").[‖]

But the killing of the vampire has a purely mechanical aspect: he may be killed by methods that would kill a living person as well. Thus he may have a nail driven into his head.[27] The Orthodox Gypsies of Stari Ras "consider that a sharp knife is as efficacious as a thorn stick for killing a vampire."[28] And we have seen that impaling (in this case with a sword) was among the various methods used to kill de Tournefort's vrykolakas.

The equation of the ideas of "killing" and "giving peace," which I mentioned earlier, is often present (see the quotation heading this section, for example). According to Cozannet, certain Gypsies pierce the heart of the dead person after a time to permit the departure of the soul.[29] Usually, however, such measures—among the Gypsies as well as among other cultures—are not needed. The body has its own mechanism for

---

[‖] This notion—that both vampires and souls can be transformed into butterflies—seems at first glance to be hopelessly opaque. Probably some form of analogy is functioning here, as in so much of mythopoeic thought. Perhaps the transformation into a vampire is seen as akin to that whereby a caterpillar is transformed into a butterfly.

ensuring the expulsion of the soul, or even scaring it away should it attempt to return: that is what decomposition is all about.[30] More often than not, the heart was the target of the stake, but sometimes it was driven in through the mouth (Russia/northern Germany) or the stomach (northeastern Serbia).[31]

As a rule, staking the revenant seems most typical among the southern Slavs; the Greeks preferred cremation, the Russians disposal in a desolate area or in a body of water, and the Germans and western Slavs favored the sort of decapitation mentioned in the account from Poland quoted above.[*] The head might be cut off with a sexton's spade, then placed at the feet or behind the buttocks, and often it was separated from the rest of the body by a layer of dirt.[32] Usually this procedure was, at best, messy, since blood was apt to spurt out of the revenant's wound. Such blood is dark,[**] according to a (modern) Kashube informant from Canada.[33] The view of blood in these beliefs is complicated, because it can be both a charm and a curse. In some areas we are told that it has an apotropaic quality and is actually to be drunk to ward off revenants; in others, that its touch is dangerous. Knoop, for example, in a study of the beliefs in the province of Posen, quoted an informant who gave the following account of the killing of a revenant: "Now a sharp spade was put on its neck and earth was put over it, so that the blood would not spray onto anyone, for that would have had a fatal effect."[34] In parts of Yugoslavia, among the Gypsies, the vampire must be covered with a hide or a piece of cloth before being staked, because "if anyone were splashed with the vampire's blood during its destruction he would go mad. Others think he would die instantly."[35]

As we saw in de Tournefort's account, sometimes the heart of the suspected vampire is cut out. In 1874 such an operation was proposed— to be performed on himself, on the occasion of his death—by a Romanian prince living in Paris who had been forced into exile because the members of his family were believed in their homeland to turn into vampires at death.[36] It is evident that he himself believed this.

Few vampires appear to have made their way across the Atlantic, but in New England in the nineteenth century there were a number of ac-

---

[*]Keep in mind that these beliefs are in constant flux. Such generalizations obtain for modern history, considered over a period of centuries, but are not necessarily in force now. Today, in fact—and here is another generalization—the lore of vampires is clearly becoming less common, even as the movies continue to exploit the subject.

[**]Presumably because it lacks oxygen, which is what gives blood its bright red color (that the blood is liquid is unexpected but not unusual).

counts of supposed vampirism, some of which were dealt with by excoriation. The following account appeared in *American Anthropologist* in
1896:

> In the same village resides Mr. ———, an intelligent man, by trade a mason,
> who is a living witness of the superstition and of the efficacy of the treatment of
> the dead which is prescribed. He informed me that he had lost two brothers by
> consumption. Upon the attack of the second brother his father was advised . . .
> to take up the first body and burn its heart, but the brother attacked objected to
> the sacrilege and in consequence subsequently died. When he was attacked by
> the disease in his turn, ———'s advice prevailed, and the body of the brother
> last dead was accordingly exhumed, and "living" blood being found in the heart
> and in circulation, it was cremated, and the sufferer began immediately to mend
> and stood before me a hale, hearty, and vigorous man of fifty years. When
> questioned as to his understanding of the miraculous influence, he could suggest
> nothing and did not recognize the superstition even by name. He remembered
> that the doctors did not believe in its efficacy, but he and many others did. His
> father saw the brother's body and the arterial blood.[37]

This author recounted other instances in which bodies were dealt with
in this manner—the hearts taken out and burned—and cited a doctor
involved in one: "Dr. ———, who made the autopsy, stated that he
found the body in the usual condition after an interment of that length
of time."

As has been mentioned, in Russia the treatment of the revenant was
somewhat different from that practiced by other Slavs. Vampires were
apt to be disposed of in a desolate area, but not buried, and often were
thrown into a body of water. The latter practice appears to have been
derived from the vampire's habit of causing droughts.[38] Löwenstimm
gives three accounts of exhumed bodies on which water was poured in
order to end a drought.[39] Presumably throwing the body into water was
intended to accomplish the same thing. In Russia even normal souls have
a need for water after death, and it is provided for them to bathe in.[40]

The relation of the dead person to water is remarked on elsewhere: in
one part of Albania it is reported that, if a funeral procession comes by,
any containers of water must be emptied; in Romania, that they must
be covered up, since the soul, being hydrotropic, might otherwise fall
into one and drown.[41] Here the soul is shown to seek water but also to
be endangered by it. (As mentioned elsewhere, an offering of water is
made to the corpse seven weeks after burial.) In Bulgaria, after a death,
containers of water are either covered or emptied; the water is no longer
suitable for drinking. Various explanations are offered: the soul had

bathed in the water, the dead person had drunk from it, or the archangel had bathed his sword in it.[42]

Some of these practices may reveal an awareness of contagion. They have another aspect as well. The Bulgarian soul, like the Russian, has a craving for water, a pitcher of which is likely to be left leaning against the cross at the grave.[43] Vakarelski does not mention what would happen if this custom were neglected, but in eastern Prussia in the nineteenth century, water was directly related to the body's potential to return from the dead. There the water used to wash the body had to be saved up until the burial day, because if it were poured away earlier, the corpse could not rest.[44] (I shall consider the function of water in greater detail in chapter 18.)

The disposal in a desolate area presented certain difficulties, for the body was thought to be preternaturally heavy. In the late nineteenth century, Lemke quoted an informant from eastern Prussia who, in remarking on a dead man who came back to haunt, said that it had taken many men to carry his coffin, taking turns, and that they had barely been able to move it.[45] Glam, the revenant in *Grettir's Saga*, was similarly burdensome: "They tried to carry [his body] down to the church, but they could drag it no farther than down to the edge of a ravine a little distance away."[46] And Vakarelski says that in Bulgaria, if a body is to be moved on a cart, one must whisper to the oxen that they are drawing a load of dirt or a living person, because otherwise the burden would be too heavy.[47]

Methods of killing revenants often occur in clusters: if one method does not work, another is tried. De Tournefort's vrykolakas was in this respect unexceptional. Mannhardt describes a supposed revenant who was dug up, decapitated, and then buried at a crossroads, her head under her arm and her coffin full of poppy seeds.[48] And Löwenstimm tells of a couple who, during a cholera epidemic in Russia in 1851, were dug up and decapitated, after which the heads were cremated and the bodies pinned to the earth with ashen stakes.[49] And Tallar tells of a body that was taken to a border and decapitated. A stone was then inserted into the mouth, and the body was cut open, washed out with boiling wine, staked through the heart, and left for the animals to eat.[50] In that order.

When a revenant is unusually tenacious, so that a series of attempts are made on its "life," the last method used is usually cremation, which seems always to be effective. This being the case, one might ask why the body was not simply burned at the start, without the preliminary beheading and staking (the Bulgarians hedge their bets: they use a glowing stake!).[51] The answer is that in some areas, notably Greece and Albania, this was done. Some scholars suspect that the custom of cremation may have originated as a preemptive strike against the revenant.[52] But because of the high water content of the average adult human body, the energy requirements for cremation are high: "An adult body of about 160 lb. (73 Kg.), cremated in a purpose-built furnace fired by gas, and with re-circulation of the hot gases, is destroyed to ash in three-fourths to one hour of steady burning at a temperature around 1,600 F. (870 C.)"[53] According to Polson, in his discussion of coke-fired furnaces, "In earlier types of furnace air was admitted cold and uncontrolled; fuel consumption was then high and each cremation required from 10 to 15 cwt. of coke."[54] (A hundredweight is usually 112 pounds to the British.) When gas is used, the time required ranges from 79 to 96 minutes, depending on the type of furnace, and the average fuel requirements range from 1,144 cubic feet to 1,964 cubic feet. An electric furnace—again, according to Polson—uses about 180 kilowatts to reach operating temperature. If oil is used to heat the furnace, and if the furnace has to be heated for each cremation, the average oil consumption "may be as high as 24 gallons."[55]

Without such a special furnace it becomes quite difficult to burn a body at all, because combustion can take place only in the presence of oxygen, and this means that the body will not burn on the side that it lies on or where the combustible material is actually against it.[††] Evans provides an analogy to illustrate this principle: "The individual pages of a book blaze readily, but the closed book hardly burns at all."[56] On early pyres, according to Polson, "Complete destruction of the body was impracticable, and, at a later date, these wooden pyres were treated with pitch and oil to effect better combustion of the remains."[57] The problem, in brief, lies not in creating a hot enough fire—that is easy—but in conveying enough of that heat to the body and for a long enough time to bring about its destruction. It is a problem similar to that of smelting metals: the Iron Age was obliged to await the development of a furnace that could conduct great amounts of heat to the iron ore.

This problem may explain the practice, attested for both early Greece and India,[58] of wrapping the body in (combustible) animal fat before cremating it. Achilles (*Iliad* 23.166–69) gathers the fat of many sheep and

---

[††]Eylmann (p. 228) claims to have had personal experience with cremation and says that if one lays a body onto a pile of wood composed of just a few dozen loads of dry sticks (*Knüppel*) and sets this on fire, the flames will simply scorch the outside of the soft parts of the body. People who cremate inevitably learn to provide the fire with good circulation, usually by means of a framework of some kind to keep the fire and corpse up: see Habenstein and Lamers (p. 123) for a photograph of an attendant stoking a fire in such a framework.

cattle and wraps the body of Patroclus in it before attempting (and failing at first) to get the pyre burning. Similarly, the use of ghee, or clarified butter in cremation may derive ultimately from its function as a fire-accelerant.[59] Early humans, after all, did not have gasoline at their disposal. This is, incidentally, the accelerant-of-choice for modern murderers, who frequently pour gasoline on a corpse in the expectation of destroying it, not realizing that the gasoline will burn away long before it does much more than char the corpse, while it will not even char those parts of the corpse that touch the ground and exclude oxygen.

Cremation, which seems to us so tidy a form of body disposal, is actually not tidy at all, and certainly not quick if you are using a furnace without good circulation of oxygen. Klapper cites several accounts of vampires whose bodies proved suspiciously hard to burn, one of which could not be destroyed even though the hangman used "an enormous amount of wood." The hangman was finally obliged to cut the body into "nothing but little pieces," but even then he found it difficult to burn it.[60] The Silesian shoemaker was cremated with about 21 cubic meters of wood, and yet another revenant required an entire day's work on the part of the hangman before he would burn completely.[61] Finally, the revenant Cuntze, of whom we shall have more to say in a later chapter, required 217 pieces of wood (*Bränn-Scheite*) to burn completely.[62]

When you add to this a consideration of the human element involved— the feelings people would have as they constantly turn Uncle Fred on the fire so that he roasts evenly—the limitations of cremation become clear. It is both expensive and unpleasant—hence most common among the rich, who can both afford the expense and oblige others to endure the unpleasantness for them. In ancient Rome, for example, cremation was most common among the patricians.[63] And according to Filipovic, it was usually warriors and rich or important people who were cremated in the Balkan and Slavic past.[64] In India, cremation is performed by a hereditary caste, the Doms, "a low-caste but very wealthy group who arrange and supervise cremations (an 'unclean' occupation)," and who receive a minimum of five hundred rupees for their efforts.[65] According to Rau, "Sometimes, if a family can't afford enough firewood, a half-burned corpse is thrown into the river. The very poor place their dead in the Ganges with no cremation at all."[66]

Besides explaining why revenants are not, as a rule, routinely cremated, these considerations may account for some of the "mixed rites" of the sort described by Audrey Meaney in *A Gazetteer of Early Anglo-Saxon Burial Rites*:

The excavators noticed that in the graves 'some of the earth appeared burnt', or 'the stones lining the grave were reddened by fire'. An isolated incident of this kind would not be remarkable; it is the frequency with which such statements occur in the excavation reports dealing with sites in the central part of England which helps to convince that the traces of fire are not merely accidental. Moreover, at times the signs are clearer. At Kempston Bd [sic] and Woodstone Hu a few skeletons were partially consumed by a fire which had been lit in the grave either before or after the body was laid in. Presumably after the fire had burnt itself out, the grave was filled in as usual.[67]

The discovery that it is difficult to burn a body completely, and quite messy to remove a partially burned body to a gravesite, may have led to the practice of attempting a cremation within the grave itself (a practice attested for the ancient Romans[68] and Greeks[69]). The advantages and disadvantages of such a procedure are clear: the remains would not have to be moved—an important consideration if they are believed to be dangerous—but it would become even more difficult to ensure an adequate suppy of oxygen to the fire, so that you could scarcely expect anything but "partially consumed" skeletons. If the body could be burned to ash, the problem of removal would be solved, of course, but as mentioned, this is a difficult undertaking, especially in a damp climate or where the fuel supply is limited.

Yet another problem must be considered. Burial and cremation are both extremely time-consuming procedures. In normal circumstances—when people are living out their appointed years and dying in an orderly fashion—both means are adequate to dispose of bodies. But in times of plague, which in Europe was sometimes blamed on vampires and revenants,[70] the survivors cannot dig enough holes or build a fire big enough for all the bodies, even assuming that they do not flee for their lives. In the Middle Ages, during one epidemic the bodies became such a problem that "in Avignon the Pope saw himself obliged to consecrate the Rhône, so that the bodies could be thrown into it without delay, when the churchyards were no longer sufficient."[71] Quicker methods are needed, hence the staking and decapitation. Though known to be less effective than cremation, they do not prove unusable just when they are most needed.

The most striking characteristic of these methods of dealing with the dangerous dead is their great antiquity and wide geographic range. Ludwig Pauli mentions a number at Celtic sites from the Iron Age: tying the body, prone burial, displacing parts of the skeleton, partial cremation, weighing the body down with large blocks of rock, orienting or positioning the grave differently, special burial places, placing wooden stakes across the body, including charms in the grave.[72] He notes one burial site at which thirty-two of eighty-nine skeletons were missing the skull, and others in which the skull was present but separated from the trunk, where there was no reason to believe that the grave had been disturbed (by grave robbers, for example). He suggests, in fact, that in the Hallstatt and La Tène cultures the danger from the corpse was often perceived only after burial, so that the grave had to be opened again.[73] As we have seen, this is common in modern times in Europe.

Paul Ashbee gives an example of a "butchered skeleton" from Neolithic Britain, saying that "decapitation was followed by an assault, first on the legs and then on the arms. Cannibalism was originally suspected . . . but there is little evidence for this practice."[74] And Ange-Pierre Leca tells of Neolithic tombs in Egypt where "in the intact tombs which have not been disturbed at all there can sometimes be found skeletons which are either completely broken up or which have parts missing."[75] He adds that another scholar had "postulated that it was fear of the dead person returning which lay behind the barbarous custom of dismembering his body, which would prevent him from coming back to haunt the living."[76]

Meaney also gives evidence of early examples of such methods in Britain, including some that she finds hard to account for (separate burial of the skull, for example). She says that it is impossible to guess "what the idea behind the throwing down of heavy flints on to the heads and bodies of children" might have been.[77] This practice is reported fairly often. In 1879, Bartsch reported, "In the villages [in Mecklenburg] it is pretty commonly the custom, at burials, to lay a flintstone at the head."[78] Wilhelm Hertz cites a similar account, adding that this is done in order to prevent the return of the dead,[79] a view that Karjalainen reports from the far north.[80] Hellwald reports that in Krain it was the custom to throw a heavy stone onto the head of the suspected vampire,[81] and Plato recommends, in the *Laws*,[82] that certain criminals should be buried at a crossroad with a stone over their head. The archaeological record of such practices is extensive,[83] and their purpose is usually to keep the body from coming to the surface and to keep animals from digging it up.

Flint may be specified because it was known that flint is a source of fire, and fire is a particularly effective apotropaic. The fire may be viewed as contained within the flint, as when Virgil (*Aeneid*, 6.6–7) refers to "seeds of flame hidden in veins of flint" (semina flammae abstrusa in venis silicis). The "burning" of the revenant is often merely symbolic. The Blums cite a Greek informant who describes people finding a grave with a hole in it (evidence that a vrykolakas was there) and putting fire in the hole to kill the revenant.[84] And they say that "'burn' is sometimes used figuratively to indicate prayers that are read."[85] Flint might also be expected, for that matter, to provide the deceased with fire in the afterlife, if this is conceived of—which it often is—as a place much like the temporal world.

Sometimes the similarities between such customs are quite striking and cross great barriers of time, distance, and culture. Modern Bulgarians leave at the grave the tools with which the grave was dug.[86] Apparently so did some of the ancient Danes,[‡‡] for Tollund Man, who dates from around 200 B.C., was found with a "short wooden spade of the Iron Age type."[87]

In such cases it seems obvious that we should look for similar conditions, similar exigencies. Both the Bulgarians and the Danes, for example, may have noticed that death is sometimes contagious and acquired the habit—a common one, as we have seen—of ridding themselves of anything that was associated closely with death.

Sometimes the dissimilarities between customs hide what they have in common. Embalming, for example, which preserves the body, and cremation, which destroys it, would seem to be intended for opposite purposes. Viewed another way, however, embalming and cremation prove to have identical functions: both reduce the body to an inert condition, a condition in which it no longer "does" anything.[§§] This is true also of excarnation and the various forms of mummification as well (drying by fire, burial in hot sand, and so forth). And in order to understand why

---

[‡‡]One could argue, of course, that this event may mean nothing more than that someone forgot the shovel. Nonetheless, the belief is common and widely distributed. A report from North Carolina, for example, states that "Tools should be left at the grave for a day or so in order to bring rest to the spirit" (Hand [1964], 7:92; see also Harva [1938], 286; Schneeweis [1961], 102; and Stora, 177–78, for examples from other cultures).

[§§]That it is the reduction to inertness that is at issue is suggested by the following account from Mecklenburg: "From the coffin to the door of the house, they strew ashes, because that which has burned no longer has anything that is living, and they sweep the floor right after the carrying out of the corpse, silently and moving backwards" (Bartsch, 95). This would seem to be a remnant—and these are common—of the idea that cremation can render the dead person permanently inert. Throwing fire and water after the corpse has, according to Bartsch (p.96), the same effect.

this is important, we shall have to find out just exactly what does happen to a body after death, if it does not turn into a spook. First, however, we shall look at some of the things the vampire is said to do.

The Vampire's Activity

Primitive thought naturally recognized
the relationship of cause and effect, but
it cannot recognize our view of an
impersonal, mechanical, and lawlike
functioning of causality. For we have
moved far from the world of immediate
experience in our search for true causes,
that is, causes which will always produce
the same effect under the same
conditions. We must remember that
Newton discovered the concept of
gravitation and also its laws by taking
into account three groups of phenomena
which are entirely unrelated to the
merely perceptive observer: freely falling
objects, the movements of the planets,
and the alternation of the tides. Now the
primitive mind cannot withdraw to that
extent from perceptual reality. Moreover,
it would not be satisfied by our ideas. It
looks, not for the 'how', but for the
'who', when it looks for a cause. Since
the phenomenal world is a 'Thou'
confronting early man, he does not
expect to find an impersonal law
regulating a process. He looks for a
purposeful will committing an act. If the
rivers refuse to rise, it is not suggested
that the lack of rainfall on distant
mountains adequately explains the

> calamity. When the river does not rise, it
> has *refused* to rise.
> —H. and H. A. Frankfort, *Before
> Philosophy*

The vampire of fiction has traditionally led an uncomplicated life, except when he wishes to travel and is obliged to take with him both his coffin and a supply of dirt from his original burial place.* For the most part, however, such a vampire lives quietly in his castle, having none but a parasitic relationship with his neighbors. The very name of the castle, when uttered by a visitor, will frequently send these neighbors into shock.

The vampire is not without energy and purpose, however. Often enough, he is shown to be engaged in an effort to do nothing less than take over the world, with the aid of an army of subordinate vampires. If one excepts his craving for blood, this power-lust is his sole passion and is seldom explained or analyzed. To be a vampire, it seems, is to be power-mad, in the grip of a compulsion not unlike that of our (folkloric) revenants counting their poppy seeds.

Sometimes his subordinates are all women, and his attacks usually have a pronounced sexual component: he is magnetic, irresistible, and deliberate in his movements, as though he knows that the lady really wants it this way. This implicit sexuality is suggested by the fact that, while he attacks men as well, he seldom does so in close-up, and both location and pace are apt to differ: women are attacked in their boudoir, in a leisurely manner, men in some dark place where they know better than to be, and quickly. The men frequently suffer their attack shortly after a well-meaning citizen has warned them. It is characteristic of such fiction that warnings are common, are uttered with the most intense earnestness—and are always ignored.

The actual attack of the vampire of fiction, deliberate as it is, can be studied at leisure in any number of movies. It is usually directed at the side of the neck and leaves two noticeable puncture marks, and it is more or less fatal depending on the importance of the victim to the story: the main characters linger on—like Lucy in *Dracula*—whereas the minor ones die quickly.

For all the intensity of his two passions, blood and power, the vampire of fiction is otherwise ascetic; in modern times he has become something

---

*Gary Larson, author of *The Far Side*, did a cartoon showing a vampire at a luggage carousel, in shock as he looks at his damaged coffin.

of an intellectual as well. In Anne Rice's *Interview with the Vampire*, for example, we see the monster in his existential dilemma, his condition problematic and agonizing, and—far from being a mysterious, evil presence in the background—he is the narrator of the story! In the past, to maintain an aura of mystery, the vampire himself has always been kept in the background, and the main character has usually been an outsider with an interest in vampires—a student or a scientist—who, by being unfamiliar with local lore but familiar with vampires, could get across a great deal of exposition in dialogue with the other characters.

However much the vampire dominated the action, it was only by being a background character that he maintained his simple way of life. He becomes more complex as he moves into the foreground, acquiring a conscience, a history (rather than merely a past), and both depth of character and richness of experience. In the past he was simpler even than the vampire of folklore. A creature of the night, flitting about in the guise of a bat, he pursued his victims until the arrival of daybreak, signaled by the crow of the cock, and then retired to his coffin to rest there quietly until nightfall. Though simple, this was a curiously effective career; often he functioned within the local ecosystem for hundreds of years, even thousands, somehow maintaining a balance between his appetites and the local blood-supply, until the arrival of the hated student of the occult or medical doctor who would slay him.

When they searched more carefully they saw Glam lying near by; he was dead, and his body was dark-blue in colour and swollen up to the size of an ox. They were horrified and shrank back from the corpse. However, they tried to carry it down to the church, but they could drag it no further than down to the edge of a ravine a little distance away. . . .
. . . A little later the people found that Glam was not lying quiet. Terrible things happened; many men fell unconscious at the sight of him, and others lost their sanity. Soon after Christmas, people began to see him walking about the farmhouse and were terrified by him; many of them fled away. Then Glam began to sit astride the roof at night and beat on it so furiously with

his heels that the house came near to
breaking. Soon he was walking about
day and night, and men hardly found the
courage to go up the valley, even on
urgent business. All this was a great
calamity for the people in the district.
—*Grettir's Saga*

The vampire (or revenant) of folklore, by contrast, while simple in some respects, is neither simple nor even coherent when considered under the aspect of his activity. If we examine the above account, for example, which contains first a description of the person of Glam, when his body is found, and then an account of his activities, we find that the two accounts differ greatly in how characteristic they are of the generic "vampire/revenant."

Glam's description is quite normal for such creatures: he has changed in color, and the change is—as usual—toward a darker color rather than "deathly pallor." His body is tremendously swollen, his appearance frightening, and he has become somewhat unwieldy, difficult to move. All this is characteristic not only of Icelandic revenants but of revenants as a class. Such creatures generally have a dark or red face.[1]

But Glam's activities have little in common with the vampire, because he robs people not of their blood but of their consciousness and their sanity, merely by appearing, diurnally as well as nocturnally, in their presence. Note the disparity between the assertion and the evidence: we are told that "terrible things happened," but they consist solely of someone walking about or beating his heels against a roof.

At the same time, while little here suggests other types of revenant—either the vampire or the Nachzehrer—Glam does have ties with other Icelandic revenants. He is not the only one, for example, who had an irksome habit of banging with his heels on a frozen sod roof.[2] Such a pattern—an unlikely event told of with great persistence—might lead us to wonder if we are not seeing a mythological interpretation of a natural phenomenon. It would be interesting to determine if a frozen sod roof does in fact make noises, perhaps with changes in temperature, much the way a frozen river does.

Among the revenant's functions is that of scapegoat for otherwise inexplicable phenomena. Since these are seldom in short supply and vary from region to region (weather, local customs, and geology all contribute to such variations), the revenant acquires different habits from one end of Europe to the other. Serbian Gypsy vampires do not bang on frozen sod roofs, while the Icelandic revenants do not turn over caravans, as do their Gypsy relatives.[3]

That the different revenants/vampires are similar, or even identical, in *appearance*, is easily explained: their description is based on evidence of a very different quality from that for their activity. For many hundreds of years (and even in this century) bodies have been dug up or found, all over Europe, declared to be vampires (of whatever type), and "killed" a second time. Such exhumations are extremely well attested, largely because they often led to legal proceedings against the "killers" of the vampire by either the local authorities or the relatives. It is only to be expected that the people of Europe knew what a vampire looked like: they were digging them up on a fairly regular basis. The seeming anomalies in the appearance of the body—the blood at the lips, the discolored face, the swollen trunk—are, as we shall see, normal concomitants of the process of decomposition.

It will come as no surprise, then, that the "historical" vampire—the one dug out of graves by concerned citizens who chopped up, staked, decapitated, or cremated his body—was a sluggish creature indeed who had little to say to his executioners and never defended himself against attack (in this respect, the fictional vampires are true to folklore). He was commonly credited with only the following responses: (1) he bled profusely when staked or decapitated;[4] (2) he moved convulsively when a stake was driven into him;[5] (3) he grunted, spoke, or squealed when the stake was driven in but not when—as in *Visum et Repertum*—a surgeon cut into him with a scalpel. Two such revenants, one from the fourteenth century, the other from the seventeenth, were reported to have spoken in complete sentences.[6] The one expressed his appreciation for the stake, because he intended to use it to ward off the dogs (dogs being hereditary enemies of vampires, for reasons that may become clear later). The best-documented revenants of this sort, however, are taciturn in the extreme: de Tournefort's vrykolakas and Flückinger's vampires offered no comment when they were killed.

> Here's a stay
> That shakes the rotten carcass of old Death
> Out of his rags!
> —Shakespeare, *King John*[†]

[†]The Bastard in act 2 of Shakespeare's *King John*. Note that Death is viewed here as a rotten carcass in rags rather than as a skeleton.

> The power of the vampire is very great
> and many-sided, even in his lifetime. He
> can kill people and even eat them alive;
> can bring into being, or remove, various
> sicknesses and epidemics, storms, rain,
> hail, and such; he casts spells on the
> cows and their milk, the crops and the
> husbandry generally; he knows all secrets
> and the future, etc. Besides this he can
> make himself invisible or transform
> himself into various objects, especially
> into animal forms.
> —Juljan Jaworskij (Galician folklore)

As we see here, when folklorists try to document the form and the doings of the vampire, they tend to end their sentences with "etc." or some equivalent.[‡] This is because of the fluid nature of the data. In other words, not only can the vampire do and become many things, but the lists expand as needed, depending on what has to be explained. A consideration of the above list, for example, will reveal that South Russian vampires typically do things that—in real life, not just in folklore—actually get done: people do die, storms do appear and disappear, cows do go dry—etc. Nothing here but the explanation—the attribution of the events to a vampire—fails to make sense, least of all the notion that a mythical creature may be invisible.[§] It might be observed in passing, by the way, that, provided the vampire is inactive, there is no difference, functionally, between the concept of invisibility and that of absence—either condition implies that you cannot see the vampire. An empty grave, for example, could mean either that (1) the vampire has departed; or (2) the vampire is invisible. In practice, the logic seems to be as follows: if something untoward happens, with no evident cause, then an (invisible) vampire was responsible. If the agent is visible (a cat, for example), and

---

[‡]Other examples: "He appears not only in human form, but also in the form of various animals: as a wolf, horse, donkey, goat, dog, cat, pullet, frog, butterfly (compare Dalmatian *kudlak* 'vampire, butterfly,' etc.)" (Schneeweis [1961], 9). The vampire can take the form of a "butterfly, frog, chicken, dog, wolf, horse, donkey, cat, goat, owl, mouse, or even a bloodfilled pod, a goatskin filled with oil, a haystack, etc." (Burkhart, 9).

[§]The vampire's appearance is consistent because dead bodies are; the vampire's activities are *not* consistent because they are mostly "scapegoat" explanations. This being so, they defy the format possible for the chapters on apotropaics, appearance, and so forth, and since I am not trying to catalog the material available, I have organized this chapter differently from the previous ones, analyzing a few events rather than listing many.

its activity seems atypical, then it may be just another visible manifestation of the vampire, who can, after all, appear in many forms. As in so many respects, here the vampire and the witch overlap: both may take other forms, both may make themselves invisible, the witch usually by applying a *Teufelssalbe* (Devil's salve) to herself.[7]

These particular Galician vampires, by the way, occur in both living and postmortem forms, and they are endowed with two souls, the proof of which is that they can sometimes be seen talking to themselves. Here again do not forget that the phenomenon observed—a person talking to himself—is scarcely unusual. It is only the explanation that requires serious scrutiny. Such instances prove to be so common in the folklore of Europe that we might do well to formulate a working principle to protect us from our own shortsightedness as we attempt to make sense of the folklore.

I propose the following:

1. In examining European vampire folklore, we shall begin by assuming that few of our informants are deliberately fabricating evidence. Either they are actually observing something or they believe that they are.

2. We shall make a sharp distinction between observed phenomena and explanation, for the one may be accurate while the other is not. The explanation will nevertheless often prove helpful to us in determining what the observed phenomena are.

3. When the "observed phenomena" make no sense to us, we shall try two further hypotheses:
   a. The language of the folkloric account may be metaphorical or inexact because the frame of reference is alien to our own. We must look for the "core event," peeling back the metaphor until we have something actual. This is less risky than it sounds, because metaphor tends both to be coherent and to reveal its secrets by how it varies from one culture to the next.
   b. We shall study the actual phenomena to determine whether it is our informants or we ourselves who lack adequate information.

Let us begin with a striking confirmation of this second hypothesis. Our informants tell us that "vampires" have blood at their lips when they are dug up because they have been out sucking people's blood. The core event here—as we have seen from de Tournefort and Flückinger—is something like this: "*A body, buried days or weeks or months before, is dug up out of the ground and examined.*" Before we conclude that the bloody lips prove that the body is not dead or that our informants are wrong, we must ask ourselves, "Do we *know* that a dead body does not have blood at its lips?" The answer is *No*. The observation—though not the explanation—was probably accurate.

The value of making a strict distinction is most obvious with such a statement as "vampires cause epidemics." Though our credulity may be strained by the explanation, no one would deny the existence of the described phenomenon. The epidemic is actual, the ascribed explanation must be discounted.

The matter can quickly become more complicated, however. Consider such a statement as "Albanian vampires eat intestines."[8] Begin by assuming that it might be correct in everything but its attribution of the act to a vampire. It seems to be excluding other events (that is, Albanian vampires do *not* eat muscle tissue). Consequently, we might ask ourselves, "What happens to intestines that does not happen to muscle tissue?" Dead bodies, both human and animal, do get eaten, because many predators are also scavengers. The next step is to try to find out what actually happens—how predators and scavengers attack bodies.

Some years ago, in a brief foray into journalism, I spent a great deal of time with a professional hunting guide, Eldon Bergman of Paso Robles, California, who at one time had hunted and trapped mountain lions for the state. Bergman showed me several blacktail deer that had been killed by mountain lions. This was evident from the condition of the corpse: the lion kills a deer by biting into the base of the spine. "The lion's first meal," according to Bergman, "is usually part of the ham, part of the loin, a few of the ribs, the heart, the liver, and a little of the lung. The next meal is the ham, shoulder, and so on. The liver seems to be his favorite food."[‖] In order to get at it, the lion eviscerates the carcass. As a result, the body cavity is empty but the rest of the deer appears to be quite intact.

Wolves attack a carcass in a similar way, except that some of the rump, which is apparently the usual point of attack, is often eaten first, perhaps because the flesh is exposed first. "The next parts of a carcass to be eaten are the heart, lungs, liver, and all other viscera except the stomach contents. The flanks and one side of the rib cage are often devoured quickly,

---

[‖]This report casts light on a Cherokee belief (reported in the late nineteenth century) that invisible witches dig up a body and take out the liver to feast upon it (Stetson, 12). Here again there is reason to believe that half of the account is true: dead bodies are dug up by predators, which often—hard as this is to understand—do have a taste for liver.

probably to allow entrance to the body cavity."[9] The members of the dog family, in fact, commonly kill by disemboweling their prey.[10] According to George Schaller, in a study of the lions of the Serengeti, "the intestines of wildebeest, zebra, and others are usually eaten before the skeleton muscles. Often a lion gorges itself on viscera alone."[11]

It is possible, therefore, that "Albanian vampires eat intestines" really means simply that bodies of dead animals tend to become eviscerated by large carnivores (small carnivores tend to attack the soft parts of the body, such as the lips, tongue, and sex organs).

Furthermore, the action of scavengers is not the only thing that could cause this to happen or seem to happen. We may have evidence of this from medieval art: a glance at the *danse macabre* figures from the late Middle Ages will reveal that, contrary to popular belief, many are not skeletons at all but decomposing bodies. Commonly they appear to be disemboweled, and sometimes worms or snakes emerge from the body cavity. Often the figures are shown emerging from charnel houses,[12] on which they were sometimes painted,[13] and it is clear that they are intended to represent bodies in a state of decay (fig. 2).

Why, though, do they appear to have been disemboweled? Here again, before dismissing our informants' testimony, we must make sure that a dead body would *not* have such an appearance. A human corpse, when left to its own devices, will typically bloat until it is close to twice its original size, through the production of gas by microorganisms that are already present, during life, in the intestines. Eventually the abdominal cavity bursts from the pressure, like an overinflated balloon, unless the pressure is relieved, as by an incision (or, of course, a staking), or unless the functioning of the microorganisms is inhibited. I observed this distressing process some years ago, when I happened on the body of a Hereford calf as it was rupturing from decomposition. Body fluids, alive with maggots, poured out of the abdominal cavity, much the way the worms or snakes emerge from the ventral area of the Death figure in the danse macabre. The latter event may, in fact, simply be a representation of the former, since medieval art is quite casual about scale.

For two reasons—the action of predators and decomposition—a cadaver will typically deteriorate in the ventral area first.* Our original statement,

---

*The matter is not quite so simple as this; not only may a corpse be embalmed or disemboweled in order to prevent this from happening, but natural processes—mummification and saponification, for example—can prevent bloating and bursting. In the case of the danse macabre figures, however, the depiction of worms in the ventral cavity suggests that the opening of the cavity was a natural process.

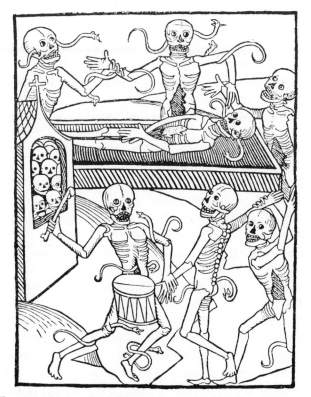

Figure 2. Totentanz figures, charnel house scene (ca. 1460). From Wolfgang Stammler, *Der Totentanz* (Munich: Carl Hanser Verlag, 1948), p. 15.

then—that Albanian vampires eat intestines—would seem to be an attempt to explain an actual phenomenon, the disruption or consumption of the intestinal area of a corpse.

It must be stressed that, our modern preconceptions to the contrary, bodies continue to act long after death. We distinguish between the two types of activity: that which we bring about by our will (in life) and that which is caused by other entities, such as microorganisms (in death). Because we regard only the former as "our" activity, we view the body as inert after death. Its movements, changes in dimension or the like, are not "real" for us, since we do not will them. For the most part, however, our ancestors made no such distinction. To them, if the body continued to change in color, move, bleed, and so on (as it in fact does), then it continued to live. Our view of death has made it difficult for us to understand earlier views, which are often quite pragmatic.

As we have seen, it can be useful to compare similar events in other folklores. From Bulgaria we have reports that the vampire eats dead animals.[14] If we disregard the attribution of the act to the Bulgarian vampire, we are left with a statement similar to the one respecting the vampire and his relationship to the plague. Dead animals are in fact consumed, just as epidemics do occur; the core event is indisputably real, even if it is attributed to a mythical creature.

Even buried corpses may be eaten by animals. Creighton quotes an account of bubonic plague from North Africa in the nineteenth century that illustrates this. "The graveyard is in the center of the village, beside a pool of standing water: the graves are shallow, and the corpses are sometimes unearthed by jackals. Both in the village and in the encampments a fall of rain was followed by a new series of attacks. The advice of the sanitary commissioner was to make graves at least six feet deep, and to cover them with lime."[15] The commissioner's advice ignores the reasons that the graves are shallow in the first place: in times of plague, deep burial is not feasible. Creighton quotes a similar account from the Arabian desert: "The deceased is buried the same day or on the morrow. They scrape out painfully with a stick and their hands in the hard-burned soil a shallow grave. I have seen their graves in the desert ruined by foul hyenas, and their winding-sheets lay half above ground."[16] Again, the shallowness of the graves is hardly surprising, in view of the fact that the grave is being dug in hard soil and with a stick for an implement.**

The correlation of a rainstorm with a new series of attacks on the graves is also not surprising. Rain has several relevant effects: it erodes the grave mound, loosens the soil, and may float the coffin (or body), while providing moisture that may encourage decay and also make it easier for scavengers to smell the body.

Since we primates tend to be diurnal, while many predators are nocturnal, people often do not see wolves and such animals feeding on carrion, unless they make an effort to study lupine behavior. In the past, however, when they did observe this, they seem to have responded in one of the following ways:

1. They would view the event as a natural one and tell of seeing an animal that ate dead bodies. Thus, in Stora's account of the burial customs

---

**Le Roux (755) has argued that the difficulty of digging in rocky soil with inadequate tools may account for disposal in trees, on platforms, and in niches in rocks.

of the Skolt Lapps, we are told of a graveyard that was moved to an island because the bodies there were disturbed by bears.[17] And Philip Tilney (1970), in an account of a Bulgarian peasant funeral, tells how long planks were placed over the coffin, allegedly "to ensure that wolves would not dig up the body and devour it."[18] And Robert Eisel in the late nineteenth century told of a body that had to be left out at night and was found in the morning to have been eaten by foxes.[19]

2. They would view the event as unnatural and, instead of altering their perception of what was natural, would conclude that the apparent animal was supernatural. Thus the werewolf is said to have been in the habit of "digging up graves and devouring the corpses."[20] Indeed, in one account this habit of the werewolf is actually used to define it: he is a "creature that dug up dead people and dragged off children" but that has now died out.[21] The French demonologists, according to Robbins, "distinguished a special variety of werewolf called *loublins*, which frequented burial grounds to eat corpses."[22] Since werewolves look like real wolves, and since real wolves do dig up and feed on dead bodies, it seems easiest to believe that such events were real—bodies were being eaten—but the animal was simply a normal wolf.

3. They would see the wolf as a real wolf, but the *corpse* as something supernatural. We have reports, for example, that wolves are "the natural enemies of revenants . . . and tear them up wherever they find them."[23] And according to Trigg, "Some Rumanian gypsy villages believe that many cemeteries are occupied by white wolves. It is only because of the vigilance and viciousness of these wolves in discovering and destroying the vampires in these cemeteries that living men are kept safe from a complete takeover of the world of the living by the world of the dead."[24]

4. They would view the event—a wolf attracted by a corpse—as a metamorphosis rather than a conjunction. Thus we are told, "By the tribe of the Kuci in Montenegro it is believed that every vampire must for some time turn itself into a wolf."[25] If an observer approached a feeding wolf, he might see the wolf leave and note that what was left behind was a typical vampire, quite inactive, and he might then conclude either that the wolf had killed the vampire or that the vampire had left its old body behind and had *become* the wolf. Among the Slavs, the werewolf typically turns into a vampire after its death.[26] Whatever else it is, the legend of the werewolf seems to be a folkloric explanation of this conjunction of wolves and corpses by people who knew little indeed about a predator that was, after all, neither easy nor safe to observe. A similar event may

be implied by Karjalainen's report that among the Voguls, "if a mother strangles her child or puts it under an overturned tree stump or a rock, to let it die, then the child transforms itself into a large-eyed dog."[27]

We will also not be surprised to see the same event—scavengers eating corpses—given different representations in folklore, some quite transparent, some opaque. Clearly this is at issue in Veckenstedt's report that in Wendic tradition ghouls are believed to dig up recent graves and eat the bodies in them.[28] A similar view seems to be implied in an Armenian prayer asking for the protection of the corpse: "Let not any filthy and unclean devil dare to approach him, such as assail the body and souls of the heathen."[29] Such unclean devils—if they are not the process of decomposition itself—would seem to be ordinary predators, many of which (foxes, wolves, and bears, for example) are used to digging: they normally bury excess food and dig it up again,[30] and Dr. Terence Allen of the Los Angeles County Medical Examiner's Office tells me that it is quite common for animals to dig up human bodies (murder victims, for example). They may even carry off parts of the body. It makes a certain kind of sense that Anubis, the Egyptian deity who presides over tombs and embalming, has the face of a jackal. Jackals would, in fact, "preside" over dead bodies. And such considerations would seem to cast some light on the question whether Apollo's epithet (Lykios or Lykeios) has something to do with wolves.[31] Apollo is portrayed as a plague god early in the first book of the *Iliad*—he inflicts an epidemic on the Greeks—and his association with death would, it seems, strengthen the view that his epithet relates to wolves, since wolves tend to appear where there are dead bodies. (They have yet another association with death, of course: in Europe they have always been viewed as man-eaters.)

One need not look far to find myths that connect wolves with death. Odin, for example, who presides over battlefields, has two wolves at his feet; Charon is shown (in an Etruscan source) with wolf's ears;[32] the Sabine priests of Soranus, the god of death, were called *hirpi*, or wolves;[33] and in American Indian (Woodlands) mythology, Wolf is the ruler of the country of the dead.[34]

The function of the raven—another carrion eater—seems to be similar: he is a harbinger of death who presides over battlefields (Odin has two ravens on his shoulders), carries off the souls of the dead, and decides who will not return to life.[35] We can get an idea of how such beliefs come into being from a Russian chronicle dating from the fifteenth century, according to which an army was presented with the following spectacle: "There were eagles and many ravens, which had flown up like a great cloud, and the birds played, the eagles screaming and swimming with their wings, and lifting themselves into the air, as was seldom—indeed never—seen; and this phenomenon was for the good."[36] Such behavior is quite common in the wild. I have seen similar scenes many times, with different birds involved, but the birds do not seem to be "playing." Rather, the smaller birds appear to be harassing the larger, which are usually predators, like hawks and owls, or nest robbers, like crows. As is so often the case, we see that if we remove the interpretations, such accounts contain accurate information. And when a creature "presides over" a particular phenomenon, often it is because that creature is actually associated with that phenomenon. Thus when we are told that in India the crow is the "bird of death,"[37] this would seem most easily explained by the fact that crows are carrion eaters. Similarly, the vultures depicted at Çatal Hüyük appear to have a ritualistic significance derived from their function as scavengers of the dead.[38]

> But the vampire does not just attack the living. Instead, just as he gnaws off his own dead flesh, he also eats from the clothing and the flesh of neighboring corpses.
> —Wilhelm Hertz, *Der Werwolf*

Now the matter grows a bit more complex. In the above quotation, we see that the vampire (actually the Nachzehrer) chews on his own flesh and on that of other corpses. By now we should be able to read out the core event easily enough—the flesh of a dead body is consumed or disintegrates—and we will presume to attribute its cause not to the vampire but to the action of either predators or invisible agents known to us (but not to our informants) as microorganisms. Bodies are found to be disintegrating, and our informants look not for the "how" but for the "who," as the Frankforts point out. A pathologist would merely revise the folklore, insisting that it is not a ghoul or vampire that eats the corpse but either scavengers or such microorganisms as B. coli, B. welchii, and so on. Why, however, in the account mentioned above, is the gnawing of flesh attributed to only one of the dead bodies? Why is it not supposed that *all* the bodies in the graveyard are Nachzehrer chewing on their own flesh?

Sometimes the situation is in fact seen in this way. Often, however, the matter is complicated by the fact that—as we have seen in chapter

5—not just anybody can be a vampire or revenant. Typically, the Nach-zehrer were dug up because people were dying of an epidemic, and the first person who died of it was regarded as the one responsible. As long as he "chewed on himself" or on his shroud, so long did the epidemic continue.[39] And while this is only one of many possible scenarios, it is usually true that the revenant is a special case—a stranger, a difficult person, "possessed of the devil," or someone believed to be a sorcerer. Whoever he is, he provides a focus, much like a scapegoat, for the apprehension of the community.

> In the dead of night stones again began
> to fly about above the houses in Lecani.
> They dropped like rain from the
> chimneys and roofs, breaking tiles and
> tumbling on to doors and windows.
> Archimandrite Leontije started to look
> for the exact spot these missiles came
> from, which could be easily seen against
> the clear sky; and, in spite of his being
> rather fat, he himself mounted on to the
> roof of the house from which,
> apparently, the stones were being hurled
> most frequently. And there he caught
> some village Gypsies in the act of
> throwing them, terrifying the
> superstitious folk who thought it was a
> vampire's doing.
> —T. P. Vukanovic, "The Vampire"

Because of the scapegoat psychology involved, the question of the vampire's activity is a very complicated one—made more difficult by the recognition, among some elements of the citizenry, that the vampire can be blamed for a variety of nuisances or criminal acts. Most of the things that vampires do happen at night and are not observed: in Bosnia and Herzegovina, for example, they "throw dirt and stones onto roofs," according to Lilek,[40] a habit that the Gypsies, in the above account, were evidently using to their advantage to frighten the populace. And de Tournefort says that the vampire scare in Mykonos encouraged people to loot the abandoned houses, knowing that their depredations would be blamed on the vrykolakas. Vukanovic gives many such examples, including one that involved his own uncle, who, representing himself as a vampire, romanced young ladies until one night a group of peasants chased him, with guns and dogs, and thereby persuaded him to end the deception.[41]

Since they did not catch him, presumably he contributed to the store of local information about the vampire and his habits. In this way the legend is constantly given new life.

In order to understand more about both the vampire's appearance and his activity, we will have to learn more about what happens to bodies after death. This should not be too distressing a prospect to the reader. How scary can a body be, after all, once it is dead?

Some Theories
of the Vampire

Almost as bizarre as vampires themselves is the principal theory with which scholars have attempted to explain the vampires. According to this theory, the "vampires" were people who were not actually dead but merely in a coma and who, on being discovered "coming to life" as they were exhumed, so frightened people that they were then killed.*

Unfortunately, this theory fails us where our documentation is strongest, namely in those accounts—such as de Tournefort's and Flückinger's—where outside observers looked closely at "vampires" that had been unearthed. De Tournefort watched the dissection of a Greek vrykolakas and insists that he barely survived the stench and that the Greeks burned frankincense to mask it.

---

*While many scholars have suggested this, the most extensive treatment of this theory is in Herbert Mayo's *On the Truths Contained in Popular Superstitions* (1851). Masters (18–22) quotes Mayo's argument at length. As Mayo himself points out, this theory has the distressing defect that it fails to account for "the universality of the Vampyr visit as a precursor of the victim's fate" (Masters, 21). The vampire is dug up, after all, because someone is attacked by him while sleeping, and since exhumations virtually always yield vampires, one is left to conclude that either (1) it is quite rare for a genuinely dead body to be buried, or (2) when a live one is buried by accident, it communicates this circumstance by appearing in the dreams of its acquaintances.

And if we use this theory to make sense out of *Visum et Repertum*, we get into similar difficulties. Flückinger's vampires had spent weeks, some of them months, in the grave, all of them—according to this hypothesis—apparently suffering from an epidemic form of coma.' And the surgeon's knife was not sufficient to bring them back to life, as the stake had done with Paole and other vampires.

Our problems do not end here. Even if we assume that the vampires were people in comas and that comas somehow occurred in epidemic form, then we still have not accounted for the reported changes in the physiognomy of the vampire—the blood dripping from the lips, the swollen, ruddy face. Surely we must dismiss the notion that these changes took place because the victim, in desperation, began to chew on himself, as has been suggested from time to time. In his book on premature burial, Hartmann cites a number of cases that were given this interpretation, including one in which it is said that a woman's lips "were bloody from the bites made by her teeth."² Sometimes it is suggested that this is done out of hunger, but there is simply no evidence that starving people chew on themselves to assuage their hunger.†

Recently scholars have attempted to account for vampires by reference to the disease of porphyria, a rare blood disease that disfigures its victims. As a universal theory (previously used to explain the werewolves),³ this explanation presents the same difficulties as the live-burial theory: it sounds plausible only so long as you do not look at it closely.‡ When one attempts to match it with our best evidence, such as the accounts by de Tournefort and Flückinger, one finds little if anything to substantiate it. Indeed, the exhumed vampires are often said merely to be unchanged from their appearance in life; we are given no information that suggests a disfiguring disease. And when Leatherdale says that porphyria "results in the teeth, hair and nails glowing fluorescently,"⁴ he gives no evidence—nor am I

---

†It is difficult to document a lack of evidence, of course, but I found no such autocannibalism mentioned in the many dismal accounts of the Nazi concentration camps—where many people starved—that I read while investigating the question of mass burials.

‡Illis's theory—that the werewolf mythology was based on the observation of porphyria victims—seems ingenious and provocative. Its principal defect, however, is formidable: in European folklore, the werewolf usually looks just like a real wolf and not like a porphyria victim at all. This is generally true of were-animals: "Not all coyotes are ghosts," according to the Jicarilla Apaches. "Some are animals. You can't tell by just looking at them" (Opler, 136). It would be much easier to find similarities between *fictional* werewolves and porphyria victims, because in fiction the werewolf looks like a compromise between a human being and a wolf. Obviously, however, Lon Chaney must not be adduced as evidence for what (folkloric) werewolves look like any more than Bela Lugosi may be used as evidence for what the vampires of folklore look like.

aware of any—that any such phenomenon was reported of the European vampire.[§]

David Dolphin, who was the first to apply the porphyria theory to the vampire lore, says that, since "a major clinical treatment for some porphyrias is an injection of heme," which would have been impossible in the Middle Ages, perhaps porphyria victims were drinking blood.[5] "If a large amount of blood were to be drunk then the heme in it, if it passes through the stomach wall to the blood stream, would serve the same purpose. It is our contention that blood drinking vampires were in fact victims of porphyria trying to alleviate the symptoms of their dreadful disease."[6] I shall defer to Dr. Dolphin's expertise on porphyria but must insist that before he relates blood-drinking vampires to the disease, he must first show us his evidence that drinking blood alleviates the symptoms of porphyria or was even believed to.[‖] His abstract, with its association of vampirism with Transylvania, suggests that his information about the vampire comes not from folklore at all, but from fiction. As we have seen, fictional and folkloric vampires have little enough to do with each other: folkloric vampires, for example, are never caught in the act, as both Georg Tallar and Johann Christian Fritsch noted in the eighteenth century.[7] When they are caught at all, they are either lying peacefully in the grave or, in their invisible mode, are chased down by a sorcerer.[8] Also, many vampires (the Bulgarian, for example) do their blood-sucking in their invisible form—their body remains in the grave[9]—and others do not suck blood at all. Vukanovic, whose study of the Serbian Gypsy vampire beliefs is one of the most detailed studies of this sort that we have, never once mentions blood-sucking. This supposed habit seems to be merely a folkloric means of accounting for two unrelated phenomena: unexplained deaths and the appearance of blood at the mouth of a corpse (see chapter 12).

Another recent explanation of the "undead" attempts to account for them by reference to our inability to conceive of our own death: "The quality of our thinking makes it impossible for us to bring about the conception of our own non-existence," according to Karl Meuli.[10] It is

---

[§]It is true that, after death, *flesh* may appear to glow in the dark because of the effect of such bioluminescent organisms as photobacterium fischeri. As I argue in an article in the *Journal of Folklore Research*, this phenomenon may have influenced two of the Greek terms for the revenant.

[‖]Dolphin, 3, also gives a clinical analysis to account for garlic as an apotropaic against porphyria victims (that is, vampires). Again, this is an interesting theory, but Dolphin has evidently made no attempt to test it, nor does he explain how the garlic can affect the porphyria victim by its mere presence—without being ingested, for example.

not his own death that is at issue, however, when a Serbian villager contemplates a "vampire," but that of someone else entirely, and Meuli finds himself obliged to patch over this difficulty by arguing that we cannot truly conceive of the death of anyone else either.[11] He makes no attempt to explain why some dead bodies come to life but others do not, nor does he try to account for the many reports we have of exhumations that yielded "living" vampires and revenants.

In the eighteenth century, when many of the famous cases of "vampirism" were publicized, a number of writers—Ranft, Meinig, and Fritsch, for example—sought to account for the vampires by naturalistic means. Fritsch pointed out that an absence of air would retard decomposition; that certain bodies—for example, those of thin people—decompose more slowly than others; and that certain conditions, such as a well-drained, sandy terrain, might be expected to retard decomposition.[12] He also argued that it is not unusual for blood to become liquid again, after death, or for hemorrhaging to take place.[13] Tallar pointed out that the "plumpness" of the vampire was merely the bloating of a dead body.[14] That their opinions have been ignored by later scholars would seem to be due to the inadequacy of their explanations for many of these phenomena: we no longer take recourse to the notion of the *vis vegetans*, or invigorating force, when accounting for changes after death.

Clearly we must begin by determining whether our informants—who show a remarkable unanimity—are telling us even part of the truth. Do bodies swell, change color, bleed at the lips? People who have exhumed buried bodies know more about such bodies than people who have not done so: the Serbian peasant has an edge on the folklorist. And the forensic pathologist, it would seem, has an edge on both of them and will be our constant companion through the next chapters.

The Body after Death

After they had opened said Cuntze's grave, as well as the graves and coffins of other people, there was found a suspicious difference in his body. For all the other bodies, which had come under the earth before and after Cuntze, were already largely decomposed, or completely putrid, but with Cuntze the corpse was undamaged, fresh, and complete—only the skin of the chest and head looked blackish, because in putting him into the coffin, they had strewn him with quicklime, so that he would be consumed faster. Under the topmost skin, which could easily be scratched away, another stronger [layer] was fresh and reddish. All his joints were flexible and the limbs moveable. As an experiment, they put a stick in his right hand, which the corpse held quite tightly with his fingers. His eyes were now open, now closed, and when they raised up the corpse, he turned his face first toward midnight, and on the following morning toward midday. Someone dared to pull off his stocking, under which everything was undamaged, the skin reddish and the

veins visible. When they opened the
other calf with a knife cut, the finest red
blood ran out, as from a living person.
The nose, which falls in first on dead
people, was completely undamaged and
not shrivelled. Cuntze had during life
been small in his person, and gaunt, but
his corpse was now much sturdier. The
face was swollen, the cheeks puffed up,
and everything in a vaporous state, much
like fattened pigs, so that the bulk of the
body hardly had room any more in the
coffin, which it had lain in from February
8 to July 20.
—Silesia, 1592 (J. Grässe, *Sagenbuch des
preussischen Staats*)

The body swells, and blues, reds and
dark greens tint the skin. Discoloured
natural fluids and liquified tissues are made
frothy by gas and some exude from the
natural orifices, forced out by the
increasing pressure in the body cavities.
The eyes bulge and the tongue
protrudes; skin blisters burst and the
bloated trunk disrupts. Little wonder
that Bacon was convinced that
purposeful dynamic "spirits" wrought
this awful change, and that some sects
have believed that putrefaction meant
"death pangs" to the deceased, and
therefore that any shortening of the
period of putrefaction conferred greater
comfort to the departing soul.
—W. E. D. Evans, *The Chemistry of Death*

The body undergoes remarkable changes in both size and color after
death, and these are unlikely to enhance its attractiveness. The quotation
from Dante's *Inferno*, therefore is intended as a warning label for this
chapter, like the ones on packages of cigarettes, to suggest that one's peace
of mind and of stomach may be at risk here. But, however distasteful it
is to do so, one must learn about the reality of death and decay in order
to understand the folklore of death and decay.

For the moment, then, our question is this: if a body does not become a vampire, what does happen to it? Within the context of our study, we must distinguish between the body's actions— the subject of this chapter—and its reactions, which I shall discuss later. The first category contains all those events, most of them really rather nasty, that occur in decomposition. These prove to be quite complex, because many variables are involved. We must also consider, however, what a body would do if it were treated as the vampires were. We know, for example, that a vampire is apt to cry out or groan when a stake is driven through his body. But what would a real body do in this predicament, if anything? Needless to say, experimental evidence is hard to come by in these matters—I have not driven a hawthorn stake into a body—but we may come to some conclusions nonetheless.

CHANGES IN COLOR

The blood, after death, gravitates into the capillaries of the dependent parts, to impart a pinkish-purple discolouration to the skin, called "hypostasis." If the body is laid supine, the back of the body becomes discoloured. It does not appear in those parts of the body in actual contact with the surface upon which the body rests, for example upon the back of the shoulders, the buttocks, and the back of the calves. The weight of the body is sufficient to close the capillaries in these areas and prevent them from filling with blood. . . .

. . . If the body has been lying face downwards, hypostasis affects the front of the body, or, in bodies which are suspended, as in hanging, hypostasis first appears in the lower limbs.

Hypostasis becomes apparent about half an hour after death, but it is not complete until some six to eight hours have elapsed. During this time it is possible to change its distribution by altering the position of the body, but, thereafter, the discolouration is usually

permanent because the blood has
coagulated. Although pink at first, the
colour rapidly darkens. When fully
developed, hypostasis is dark purple in
colour due to the fact that the blood is
no longer oxygenated.
—C. J. Polson, *The Scientific Aspects of*
Forensic Medicine

Because the oxygen in the blood is used up, and the blood, as a consequence, becomes darker, one might expect the corpse to become darker
as well. As the above quotation attests, however, the matter is complicated
by the end of circulation, which causes the blood to move downward,
impelled by gravity, toward whatever is the lowest part of the body. The
face of the body, then, is likely to be pallid if the body is supine but
dark in color if it is prone. Moreover, other variables are involved: if the
temperature is low enough, the oxygen may not be used up, causing a
hypostasis (also called "livor mortis") that is bright red, not livid, and
can be mistaken for the coloration that results from carbon monoxide
poisoning.[1]

Such changes in color result from a mechanical phenomenon—blood
seepage into the dependent parts of the body—but with decomposition
a variety of changes in color also result from "blood changes due to
bacterial action."[2] Hence the "blues, reds and dark greens" mentioned
above. Also, when putrefaction is rapid, as when death is brought about
by a septic infection, "the veins beneath the skin of the body generally
become prominent as a bluish-brown network."* And if the body is in
the open, the skin becomes darkened by the action of the sun, much the
way it does during life.[3] Finally, changes in color can take place with the
process known as saponification, which preserves the body: "The epidermis
vanishes as adipocere forms, presumably from a combination of decomposition and shedding, and the dermis becomes darkened in bodies interred in coffins, shades of brown and occasionally black appearing."[4]

---

*Polson, 224. The dendritic structure of veins is quite visible when they are outlined in this
way (see the epigraph above). In Switzerland, according to Bächtold-Stäubli, a visible vein on
a person's forehead (during life, that is) is called a "Totenbäumli" and is regarded as a presage
of death, and it is suggested that it is so called because of the ancient practice of burying the
dead in a hollowed-out tree trunk. It seems more likely that the name and the association with
death derive from the arborescent pattern of the veins of certain corpses.

DECOMPOSITION

Hamlet: How long will a man lie i' the earth ere he rot?

First Clown: I' faith, if a' be not rotten before a' die—as we have many pocky corses now-a-days, that will scarce hold the laying in—a' will last you some eight year or nine year: a tanner will last you nine year.

Hamlet: Why he more than another?

First Clown: Why, sir, his hide is so tanned with his trade that a' will keep out water a great while; and your water is a sore decayer of your whoreson dead body.

Glaister and Rentoul list the following external signs of putrefaction:[5]

- Greenish coloration over the right iliac fossa [depression at lowest part of small intestine].
- Extension of greenish colour over the whole of the abdomen, and other parts of the body.
- Discoloration and swelling of the face.
- Swelling and discoloration of the scrotum, or of the vulva.
- Distension of the abdomen with gases.
- Brownish coloration of the surface veins giving an arborescent pattern on the skin.
- Development of bullae [blisters], of varying size, on the surfaces.
- Bursting of bullae, and denudation of large irregular surfaces due to the shedding of epidermis.
- Escape of blood-stained fluid from the mouth and nostrils.
- Liquefaction of the eyeballs.
- Increasing discoloration of the body generally, and greater and progressive abdominal distension.
- Presence of maggots.
- Shedding of the nails, and loosening of the hair.
- Facial features unrecognisable.
- Conversion of tissues into a semi-fluid mass.
- Bursting open of the abdominal and thoracic cavities.
- Progressive dissolution of the body.

Only in detective novels does decomposition proceed at a predictable rate; in actuality, since a number of variables obtain, a body may either decompose very quickly, so that it is reduced to a skeleton after only a few weeks,[6] or it may be preserved indefinitely. The Cockburns mention a Chinese mummy, two thousand years old, of which "The tissues were still elastic and the joints could be bent."[7] Decomposition is aided by the presence of air, moisture, microorganisms, moderate temperatures, and insects and is hindered by their absence. It might be noted that in fiction—especially in old pirate movies—decomposition is often shown to be complete, with the skeleton remaining nicely articulated and brilliantly white. In nature, however, such a skeleton is all but unknown, not only because the different parts of the body decay at different rates but also because of the action of predators. I have observed a number of mountain lion kills (blacktail deer) that ended up, over a period of time, as scattered bones. Eventually, in fact, even the bones are likely to disappear, gnawed away by rodents.

The body may be preserved in a variety of ways, one of which, curiously enough, is burial in lime. According to Mant, "When a body is buried in lime, decomposition is retarded, and soft tissues are largely preserved."[8] In popular belief, as we see from the account heading this chapter, lime is thought to speed up decomposition. (The effect of quicklime on the corpse evidently has to do with how the lime is slaked.)

The body of the supposed revenant Cuntze, therefore, was presumably well preserved merely because, unlike its neighbors, it was covered with lime. Its other characteristics were generally quite usual for a dead body: the separation of the top layer of the skin; the "fresh and reddish" appearance of the skin beneath it; the lack of rigor mortis (see below); the bloating of the face and trunk; and the liquidity of the blood in the limbs, of which I shall say more in a moment. According to Dr. Thomas Noguchi, even the grasping of the stick would not be unusual, since the hands, being dehydrated, would remain in whatever position they were placed. As for Cuntze's "turning his face toward midnight," I am at a loss to interpret the writer's expression: for one thing, I am not at all sure I know which way midnight is. But it seems clear, because Cuntze turns his head when he is picked up, that the impulse involved is gravity rather than the volition of the corpse. And presumably its direction is interpreted thus because midnight is, after all, the time when the spirit world is at its most powerful.

There are some remarkable examples of the preservation of bodies. Some of the so-called bog bodies of Northern Europe—notably Tollund Man, who dates from the Iron Age—remain quite intact. According to Christian Fischer,

The reason for the preservation of the bog bodies (and of other organisms also) lies in the special physical and biochemical makeup of the bog, above all the absence of oxygen and the high antibiotic concentration. The manner in which the body was deposited is also of great importance—for example, placed in the bog in such a way that air was rapidly excluded. It is important not only that the bog water contained a high concentration of antibiotics but also that the weather was cold enough (less than 4° C) to prevent rapid decomposition of the body. If the body had been deposited in warm weather, one can assume that the presence of anaerobic bacteria in the intestinal system would have had a destructive effect on the interior of the corpse before the liquid of the bog could penetrate the body."[9]

What the clown in *Hamlet* proposes in jest actually happens to bodies buried in bogs.

When a body that has failed to decompose comes to the attention of the populace, theories explaining the apparent anomaly are likely to spring into being. Such theories will either assume that the events were natural and try to account for them by scientific or pseudoscientific explanations or view them as supernatural. Historically, at least in Christian tradition, supernatural explanations have tended to be of two varieties: either the body had been reanimated somehow—it was a vampire or revenant—or it was the former dwelling place of a saint and so was immune to decay. From the point of view of the body, the former explanation involved more risk than the latter: the vampire would be destroyed. But the saintly version of the intact corpse was unlikely to be left alone either, for relic hunters might well disassemble it; at the very least it would be put on display, chivied about, and perhaps stolen by someone who felt a need for its aura of sanctity. Thus the body of Saint Cuthbert had a long and varied history after his death in A.D. 687, and this history included a visit from the bones of the Venerable Bede, which were placed in the coffin by Aelfred. For at least 850 years, however, the body apparently remained intact, until eventually, in the nineteenth century, it was found to have been reduced to a skeleton.[10]

Presumably Saint Cuthbert was preserved by saponification, a form of postmortem change "in which there is alteration of the appearance and consistency of the fatty tissues of the body consequent upon the trans- formation of the neutral fat into new compounds, mostly fatty acids."[11] The compound itself is known as adipocere. According to Evans, "In bodies with complete conversion of the fat to adipocere, a pink-to-red colour is present in the depths of large muscles and it is occasionally, though not often, seen throughout some muscles. . . . In a few instances the reddish colour seen immediately on cutting into a muscle has been bright enough to give the impression of muscle freshly dead, even though the death occurred more than 100 years previously."[12]

It is clear that such bodies—preserved by saponification or mummification—contributed to the vampire lore. But both processes do quite distinctive things to the corpse, and our best-attested vampires were clearly not mummified—the presence of liquid blood excludes that possibility—and were not buried long enough for saponification to have taken place.

What then was inhibiting decomposition?

The answer to that question is twofold: First, while our informants invariably say that "the body had not decomposed,"[13] they almost always present evidence that it really was decomposing. A comparison of Glaister and Rentoul's list, for example, with the descriptions of vampires, will reveal that the events of decomposition and those of the folklore correspond nicely. Flückinger's Miliza, for example, had in common with countless other vampires the fact that she had "come to [a] surprising plumpness in the grave." Our Silesian shoemaker was found "undamaged, greatly bloated," and it was noted that the skin of the body's feet had fallen away and that new skin had grown. Indeed, in the Kosova District in Yugoslavia, according to Vukanovic, the Orthodox Gypsies believe that, if a corpse swells before burial, it will probably become a vampire.[14] Here the bloating is viewed as prognostic of the condition of vampirism. And Schmidt cites the belief that, in Greece, the swelling of the body is viewed as an "unmistakable sign" that the deceased is a vrykolakas.[15]

The bloating occurs because the microorganisms of decomposition produce gas, mostly methane, throughout the tissues, and this gas, lacking an escape route, collects both in the tissues and in the body cavities. According to Fisher, "It is not uncommon to see advanced decomposition within twelve to eighteen hours, to the point that facial features are no longer recognizable, most of the hair slips away from the scalp, and the entire body becomes swollen to two or three times normal size."[16] That this is a normal event in decomposition was pointed out in 1732 by the Royal Prussian Society of Science, although without leaving the slightest trace, as near as I can tell, in the literature of vampirism.[17]

The sloughing away of the outer layer of skin—as we have seen with several vampires—is also a normal event, known as "skin slippage," and the skin underneath is not "new" but simply raw-looking. The same is true of the nails that were said to have fallen away, leaving "new" nails. (The embalmers of ancient Egypt were aware of this phenomenon and dealt with it either by tying the nails to the fingers and toes or by putting metal thimbles over the tip of each finger or toe.)[18] Sometimes the revenant is believed to have chewed on his nails—causing them to fall off.[19] Similarly, the discoloration of the face (attested for countless vampires and revenants) is a normal event, as is the emission of blood-stained fluid from the mouth and nose.

Another factor is also present, however. Of all of Flückinger's vampires, only Miliza was said to be bloated. How did she differ? A comparison of the cases reveals two differences: first, according to Flückinger, she had died after a three-month period of illness, whereas the others, with one exception, had been ill only briefly. And the exception, the young man named Rhade, had remained buried for a shorter time (five weeks as opposed to her three months). Again, the medical facts seem to fit nicely, for, according to Glaister and Rentoul, "bodies of persons dying suddenly in apparent health decompose less quickly than those of persons dying from acute or chronic diseases, especially infective diseases."[20]

Miliza had also been buried longer than all but one of the others (a child who had also been buried for three months),[†] and had therefore had more of an opportunity to decompose. If that still seems like a long time for her body to have remained more or less intact, it must be remembered that burial alters considerably the factors that influence decomposition: the presence of air, moisture, microorganisms, moderate temperatures, and insects. It is because of this that, according to Glaister and Rentoul, "It may be accepted as a general principle that a body decomposes in air twice as quickly as in water, and eight times as rapidly as in earth."[21]

When we add to these considerations the fact that the bodies were almost certainly kept cool—Flückinger's report is dated January 26, 1732—it seems clear that nothing untoward had taken place with them at all. They were simply decomposing on schedule, showing various symptoms characteristic of bodies in a state of decay: the falling away of nails and skin, bloating, and—yes—even *obvious* decomposition, in the case not only of several nonvampires but of Stana (a vampire) as well.

Curiously enough, the awareness of the variability of decomposition actually made its way into a standard book on the subject of vampires.

[†]The child was only eight days old and might mummify merely because the surface-to-volume ratio of the body would favor rapid cooling and dehydration. Also, newborn babies tend to mummify because they have not acquired the intestinal flora that bring about decomposition. Rather than dismiss such possibilities merely because they seem, at first glance, to be anomalous, we must find out what would happen in the circumstances described, always keeping in mind Smith's Law: "Anything that did happen, can happen."

Montague Summers, the collector of occult miscellany, maintained three distinct views of one event:

1. That it is not unusual for great variations to obtain in normal decomposition. He quotes three doctors on the matter, one of whom says, "I have seen bodies buried two months that have shown fewer of the changes produced by putrefaction than others dead but a week."[22]

2. That when a *saint's* body fails to decompose, however, it is a great miracle: "It must then be carefully borne in mind that the preservation of the bodies of saints is a very remarkable miracle, and is in no wise to be compared with that preservation of bodies which may occur from time to time under conditions with which we are imperfectly acquainted."[23]

3. That when a *vampire* fails to decompose, another great miracle is taking place, this one of a quite different type: "The vampire has a body, and it is his own body. He is neither dead nor alive; but living in death."[24]

This blithe indifference to coherence will serve us as a good example of mythopoeic thought, which does not insist on consistency but considers events separately, allowing each an independent existence. This is not an entirely incomprehensible position: dead bodies do, after all, differ, if only because their development is subject to many physical laws. It is because of this, also, that a seeming anomaly of folklore occurs: the reader will have noticed, by now, that the "undead" are not necessarily evil—often they are themselves victims: they include people who have been murdered, struck by lightning, drowned, or have committed suicide. All such dead bodies have something in common, but it is not their attitude toward their fellow man: it is these people, rather than those who die peacefully in bed, who are apt to be left undiscovered long enough to develop into monsters, growing in size, changing color, shedding their skin—in short, undergoing all the diverse changes that we have seen in the "vampires" and doing so in full view rather than under the ground. They are the ones, as Joachim Sell has said, who have lost their human form.[25] Needless to say, this is true also of those bodies that are exhumed after burial.

I mentioned that most "vampires" were dug up quite soon after burial—Flückinger's vampires, for example, had been interred for three months at the longest—and the reason for this is close at hand: it was only because the "vampire was killing people" (that is, people were dying) that the body was dug up at all: if no one died, then the deceased was presumably not a vampire. The following factors would seem to determine the time limits involved:

1. Until others died of the disease, or other distressing events were noticed, there would be no need to kill the vampire.
2. Normally a lag would be caused by the reluctance to take such a drastic step as that of digging up a dead acquaintance and mutilating the body. Phillip Rohr (*de masticatione mortuorum* [1679]) mentions this problem, saying that, typically, the relatives of the deceased "most strongly oppose any scheme of disinterment. Hence arise numberless quarrels, blasphemies, and much false swearing not unmixed with violence."[26]
3. Sometimes there is a lag caused by an attempt to get the local authorities involved. We have seen this with both Flückinger's vampires and with Peter Plogojowitz.
4. Eventually an epidemic runs its course. After it had died out, presumably there would no longer be a need to end it by killing the vampire.
5. Also, eventually the grave site would become stable, thereby ceasing to draw attention to itself by cracks, holes, and the like. Swedish law assumes that this happens within six months, for only after that time is the grave considered stable enough to erect a headstone on it.[27]

But if there were natural limits to how soon and how late the vampire would be dug up, there were apparently no limits at all to what was considered suspicious behavior on the part of the dead body. Elwood Trigg, in a discussion of Gypsy beliefs, says, "If, after a period of time, [the body] remains incorrupt, exactly as it was buried, or if it appears to be swollen and black in color, having undergone some dreadful change in appearance, suspicions of vampirism are confirmed."[28] Note that what is being said here is that if the body remains as it was, then it is a vampire, whereas if it changes—then it is a vampire. Since these are the only options available to the body—decomposition and lack of same—and since both are considered presumptive evidence of vampirism, there is a strong likelihood, if it is dug up at all, that it will be viewed as a vampire and "killed."

The evidence from exhumations seems to bear this out: in the entire literature, I have so far found only two instances of exhumations that failed to yield a "vampire,"[29] although in some instances an observer saw a dead body while others saw a revenant or vampire (de Tournefort's, for example).[30] With so many options at its disposal, the body is almost certain to do something unexpected, hence scary, such as showing blood at the lips. Note, however, that most of the material on the subject was collected in past centuries and shows a natural bias for the dramatic and the exotic, so that an exhumation that did *not* yield a vampire could be expected to be an early dropout from the folklore and hence from the literature.

The fluid blood flowing through the canals of the body seems to form a greater difficulty; but physical reasons may be given for this. It might very well happen that the heat of the sun warming the nitrous and sulphureous particles which are found in those earths that are proper for preserving the body, those particles having incorporated themselves in the newly interred corpses, ferment, decoagulate, and melt the curdled blood, render it liquid, and give it the power of flowing by degrees through all the channels.

This opinion appears so much the more probable from its being confirmed by an experiment. If you boil in a glass or earthen vessel one part of chyle, or milk, mixed with two parts of cream of tartar, the liquor will turn from white to red, because the tartaric salt will have rarified and entirely dissolved the most oily part of the milk, and converted it into a kind of blood. That which is formed in the vessels of the body is a little redder, but it is not thicker; it is, then, not impossible that the heat may cause a fermentation which produces nearly the same effects as this experiment. And this will be found easier, if we consider that the juices of the flesh and bones resemble chyle very much, and that the fat and marrow are the most oily parts of the chyle. Now all these particles in fermenting must, by

the rule of the experiment, be changed
into a kind of blood. Thus, besides that
which has been decoagulated and melted,
the pretended vampires shed also that
blood which must be formed from the
melting of the fat and marrow.
—Dom Calmet, *The Phantom World*

Calmet's theory, however imaginative it is, has been ignored by the world of science, and I quote it only because it illustrates dramatically how very puzzling it was to people that a body full of blood would bleed when cut open. Presumably the vampire-killers expected the blood to remain coagulated. I say "presumably" because we are never told what our informants expected the blood to do, only that they were astonished to find that it was "fresh," a finding that de Tournefort disputes rather vigorously.

That the blood is liquid, however, is no cause for surprise. Blood does coagulate after death, but then, depending on how death occurred, it either remains coagulated or liquifies once again. Its tendency to reliquify shows a remarkably neat correlation with our evidence concerning vampirism, because it tends to do so when death has been sudden, as from concussion, suffocation, electrocution (worldwide, people struck by lightning tend to be among the dangerous dead), or following a short attack of angina pectoris.[31] The decisive event, according to Ponsold, is the sudden removal of oxygen, which is characteristic not only of death by smothering but also of deaths that involve a sudden end to the functions of either the heart or the central nervous system.[32] According to Mant, in fact, "It is clear that uncoagulable fluid blood is normally present in the limb vessels and often in the heart of any healthy person who dies a sudden natural or unnatural death from almost any cause."[33]

Here we see another reason why, as we have already noted, vampires and revenants tend to be those who have died "before their time," such as murder victims, suicides, and those struck by lightning.[‡] Presumably the suddenness of their death, not its timing, is the relevant factor. Not only do they decompose differently (more slowly), but their blood reliquifies. The liquidity of the blood, not surprisingly, has other reflexes in folklore besides those associated with vampirism—most notably, the be-

---

[‡]According to Plutarch, the bodies of those struck by lightning were believed to be incorruptible (*Mor.*, 665c, quoted in Garland, 99). Because of the suddenness of such a death, decomposition should be slowed down.

lief that a corpse will bleed in the presence of its murderer, which I shall discuss later.[34]

The appearance of blood at the mouth, which was so distressing to the exhumers of Peter Plogojowitz, is also normal. As noted above, once blood is no longer circulating, its movement is determined by gravity. Consequently it tends to pool, and Ponsold observes that pooling in the intestinal cavity can be mistaken for hemorrhaging.[35] Flückinger remarked on this phenomenon several times and was clearly puzzled by it: it is sometimes taken for more evidence that the vampire has been gorging on blood. If the body is lying face down, then the trachea is apt to be in the vicinity of pooling blood, which tends to seep out through the mouth and nose. Ponsold remarks that this seepage should not be mistaken for evidence of an inflammation of the lungs—yet another source of blood at the lips and nose.[§] Here again we have a remarkably close fit with the folklore of vampirism, for, as noted in chapter 7, the putative vampire was typically buried face down.

But blood migrates to the mouth and nose in the course of decomposition as well. According to Mant, "The gases in the abdomen increase in pressure as the putrefactive processes advance and the lungs are forced upwards and decomposing blood escapes from the mouth and nostrils."[36] Such blood, appearing at the mouth of the corpse, was apparently a principal cause of the belief that the vampire sucked blood (as we have seen with Peter Plogojowitz). I have found one account in which the blood-stained fluid is regarded as a natural part of decomposition: according to Bartsch, in Mecklenburg it was considered important to keep any cloth away from the mouth, "so that the moisture that issues from the mouth, with the decomposition of the body, does not directly touch the shroud."[37] As we have seen, if any cloth touches the mouth of the corpse, the corpse is apt to begin to chew on it, thereby bringing about the death of the friends and relatives of the deceased through an agency that is never really explained. If a corpse does not really eat its shroud—or its extremities, as is also reported—then we are left with the following question: what, if anything, was being observed? Bartsch's observation suggests that they were observing the effect of capillary attraction on the shroud. The moisture would presumably cause the shroud to be plastered against the

---

[§]Ponsold, 292. Any disease that causes disintegration of the lung tissue can cause blood to appear at the lips. Both pneumonic plague and tuberculosis do this, and both have been associated with vampirism, presumably by analogy with the tendency of the corpse to exhibit blood at the mouth.

mouth, so that it would adhere to the mouth as it dried. The plausibility of this supposition is suggested by the fact that, according to our sources, the event could be prevented by the simple expedient of keeping any cloth away from the mouth of the corpse.

As for "chewing" its own limbs, this would seem to be merely a typical interpretation of decomposition of the sort that I have discussed in chapter 10. Sometimes, as we have seen, the supposed revenant is even held responsible for eating the bodies in nearby graves.[38] In folklore, decomposition tends to be explained as the action of demons. Any demons shown in art, with form and color, were generally conceived as analogies to actual consumers of dead bodies. Thus Pausanias, the Greek travel writer of the second century, tells us of a painting of the demon Eurynomus, "said by the Delphian guides to be one of the demons in Hades, who eats off all the flesh of the corpses, leaving only their bones. . . . He is of a colour between blue and black, like that of meat flies; he is showing his teeth and is seated, and under him is spread a vulture's skin."[39] Here we see that both Pausanias and the artist relate the conception of Eurynomus ("wide-pasturing"? Because he goes far and wide to eat corpses?) to actual corpse-eaters, the meat flies and the vultures. Similarly, in a second-century Greek manuscript, Hades is conceived of as a place where dogs devour dead bodies—a common event, and one frequently proposed in curses hurled across the Homeric battlefield.[40] It is not going too far, perhaps, to see Cerberus as a reflex of this mysterious consumption of corpses: a dog who allows you into the kingdom of death but devours you when you try to leave.‖

> In the opened grave they found the
> body complete and undamaged by decay,
> but blown up like a drum, except that
> nothing was changed and the limbs all
> hung together. They were—which was
> remarkable—not stiffened, as with other
> dead people, but one could move them
> easily.
> —*The Shoemaker of Breslau*

‖When Herakles goes into Hades, he throws Cerberus a honey-cake—a typical offering to the dead—by way of providing a substitute meal, so that he himself is not eaten. According to Garland, "In general we know very little about what food was served to the Classical dead and about how it was prepared. Lysistrate (Ar. *Lys.* 601) speaks of a honey-cake called *melitoutta*, which the scholiast fancifully explains was given to the dead in order to ward off Kerberos" (p. 113). This explanation makes perfect sense, of course, if Cerberus is intended as a represention of how the corpse is consumed after death, thereby preventing a return to life. The reasoning seems to be that if you offer him a more attractive food, he will leave the body alone.

Our misfortunate shoemaker, a classic revenant, is typical in many respects, not the least of which is that, after death, he dutifully decomposed as best he could, only to be accused of remaining altogether too intact. His decay would have been hampered, according to Dr. Thomas Noguchi, by his exsanguination. It will be seen that he exhibits normal symptoms of a dead body: his skin is peeling away and he is bloated. Moreover, once exposed to the air, his body becomes "much fuller of flesh"—that is, bloated—in a period of about two weeks. Finally, when he is "killed" for the second time, a great deal of wood is required to burn his body, an observation frequently made, by the way, by people who do not maintain the technology of cremation. Not only are bodies composed largely of water, but a buried body functions like a sponge, according to Dr. Noguchi, soaking up water because its salt content is greater than that of its surroundings. We do not know, of course, whether the shoemaker's body was exposed to water, as it lay in the grave, but the possibility is suggested by its preservation: the simplest explanation for this would seem to be that the body underwent saponification, which requires an abundance of moisture.

This would not be an unusual event in Lower Silesia: "low German" and "high German" are geographical terms, and Breslau is in fact located in low, flat country. In a Latin description of Breslau published in the sixteenth century, Barthel Stein remarks on the country's swampiness and the Oder's habit of flooding the surrounding territory.[41] In Breslau, as in New Orleans, it would not be unusual for burials to have taken place in damp or water-logged earth.

That his body did not exhibit rigor mortis was evidently a source of great concern to his exhumers. We have seen this with de Tournefort's vrykolakas as well, and it is something of a standard plaint of the people who dig up revenants. Klapper gives an account of a distraught family who revealed that the body of their deceased was not rigid (and that therefore someone else in the family would die).[42] In fact, since rigor mortis is a temporary condition—caused by, and ended by, decomposition—there is simply nothing unusual about this. As with so many of the phenomena of death, however, the rate at which rigor arrives and departs is subject to great variation. According to Glaister, "In the majority of cases rigor will have commenced to pass off in about thirty-six hours, but, in cold weather, and for other reasons, a much longer interval may elapse."[43] (Its onset and duration can also be shortened greatly, as by heat and adrenalin. Also, bloating can cause a stiffness in the corpse that may be taken for rigor mortis.)[44]

That people did not understand the temporary nature of rigor mortis is not surprising. In a normal death, the body might actually be in the ground, or at least in its coffin, before it came out of rigor. In any case, it would not usually be handled a great deal after it had been washed and placed on a bier or in the coffin. The abnormal death, on the other hand—the murder victim or suicide, whose body was not discovered immediately—might draw attention to itself by failing to show rigor mortis.

It must be stressed, however, that how quickly a body is laid to rest varies greatly. One might assume that, in the past, when bodies were not embalmed, it was important to get them into the ground before they began to decompose. In fact, however, the contrary was often true: they might not be buried *until* they were well into decomposition, since that was the proof that the body was "normal." We are told that in Stralsund, in the eighteenth century, burial usually occurred four to seven days after death but that in the past the determining factor had been simply the onset of decomposition.[45]

Not only are the variables of rigor involved here but also the variables in the entire belief system of the people observing the corpse as well as the current events in their lives. Bodies become suspect when something goes wrong—when people are dying, for example—and at such times almost anything the body does may be seen as evidence of its potential for returning from the dead. Thus we are told that Peter Plogojowitz's nose had sunk in somewhat, a normal enough event but not sufficient to persuade his exhumers that he was decomposing. In the case of the Silesian Cuntze, on the other hand, we are told that since his nose had *not* sunk in, and since this was expected of a corpse, he must be a revenant.

The sad condition of Peter Plogojowitz's nose would not be unusual, according to Dr. Thomas Noguchi. With a buried body, anything that protrudes—nose, ears, elbows—may be damaged by contact with the soil as a result of pressure and/or dehydration. If Plogojowitz was buried in a shroud rather than a coffin (and this is likely), and especially if he was buried face down, as potential vampires were, then his poor squashed nose acquires a raison d'être. Prone burial would presumably focus the weight of the dirt on the part of the face that protrudes, namely the nose. We are told, by contrast, that Cuntze was buried in a coffin, which would have protected the body from the weight of the earth and allowed his nose to remain intact, to the surprise of his exhumers.

Such considerations may seem grotesque, if not comical, yet they illustrate an important point: our descriptions of revenants and vampires match up, detail by detail, with what we know about dead bodies that have been buried for a time.

Besides such actual events that, by their variability, distress the exhumers of the body, a variety of pseudoevents occur. The most noteworthy of these is the belief that the hair and nails of the vampire, or of the dead in general, continue to grow—a belief that, to borrow a saying from the Yugoslavs, wouldn't die if you drove a stake into it. Sometimes, in the case of the vampires, the teeth also continue to grow. In actuality, neither hair, nails, nor teeth grow after death, they merely *appear* to do so. This is because the skin shrinks back as it becomes dehydrated. The toothy appearance of a skull is similar: it does not have longer teeth than it had in life, they are just more evident.

In China, incidentally, the revenant may have a rather shaggy growth of white or greenish-white hair, a circumstance that de Groot attributes, plausibly enough, to the growth of fungus on the corpse.[46]

Medical examiners are also taught to look out for pseudo-events. Ponsold, for example, says that a body can appear to be in rigor mortis either because of dehydration or because—in the case of a body that is only apparently dead—of the stiffness brought about by cold.[47] He mentions a variety of such sources of confusion, in fact, and I bring them up only for what they tell us about how difficult it is, even now, to be sure of what we are seeing when dealing with a corpse. Consider how much harder it would have been for a Serbian peasant in the eighteenth century to know what to expect of a body, which has so many resources at its disposal. It can stiffen and relax, bleed at the mouth and nose, grow, shrivel, change color with dazzling versatility, shed its skin and nails, appear to grow a beard, and even burst open. Indeed, since the penis and scrotum undergo bloating, it can even show the "wild signs" remarked on with such pained circumspection in the account of Peter Plogojowitz.[48]

We can now account for the anomalies in the appearance of the corpse. But why were vampires thought to emerge from the grave? Why did they allegedly cry out, groan, or squeal like pigs when staked? Or, rather, why did some of them? Flückinger's vampires apparently lay there in a docile-enough state under the scalpel, but Arnold Paole groaned audibly when he was staked—a circumstance remarked on commonly enough, and with sufficient testimony, that we will want to consider it seriously.

Actions and Reactions

We have seen that much of what a corpse "does" results from mis-understood processes of decomposition. A close study of the data reveals not only that the bodies of supposed vampires were quite obviously dead but also why they were believed to do such diverse and bizarre things. If we consider these carefully we may find that the events have a certain logic.

Fortunately, we have sufficient information to do this. Vampires differ from other monsters of folklore: although they have an active life in legends and tales, there is an endless array of evidence—folkloric, ar-chaeological, and even legal—of what they were believed to do and how it was explained. Vampires were often dug up and "killed," and both the appearance of the bodies and the reasons given for the actions of both the corpses and the living are recorded. We can, therefore, ask questions about these beliefs and how they arose with considerable hope of finding reasonable answers.

The vampire sucks blood

This is the best-known belief about vampires in European countries and one of the most easily understood. We have already seen the phenomena that gave rise to it: (1) the corpse, when exhumed, has blood at its mouth;

(2) it is bloated; and (3) it bleeds when cut. We have also seen, in chapter 12, that these are normal processes—but we cannot expect the exhumers of the body to know that. Observing that he has blood at his lips, that he is full of something that was not there before his burial, and that he bleeds profusely when they stake or decapitate him, they conclude that he has got the blood from outside the grave. "Not without astonishment," says Peter Plogojowitz's chronicler, "I saw some fresh blood in his mouth, which, according to the common observation, he had sucked from the people killed by him." Where could he have found it if not in the veins of other people? And how could he have got it if he were not still alive?

A search easily reveals the causes of such reactions on the part of the living. The scapegoat phenomenon is prominent among them. This need to find a "cause," especially one that is preeminently blameworthy and can be exorcised in a satisfyingly physical manner, is clearly strong in the pursuit of vampires, much as it was in that of witches—except that the witches did not have the good fortune to be already dead when they were tortured and killed. Nightmares, too, played a part in the vampire phenomenon. They seem to provide a plausible explanation of the striking tendency of vampires to attack their victims while they sleep, as in *Visum et Repertum.**

Perhaps foremost among the reasons for the urgency with which vampires were sought—and found—was sheer terror. To understand its intensity we need only recall the realities that faced our informants. Around them people were dying in clusters, by agencies that they did not understand. As they were well aware, death could be extremely contagious: if a neighbor died, they might be next. They were afraid of nothing less than death itself. This is hard for us to understand, for, though death is as inescapable today as it was then, epidemics do not usually rage out of control, at least in industrialized countries. Moreover, we have well-established methods to control them. We are no longer obliged to mythologize them in the same way.

It is hardly surprising that we find other folkloric reactions to the bleeding of the corpse, such as the common European belief that it occurs in the presence of the victim's murderer. We know that a corpse can bleed, but what would cause it to bleed specifically in the presence of its murderer? The answer seems to lie in the way in which the corpse is manipulated when the murderer is led into its presence. In 1815 a scholar by the name

---

*In the eighteenth century, several authors pointed this out—that the attack took place in her sleep (Ranft, 186–87; see also Fritsch, 32, and Meinig, 35ff.).

of Friedrich von Dobeneck published a collection of folklore, mostly from the Middle Ages, that contained the following account:

Since, after intense questioning, the killer was not to be found or revealed, they were forced to set up a bier-right, at which Nicholas and Baltas, who stayed, *satis confidenter*, with their original statement, did not cause the corpse to make any sign. The corpse had been murdered 36 hours before and had lain partly in a building, partly—a few hours before the trial—under the open sky, in quite cold weather, chest and stomach exposed.

N. B. Four [men] lay in wait for the deceased, but since he arrived [armed] with a halberd, the abovementioned two ran away.

When Jörg was brought forward, the corpse gave out bloody foam from the mouth. (N.B. He was present when the deceased was stabbed, but did not lay hand on him.) He was led away and after Claus, the guard, was brought in— he had run to [the dispute] out of *ratione officii*, and because he was asked, and had tried to make peace, and had taken the halberd from the deceased: the corpse bled from its wounds, and this blood (which was over the heart) trembled no differently than if the heart were still alive.

Nonetheless, the guard did the *formulam juris jurandi* three times, as he was asked: (N.B. He put 1) two fingers on the mouth of the deceased, 2) on the wound and 3) on the navel, and also had to repeat after the pastor, who reminded him of his conscience, but he did not want to admit the deed.

In the presence of Lawrence—with whom the deceased, when he was stabbed, had had a dispute and had struggled—the corpse again gave out bloody foam from the mouth, as well as some blood from the wounds. The next day the guard revealed himself to be one of the killers.

Ex hoc apparet, vulnus, corpusque mortui gradus culpae observasse. [From this it is evident that the wound and the corpse of the deceased took into account the degree of guilt.]

Since Jörg was present, quite naturally red blood foamed from the mouth. (N.B. He was the one who all but began the dispute. Therefore the mouth foamed *ex rancore; sed non vulnus* [from rancor, but the wound did not] because he was not the killer. When the guard was present, nothing was produced at the mouth. But when he put two fingers on the wounds, blood flowed over the sides, quite naturally, so that the *chirurgus* had to wipe it away. When he put two fingers on the navel, the wounds again bubbled up, in a ferment, and twitched just as though the arteries were beating. Lawrence had struggled with the deceased, and while repeating [after the pastor?] bloody foam ran out of the mouth of the deceased, and when he put his fingers on the wound, it twitched again and moved. When he left, it did not twitch any more.[1]

Here we see that the accused was obliged to manipulate the corpse and that, as with the vampires, it was a source of wonder that the blood was liquid, although we now know that to be a normal event when death is sudden. The bloody foam results from the puncturing of the lungs, which are both rich in blood and have access (via the trachea) to the mouth. As is so often the case in such accounts, the author tries very hard to give details, yet fails to give us the details that *we* need. Were the men obliged to press down on the body, for example, or did they just touch it? The author does not say. It is important to note, by the way, the functioning of analogy in this account. With Jörg the blood flowed only from the mouth. In the opinion of our source this demonstrated that he incited the dispute by the use of his mouth. Blood did not flow from the wound because Jörg had not stabbed the deceased. We have also seen such sympathetic phenomena in our accounts of revenants, especially with the German Nachzehrer, whose "actions," while in the grave, are taken to be related to deaths among those he left behind.

A woman had lost her child through death. A few days after the burial they noticed an opening in the grave, which went as far down as the coffin lid. This was covered up, but the next day it was there again. Again it was covered up, but a man hid himself behind a bush and observed the grave. In the evening he noticed a black dog that stopped at the grave and then dug a hole. He told the mother of the child what he had seen, and she asked the pastor for advice as to how she could secure the peace of her child. The pastor told her that she should take earth from the track of the cart that had carried the body of her child to the churchyard, and fill up the hole with it. The mother followed the advice, and since then the grave remained undisturbed.

—Otto Knoop, *Sagen und Erzählungen aus der Provinz Posen*

The earth is disturbed at his grave

Several events may disturb the earth at a grave, whether or not it contains a vampire. When a grave is dug and then filled again, the earth is loosened considerably, so that it takes up more space than it had before. As it packs down, the grave mound slumps and may develop cracks. In order to deal with this, the grave is often tamped down thoroughly, as Hellwald reports for Bulgaria.[2] Sometimes it is wetted in order to compact it further and encourage decomposition, which is hastened by the presence of some moisture.[†]

Decomposition is retarded by deep burial. According to Mant, "generally speaking the greater the depth of the grave, the greater the degree of preservation. In shallow graves the soil is aerated, and the body itself will become the prey of a far greater variety of insects and animals; also in summer these shallow graves, and consequently the body, will become warmed by the sun."[3] According to Strackerjan, the people of Oldenburg in Lower Saxony believed that vampirism could come about merely because of a shallow burial.[4] Presumably only such bodies would draw attention to themselves, because only they would be the ones uncovered through any of a variety of means I will discuss in chapter 14.

Also, however, they might be expected to cause—without help from outside agencies—yet another type of disturbance. As the body decomposes, it changes size radically, first becoming much larger (by bloating), then becoming smaller as it collapses. This process could disturb the grave. The weight of any significant amount of earth would presumably inhibit bloating, causing the tissues to rupture rather than raise the dirt above the body.

But corpses, especially those of murder victims and victims of plague, are often buried in very shallow graves: the typical murderer is in a great hurry, and in times of plague, so many people are dying that the living are unable to do much more than stack them and cover them with a layer of dirt. In Erfurt, for example, in the Middle Ages, it is said that, after the churchyards had been filled, twelve thousand bodies were thrown into eleven large trenches.[5] This may explain why our sources insist that murder victims and victims of plague have a particularly pronounced tendency toward vampirism. Not only are both apt to undergo shallow burial, but, like suicides, not having died in the presence of friends and

---

[†]Because the dirt is loosened by digging, and because the coffin (or body) displaces a considerable amount of dirt, it is impossible to bury a body without ending up with far too much dirt to fill the hole. The grave proves to be a convenient place to leave the extra dirt, and this practice has the advantage of outlining the location of the body, for the convenience of both mourners and future grave diggers. Because of grave robbers, however, sometimes the grave is leveled to conceal it. (For an example of this from the African Congo, see Habenstein and Lamers, 277.) For reasons why graves are robbed, see chapter 14.

relatives, they may be found showing signs of vampirism—that is, decomposition—even before burial: blood at the mouth, swelling, and so on.[‡]

Richard and Eva Blum, in a valuable study of Greek folklore, quote an informant who actually defines the vrykolakas as an unattended dead body: "These were dead people who had died alone and had no one there to take care of them."[6] This seems to be a further reduction of categories, because murder victims, suicides, and victims of plague do, of course, have in common the fact that they are often left unattended.

It is probably not going too far to suggest that a vampire might be defined as a corpse that comes to the attention of the populace at a time of crisis and is taken for the cause of that crisis. The disturbance of the grave is merely one means whereby the body makes itself noticed.

Frequently the grave is said to have a hole in it, which is presumably due to the action of scavengers, as would seem to be the case in the account from Poland heading this section. If we consider that account carefully, we find nothing even out of the ordinary, let alone supernatural: a dog finds a grave, presumably by scent, and digs down to the body, only to be stopped by the coffin.[§] The next day, the dog comes back, only to find that someone has mysteriously filled in a perfectly good hole. In the accepted manner of dogs it digs a new hole where the dirt is loose—that is, where the old one was. The next day, this too is filled in. This particular dog was observed at these labors and, being black, was apparently seen as a supernatural being (Mephistopheles appears to Faust in the guise of a black dog). As Swieten pointed out in 1768, "a dog, a cat—especially when they are black and seen by night—are always the devil or a ghost that is creeping around in the graveyard or elsewhere."[7]

It is ironic that one reason we use coffins is to prevent animals from digging up corpses. Here the coffin functions as it was intended. If the

[‡]The swollen body is often so unrecognizeable that relatives are unable to identify it (Mant, 151; Parikh, 156).

[§]While it may seem superfluous to point out that dogs are carnivores and dig into graves to feed on bodies, this is sometimes forgotten by people who are used to feeding their dog out of a can. Several coroners have told me gruesome stories of dogs that, cooped up in a room with their dead master, fed on his body, causing investigators to assume at first that these wounds caused the death rather than, say, a heart attack. (See Spitz and Fisher, 31, for a photograph of such a body.) In the eighteenth century the carnivorous nature of dogs was evidently forgotten by those who embalmed the duke of Orléans: "During the evisceration there was a Great Dane belonging to the prince in the room. Before anyone could stop him, the dog pounced on the heart and ate a good quarter of it" (Journal de Barbier [1723], quoted in Ariès, 388).

observer had been less inclined toward superstition, he might have de-duced the function of the coffin from the event. In that case, of course, the event would have lost its remarkable character and would never have been recounted in a book on folklore.

In the absence of detailed information, one can only speculate on why this event was regarded as supernatural at all, especially since the su-pernatural dog was stopped by a natural barrier. Perhaps the dog's ability to locate the grave was considered a suspicious circumstance. But we should eliminate the natural explanations first by asking ourselves, "Can a dog find a buried corpse?" Over a period of years, I have conducted a number of inadvertent experiments on this question, with the aid of my own dog. In a spirit of scientific curiosity, she dug up, or tried to dig up, various cadavers of buried pets, including a chicken, and a large channel catfish from my pond. I had been unwilling to commit these to the trash can, so as not to rout my neighbors from their houses. Rotting flesh has an extraordinarily powerful smell, which dogs can detect if it is not buried too deep.

On first learning this—years before I began to study the vampire lore—I conceived of a simple way to thwart the process. From then on, when I buried a pet in my yard, I put a rock over the grave to prevent the dog from bringing me a grisly little corpse in triumph. Later I learned I was not the first to invent the technology: where coffins are unavailable for burial, rocks and boards are frequently used to protect the corpse from preda-tors.[8] Sometimes, as in the Tigre Province of Ethiopia, a stone slab is used.[9]

People have noticed, in times of plague,
that dead people—especially women—
who had died of the plague, engaged in a
smacking [sound], like a sow when it
eats; and that during such smacking, the
plague increased strongly, and people
died often, usually of the same sex, one
after the other . . . Anno 1553, when the
plague ruled here in Lauban, this
happened also: a woman made smacking
[sounds] in her grave.
—Martin Böhm, *Sermons*, 1601

This is said of the Nachzehrer, a north German type of revenant. As we have seen, once he finishes munching on himself, he often begins on other corpses buried in the vicinity. The smacking or chewing noises he makes, according to Klapper, always occur in connection with epidemics.[10] This noisiness he shares with yet another revenant, a woman who has died in childbirth and can be heard suckling her child.[11]

This is a classic opportunity to separate the core event from its explanation. Since the chewing and suckling are interpretations, not facts, we should look for noises caused by dead bodies that could suggest such sounds.[‖] We might be tempted, of course, to deny such an outlandish possibility outright, except for three facts. First, there is a lot of evidence that people thought they were hearing such noises. Second, we are told of specific instances, in specific places, where such "chewing noises" were heard. Finally, living in an age relatively free of epidemic disease, we lack the firsthand experience with mass burials that our informants had. In short, there is a possibility that they knew something we do not, even if their interpretation of the event was fanciful.

I know of only one mechanism whereby a corpse can make a noise. When it bursts, as a result of bloating, the emission of gases, body fluids, and maggots—often present in astonishing numbers—may be audible. According to Brouardel, "Grave-diggers sometimes think that they hear a noise in the grave three weeks after burial; this noise is due to the bursting of the abdominal wall when distended by gas."[12] Only once have I heard this, on a hike in Monterey County, when I came across the body of a Hereford calf as it burst, emitting quantities of fluids and gases. Unfortunately, it is difficult to get accurate information on situations roughly parallel to those described by our sources. We can only delineate, as closely as possible, the circumstances that our informants were describing, which included the following conditions:

1. We are told that the waxing and waning of the "chewing" sounds corresponded to the waxing and waning of the plague.
2. We know that the waxing of the plague corresponds to shallowness of burial. The grave diggers cannot keep up with their work. And because of the presence of real or supposed contagion (they did not know about plague vectors), they do not choose to linger over it. When large numbers of plague victims must be buried, mass graves are dug, and the bodies tend to be put in layers that alternate with

---

[‖] Frequently the sound is compared to that of a pig when it eats. Rohr refers to it as a "sonus porcinus" (p. 12). See also Lauterbach, 25.

layers of dirt. The layers of dirt are usually shallow because more bodies are arriving for burial.

3. In Western Europe, according to Gottfried,[13] the plague generally came in late summer and early autumn, because one of its vectors, the rat flea, is most active in warm weather. The events occur, then, during warm weather when the bodies are in a shallow grave. Such conditions are conducive to rapid decomposition because of the aeration of the soil, the action of insects and animals, and the warming effects of the sun.

What was being heard, clearly, was the same thing that Brouardel's grave diggers heard, except on a much larger scale: the disruption of large numbers of bodies bloating and bursting, causing a sound rather like an epidemic stomach-rumbling. As it happened during the plague, it would be related causally to the plague: *post hoc, ergo propter hoc*. Once the sound was noticed, moreover, people would presumably begin to listen for it, as it betokened (and did correspond to) an increase in the virulence of the epidemic.

The plausibility of this argument is enhanced by other accounts, from both folklore and history, that seem most easily explained in this manner. The classic form of these is as follows: a body is heard in its grave (sometimes a dog is seen listening at the grave), whereupon the grave is opened and the body is found, quite dead, but in a different position from when it was buried, which suggests to its exhumers that it had been buried alive. Moreover, its flesh is lacerated, and this is taken for evidence that, since the person was starving, he had chewed on himself by way of satisfying his hunger. Sometimes the body is determined to be still warm, suggesting that it had just died.

As I have mentioned elsewhere, there are problems with this interpretation, the most obvious of which is that it supposes that the body was able to remain alive—in some cases for weeks or months—without oxygen, food, or water. On the other hand, none of these phenomena is inconsistent with the events of decomposition. Corpses do make a certain amount of noise when they burst; dogs do have exceptional hearing and show a great deal of interest in graves; corpses do change position because of their internal pressures (and because when rigor mortis ends, gravity takes over; see Bartels, 136, for an illustration of how this would happen); and a variety of forces, such as the bursting of the corpse, cause lacerations. I have also been told by a medical examiner that the action of maggots can cause lacerations that mimic stab wounds.[14] Finally, the warmth of the corpse is not anomalous. According to Albert Ponsold, it may actually increase after death because of the action of the micro-organisms of decay.[15] Decomposition generates heat.[#] More commonly, the corpse is viewed as warm because people judge its temperature by touch, not with a thermometer, and if their hands are cold, the corpse appears warm by comparison.[16] The warmth of a corpse can scarcely be taken for proof that it was still a living body, let alone that it had died and come to life again.

Not surprisingly, there is considerable variety in the *explanations* for the sounds emitted from graves. In the Philippines, according to Ramos,[17] ghouls can be heard eating newly buried bodies, an interpretation that would seem to be designed to account both for the sounds emerging from the grave and for the disintegration of the body.[**] One of the most imaginative interpretations of this sort—reported from Mississippi—is that "A woman's hair is never plaited (for burial) for the devil will send his blackbirds to unplait it and they will be heard at work inside the coffin even after it has been placed in the ground."[18]

Whether Brouardel is right in attributing such sounds to the rupturing of the corpse, there is no doubt that mass burials can bring about dramatic effects. In June of 1986, UPI ran the following story—which illustrates, incidentally, one of the ways in which bodies "emerge from the grave":

> Larry Mohler, a Sheridan [Oregon] chicken grower, thought he had seen the last of 26,000 chickens that had died of heat prostration over the weekend when he had a bulldozer shovel their carcasses into a 20-foot hole.
> Not so.
> Twelve hours later, gasses produced by the corpses caused the pit to explode.
> "We had a miniature St. Helens," Mohler said. "The dirt we piled on top started bubbling and moving. And then the whole thing just blew up."
> The 'explosion' spread bits of chicken over about 40 feet. Friends and neighbors showed up to help him rebury the carcasses.[19]

As it happens, this account serves also to show how newspapers create folklore. I asked the Mohlers how an explosion would have been touched

---

[#]In chapter 4 we saw that de Tournefort explained the warmth of the Greek vrykolakas thus, at the beginning of the eighteenth century.

[**]When the body was not buried quickly enough, according to a nineteenth-century West Bisayan source, such ghouls might also cause the belly of the deceased to burst, whereupon "a very strong and fever-bearing stench would be emitted" (José Maria Pavon, cited in Ramos [1968], 187).

off, and Mrs. Mohler was kind enough to tell me what really happened. About thirty thousand chickens had been buried in fourteen-foot holes and covered with two feet of dirt. There was no explosion (the press had apparently derived this fiction from Mr. Mohler's speculation as to what would happen if he threw a match on the pit). Rather, according to Mrs. Mohler, "it looked kind of like a lava flow." The ground cracked, and the mass of dead chickens flowed out into the driveway. The Mohlers discovered—as many people have—that bodies have a much greater displacement when they decay, but, unlike our folkloric sources, they did not attribute this to the volition of the bodies. They simply miscalculated how deep a layer of dirt was needed to keep the bodies down. This is, as we have seen, a very common miscalculation.

> When they [vampires] have been taken
> out of the ground they have appeared
> red, with their limbs supple and pliable,
> without worms or decay; but not without
> great stench.
> —Dom Calmet, *The Phantom World*

> Bearing in mind the anal-erotic origin of
> necrophilia . . . we are not surprised to
> observe what stress many writers on the
> subject lay on the horrible stink that
> invests the vampire.
> —Ernest Jones, "On the Vampire"

By now the reader will recognize that Calmet's account contains a rather accurate description of the characteristics of an exhumed body. Its color is likely to have darkened, it will lack rigor mortis, and it may even be free of maggots, provided that flies did not get to it before burial—and people usually try to protect the body from flies. Moreover, it may show little obvious decay, since decay is slowed down by inhumation. But because a body decays from the inside out, as the microorganisms in the intestines attack it after death, it has a strong, not to say overwhelming, odor. Hence our informants give us conflicting information: they say that the body is not decaying but give clear evidence that it *is*, as is evident from its altered color and its stench. Clearly they define "decomposition" rather differently from us, presumably because in the early stages most of the decay remains internal.

Once again we would do well to trust their descriptions rather than their interpretations. For one thing, they frequently have alternative explanations for phenomena. An ordinary dead body is supposed to have an abominable stench (Peter Plogojowitz had too little for a proper corpse); but if it does, then this too may be evidence of a diabolical presence, perhaps because it suggests the sulphurous ambience of the Devil.

Such misinterpretations may remain stable as long as the phenomena are being observed continually, as was true of the vampires among the peasants of Europe. When the folklore broke loose from its moorings, however, and spread into areas where it was no longer associated with specific activities—that is, the exhumation of dead bodies—then a series of reinterpretations took place. We got the fictional vampire, who became somewhat streamlined, losing the distinctive chubbiness of the vampire of folklore, while acquiring longer teeth and a far more refined presence. He was invariably ambulatory, even though his predecessor in folklore often as not performed his evil while remaining in the grave. And various scholars have postulated that the bodies were in fact alive, a hypothesis scarcely less absurd than the beliefs it tried to explain. By keeping this theory firmly in mind, they managed to ignore the possibility that the vampire stank because he was, in fact, putrefying.

Because the smell of the corpse was associated with death, it tended to be viewed as a cause of death. Often the plague was blamed on foul odors. In the Middle Ages, according to Gottfried, "Some theorists, basing their arguments primarily on Galen, claimed that whether the cause of plague be astral or environmental, its transmission between men could be explained by miasma-contagion, or corruption of the air." In the late fourteenth century, he says, "many doctors claimed that foul odors were another source of air corruption."[20] This view is evident in an account by William of Newburgh, according to which "the air became foul and tainted as this fetid and corrupting body [the revenant] wandered abroad, so that a terrible plague broke out and there was hardly a house which did not mourn its dead."[21]

Such views seem to have found a home in popular belief systems. Among the Lapps, for example, it was believed even in this century that the smell of a corpse could make one ill.[22]

Yet strong-smelling substances are typical apotropaics in the lore of the vampire: garlic, incense, perfume, green nutshells, cow dung, human feces, and juniper. The idea here seems to be to "fight fire with fire." We are told, for example, that jaundice is to be cured by the use of yellow materials.[23] Or because the soul is smoke, as Grober-Glück remarks, one smokes it out of the room (after death) with incense.[24] We have seen this in de Tournefort's account in chapter 4. Similarly, if the odor of the vampire is a force to be reckoned with, then it must be opposed with similar forces—other substances with a strong smell—of which garlic is only the best known. Early in my research, I thought that such apotropaics might have been used merely to mask the smell of the corpse. Philip Tilney, in a study of Bulgarian burial practices, offers some support for this view in his remarks on the use of flowers and incense: "The use of the flowers and incense is clear. Embalming is not a technique used in small villages as a rule, and the body must be buried soon after death. The scent of the flowers and incense, therefore, is used to counteract any odors from the body, should the burial process be delayed for any reason."[25] But it is clear that such substances also have the quality of banning the vampire, for they are used even when people are not present. Garlic, for example, is often stuffed into the mouth of the putative vampire at burials, and it is difficult to see how this can be anything but a charm intended to thwart his evil purpose.

We can only speculate about motives, but we have an abundance of information about the phenomena of burial. We now know, for example, that a body does not always wait to be dug up, as so often happened to suspected vampires. It may often emerge from the grave of its own accord, impelled not by a supernatural force but by a variety of perfectly natural ones.

Hands Emerging from the Earth

"Hand of sinner sticks out of grave."
—Thompson's *Motif-Index*: E411.0.1

In the city of Stettin there once lived two spoiled children who caused their parents much heartache and in their godlessness finally went so far that they even struck them. For this, however, they were punished terribly. For after they had both died and had been buried, the hand of each one, with which they had mishandled their parents, suddenly stuck out of the grave. The most frightening part of it was, however, that the hands were fresh and bloody and could not decay. They dug them into the earth again, but this did not help: they grew out again. Then they finally decided, having consulted with the council and the clergy, that they would sever them with a spade. This was done, and they hung them, for eternal commemoration, in the church of St. Peter and Paul, in the vestry, where they are said to hang even now.

—J. Grässe, *Sagenbuch des preussischen Staats*

Hand Leads To Buried Body
A hand protruding from an incline near
the Harbor Freeway led to the discovery
of the badly decomposed body of an
adult male, Los Angeles Police said
Sunday.
The body was found in a shallow grave
after residents of the 9100 block of South
Grand Avenue reported seeing a hand
jutting through the dirt of a nearby
freeway embankment. . . .
—*Los Angeles Times*

Once we see clearly that the exhumed vampire was merely a dead body, undergoing a process of decomposition that rendered it monstrous and threatening, we find that most of our information about it begins to make sense. And that includes even the belief that the vampire leaves the grave. Bodies emerge from the earth, with or without help, for many reasons. One of these, as we saw in chapter 10, is that they may be attacked by scavengers.

It is evident that in Europe this process was mythologized into the belief that dogs and wolves were the enemies of vampires and attacked them on sight. Such animals were found at graves, especially during epidemics, digging up and feeding on bodies, and, when the bodies proved to have the usual characteristics of a vampire, the animals were seen to be *attacking* them rather than merely feeding on them.

The mythologizing does not end there, however. Remember that the body is not being observed from burial until it decomposes or is dug up by animals. Instead, it is discovered only at a particular stage of its development, so that the observer sees only the *consequence* of a group of processes that have occurred up to that moment. As a result, what is conveyed to us is not a description of a process but one of a number of possible tableaus: we may be shown the vampire as he is exhumed, lying in his grave, ruddy and swollen, with blood dripping from his open mouth. Or else (if temperatures have been low and the body has been well preserved) we are told the vampire is "just as he was when he was buried."

An observer of the tableau (that is, the outcome of a process) may then deduce that a shallow grave was eroded or dug up to reveal a corpse. If he does, then he will report an event that, as folklore, will likely have a short half-life because it is undramatic. But if he does not understand the causes, he will not report simply that an inexplicable event has occurred but will deduce a causative process incorrectly, attributing it to whatever forces are provided by his philosophy. In effect, he reconceives the events to fit them into his belief-system. Such events are attributed, then, to gods, demons, or (in the case of the vampire) the volition of the corpse itself.

The "hand of sinner sticks out of grave" theme appears to be a tableau of this sort. The event is not unusual—if it follows two other events: shallow burial and either erosion or the presence of scavengers (or both). This is because the scavengers dig down to the corpse and latch onto whatever part of it is most easily brought to the surface, which is most likely to be a hand. This could explain how the hand in the newspaper account quoted above came to the surface. Erosion could also account for this, since the dirt would have been loosened by digging, then raised higher than the dirt that surrounded the grave.

As usual, we must distinguish between the core event and its folkloric explanation. A body dug up by dogs is not unusual. But seen as a tableau, with the scavengers no longer present, there is nothing to account for the hand emerging from the earth except its own volition. Although we would reject such a notion, our informants believed that bodies continue in a kind of life after death in which anything that happened was a result of volition. This theory satisfied the observers because, like so much of the vampire lore, it seemed to account nicely for all the *observed* events—a necessary but not a sufficient condition for a theory.

> This "anger of the earth" finds its expression in various forms. First of all, the angry "Mother Earth" does not accept the unclean corpse. And indeed such a corpse always comes back to the surface of the earth, however often it is buried. But then the buried corpse does not succumb to decomposition, and thereby the dead person has the potential to escape from the grave at night. . . .
> The third sign of the "anger of the earth" is felt especially by the living. The earth shows its anger with cold and frost in the spring, which have a destructive influence on the thriving of the grain in the fields. . . . Thus, in ancient times, the Eastern Slavs did not bury the unclean

corpses in graves, but threw them out in
desolate areas, mostly in ravines and
swamps. Evidently to protect them from
wild animals, the corpses were often
covered with branches, stakes, and such.
—Dimitrij Zelenin, *Russische (Ostslavische)
Volkskunde*

Bones, hairs, nails, and teeth of the
dead, were the treasures of old Sorcerers.
—Sir Thomas Browne, *Hydriotaphia*

Two Held in Theft of Head, Ashes from
Cemetery
The partially decomposed head of a
woman, stolen from a crypt at
Hollywood Memorial Park Cemetery
early Wednesday, was found in the street
next to a man who was subsequently
arrested, Los Angeles police said.
—*Los Angeles Times*

We see in Zelenin's passage a variety of events and explanations that
bear on our problem of body disposal. As usual, we will find it most useful
to separate the two, because the explanations show an unacceptable view
of cause and effect.

The mythological version is as follows: (1) Bodies are believed to come
back to the surface of the earth; (2) This happens because either the earth
expels the body out of anger or the body, remaining alive, escapes from
the grave at night; and (3) Besides expelling the body as unclean, the
earth creates bad weather out of anger. Therefore the unclean must not
be buried, thereby preventing the earth from spewing them up and the
weather from turning bad.

Zelenin apparently does not notice that the informants give two mythological explanations of why bodies come to the surface. This should
suggest that a real event is being observed. The dead rise from their
graves in many, if not most, cultures, so we may safely disregard any
one cultural explanation of the phenomenon.

In order to understand this particular event we may first single out its
"real-life" content: (1) bodies do not always stay buried; for various reasons, they may reach the surface of the earth; (2) bodies do not always
show obvious decomposition; (3) sometimes the weather turns cold in the
spring; (4) crops require moderate temperatures to thrive; (5) the eastern

Slavs did not bury "unclean" corpses but disposed of them in desolate areas; and (6) to protect the dead from the depredations of animals, they sometimes covered them up.

Looked at this way, much of our passage is wholly factual. Bodies may indeed be unearthed, and by many agents, including the following:

1. People dig them up:
   a. Grave robbers in search of grave goods or bodies or body parts (for magical use or for sale).
   b. People who think the body should not have been buried there (a suicide in consecrated ground, for example).
   c. People who have decided the body is a vampire and wish to kill it.
   d. People who practice secondary burial, expecting the body to have been reduced to a skeleton.
   e. People who have forgotten where an unused graveyard is and dig holes or till the ground.
      (Nowadays we must add archaeologists to this list!)
2. Animals dig them up. Most large carnivores are also scavengers, and many body-disposal practices reflect this problem (covering the grave with rocks, boards, brush, and so forth).
3. Erosion uncovers bodies.
4. Flooding uncovers bodies: the coffin or body, being buoyant, sometimes pops to the surface in floods, coming up through waterlogged ground.

Obviously many of these events are unlikely to be observed by the local populace. Grave robbers and predators tend to work at night, in places that people may be loath to go even in daytime. And if the grave robbers see the opening of the grave interpreted as the body's own work, they will presumably keep the truth to themselves. Moreover, if nocturnal activity in a graveyard is noticed, it is unlikely that it will be investigated closely—indeed, it may serve to substantiate the belief in revenants rather than disprove it.

The disturbance of gravesites has generated a variety of folklore, not just the belief in vampires. In the nineteenth century, as we have seen, many people concluded that people were being accidentally buried alive, and that this accounted for the stories of vampires. The result was another (mythological) version of the same events, as is illustrated in this account from Franz Hartmann's *Premature Burial*:

> In 1866 a young and strong man, Orrendo by name, had a fit and died. He was put into a coffin and deposited in the family vault in a church. Fourteen years

afterwards, in 1880, the same vault was opened again for the purpose of admitting another corpse. A horrible sight met those who entered. Orrendo's coffin was empty, and his skeleton lying upon the floor. But the rest of the coffins were also broken open and emptied of their contents. It seemed to show that the man after awakening had burst his coffin open, and, becoming insane, had smashed the others, after which he had been starved to death.[1]

Hartmann's explanation requires that the "dead" man remained alive, escaped his coffin, and went insane—thus accounting for his smashing the other coffins. It is much simpler to suppose that someone broke into the tomb in search of valuables, or even body parts, and, having disturbed the remains, failed, with a deplorable lack of tidiness, to put them back in their coffins.

In such accounts, the informant can only rarely conquer his need to explain the events. Sometimes the bulk of the story is made up of interpretation, not data. Witness the following account from Utah:

> There is a cemetary [sic] in a town called Monroe, Utah. Many people were buried in this cemetary before the new one was made in 1946. When they were moving some of the graves, it was requested that some of the caskets to be moved were to be opened, and in about seven, people had evidently been buried alive without formaldihide [sic]. These people had turned over in their graves, scratched the ceiling of the caskets, torn their hair out, scratched themselves, jabbed their eyes out, and one had even attempted to scrawl a message on the top of the casket. In all cases, the expressions on the faces were hidious [sic] and contorted.[2]

The corpses were not, of course, *observed* to do anything at all: everything is deduced from their condition, and the deductions are offered as real events. Presumably the observers expected the corpses to lie there and quietly molder away rather than bloat, burst, change position, and stain the casket. (This last may account for the attempt to "scrawl a message." Evidently the scrawl was illegible.) Nothing is more common in such accounts than the hideous visage of the deceased, and nothing is more natural. It is clear that a process of selection took place in producing this account. Only seven corpses qualified for "buried alive" status, and these seem to have been chosen according to only two criteria: their changes were both dramatic and unexpected.

The process of decomposition probably accounts for why pregnant women are viewed as especially apt to become revenants. According to Parikh, when the body of a pregnant woman decomposes, "In about 48–72 hours . . . the foetus may be expelled from the uterus."[3] Albrecht von Haller remarked on this in 1778.[4] It will be seen how startling it would be to the exhumers of the body to find that it had given birth in the grave. Masters cites an account that seems most easily explained thus: "To the horror of the authorities it was discovered that not only had [the pregnant woman] been buried alive in a trance-like or cataleptic condition but she had put up the most incredible struggle within the coffin. During the course of this she had given birth to a child. Both had suffocated to death."[5] It seems more likely that the fetus was expelled as the body bloated. Presumably because of this phenomenon, in many cultures the fetus is removed from the womb before burial.[6]

As for the body-disposal methods mentioned by Zelenin, one can shed considerable light on them by imagining situations in which they were used. If you believe that a body is dangerous, you will presumably remove it as far from your habitation as you can, and as quickly (unless you simply flee your habitation, which also happens). If your community abuts on another, then, as we have seen, you bury the body at the common boundary of the two communities.

If there is no adjoining community, the proper resting place for the vampire is a "desolate area," in ravines and swamps. Another way of defining such an area is to say that it is uninhabitable, which means that the vampire is being removed from the presence of people. Since the body is heavy, awkward and—if already undergoing decomposition—unpleasant to transport, it is more likely to be disposed of in low areas than in high.* The object, presumably, would be to move the body as far away as possible.

Unfortunately the qualities that render the terrain uninhabitable also affect the problem of body disposal. If the body meets its fate on high ground, for example, as happens with the revenant Glam in *Grettir's Saga*, it is likely to be covered with rocks or brush to protect it from animals—that is, with whatever can be used for that purpose and is in plentiful local supply.[7]

There are several reasons not to bury the body. On high ground, burial may be difficult or impossible because the soil is shallow and rocky. This is illustrated in a report from 1876–77, dealing with plague in the Himalayas:

The custom of the country is to burn the body beside the most convenient mountain stream terminating in the Ganges. But from that good practice the

---

*Such bodies are preternaturally heavy, a reflection, one suspects, of the fear of the people transporting them; see *Grettir's Saga*, 72; Vakarelski, 37; Lemke, 3:51; and Brown, 35.

people have deviated in regard to bodies dead of any pestilence (smallpox, cholera, plague), which are buried. Of all countries the Himalaya is least suited to the burial of the dead. For, by reason of the rocky subsoil, it is seldom possible to dig a grave more than two feet deep; and, as a rule, the pestilent dead are laid in shallow trenches in the surface soil of the field nearest to the place of death, or of the terrace facing the house, or even of the floor of the house itself. This bad practice is begotten of fear to handle the body, and has been long established.[8]

This passage is worth considering for a moment. The local people normally use two typical methods of body disposal: cremation (which renders the body inert) and disposal in water, which removes the remains from their presence. In effect, they are "hedging their bets" to ensure that the dead cannot come back to, well, plague them. We are told, however, that they depart from this practice during times of epidemic, presumably because the body-disposal potential of their culture is then overwhelmed by both the energy requirements of cremation and the difficulty of persuading people to handle the bodies. Thus the mass grave comes into being—a periodic discovery of human beings in times of mass deaths.[†]

Note that, according to this source, bodies were often buried in the floor of the house if they were diseased, hence a source of fear. House burial is well attested archaeologically, for example, in Anatolia and in Babylon. According to the Turkish archaeologist Tahsin Özgüç, in the Chalcolithic period in Anatolia it was not uncommon for bodies to be buried in houses. Often a number of skeletons are found under a single room, only five to ten centimeters under the ground. It is clear, he adds, that the inhabitants went on living in the houses, a circumstance that he takes for evidence that the dead were not feared. Otherwise, why would people put up with their presence?[9]

Now according to the above quotation, house burial was used in the Himalayas precisely *because* of fear of the corpse. How are we to reconcile the two views? It seems to me that three possibilities exist. The first is that the diseased body is left in situ because no one is willing to touch it, and a grave is dug next to it, so that the body does not have to be lifted at all, but can be merely pushed—with a stick or implement of some sort—into the grave. The grave is shallow because the gravediggers

[†]It is much easier to dig one large grave than to dig many small ones. The digging of a mass grave may be achieved, or at least aided, by draft animals and implements, whereas the digging of individual graves depends on manual labor. Mass graves are also space efficient, taking up less earth surface and allowing less wasted space between bodies within the grave.

are not eager to remain in the presence of a contagious corpse. That people went on living in the house, with a corpse buried just under the earth, might seem implausible—the stench of such a corpse, in a closed space, simply defies description—but they may have moved back into the house after the corpse had been reduced, by decomposition, to an inert condition. The "life" of the corpse tends to correspond to the period during which it is still changing and developing, and it ceases to be frightening after its second "death."[‡]

Second, they may have practiced house burial in order to retain the spirits of the dead nearby, either out of fear of their anger, if they were removed from their home, or because they were viewed as potentially helpful. According to Servius, the Romans originally practiced house burial "ut lares colerentur in domibus" (so that the domestic deities might be cared for in the houses).[10]

The third possibility is suggested by more recent excavations in Anatolia at Çatal Hüyük (ca. 6,500 to 5,650 B.C.). There bodies were found buried under floors of houses, but only after having been excarnated, perhaps by vultures.[11] Such bodies, once the flesh was removed, might not be frightening because they would not continue to change.

Because of the problem of transport, one would expect low uninhabitable ground to be chosen for burial of the restless dead, and this is, in fact, attested for much of Europe in folklore. Such corpses were commonly disposed of in swamps and bogs.[12] Here again we must consider how such a choice of site influences the methods of body disposal. In a swamp, while the soil may be deep enough for burial and unlikely to be rocky, the high water-table may make it impossible to dig a dry hole deep enough to bury the body. If the body were buried anyway, or simply submerged in the water, there would be a good chance of its coming to the surface again, since eventually it would become extremely buoyant from the lightweight gases produced by the microorganisms of decay.

This is not mere conjecture. It is quite common, now as in the past,

---

[‡]People do sometimes keep their dead in their presence, and an archaeologist of my acquaintance tells of having walked by a house in Indonesia where a corpse had been lying for five months, awaiting a propitious time for disposal. He says that it was unpleasant even to walk by the house, the stench was so great. The common practice is to render the body inert—by drying, embalming, or cremation—before storing it in the living quarters. In the United States, for example, it is not uncommon for the relatives of the deceased to keep the ashes in an urn. See Bernd and Bernd, 410, and Eylmann, 230, for Australian examples.

for murderers to dispose of bodies by throwing them into bodies of water[13]—the murderers of today rediscover the problems encountered by the vampire-killers of yesteryear. According to Dr. Terence Allen, former deputy medical examiner of the Los Angeles Medical Examiner's Office, it is almost impossible to weigh a body down sufficiently to keep it submerged. He showed me a slide of a body that had floated to the surface bearing a cast-iron generator housing that weighed 145 pounds—5 pounds more than the body itself. And since the body reached the surface, we do not know its potential lift, only that it would lift at least 145 pounds (because of the specific gravity of water, the actual weight of the object would be 125 pounds).

Brouardel gives a similar account:

A druggist named Aubert was murdered in the country by a husband and wife of the name of Fenayrou, assisted by their brother. To get rid of the corpse, they threw it into the Seine, after having enclosed it in a piece of lead pipe. They hoped that thus it would stay at the bottom of the water. Three days later Aubert floated, though still enclosed in the lead pipe.

An enormous quantity of lead would have been requisite to prevent a body from rising to the surface; the only means of keeping it at the bottom would be to open the abdomen and perforate the intestines; in this way the gases would escape as soon as they are produced.[14]

The horrid image of this place is still in my mind. I cannot drive it from my imagination. The tombs are all above ground, and those who can afford it will never be buried underground. . . . This graveyard is all on a dead level and on rainy days inundated with water. It is a morass, a swamp partly rescued from its wilderness. I followed the procession to the grave. The coffin was taken from the hearse. . . . The grave was not over two feet and a half deep, I measured it for curiosity. The bottom was soft mud into which could be thrust a stick to almost any depth. The water was within a foot of the top of the grave. The clods of earth around all clay, such as earth as would be dug from a bog. The coffin was put into the grave and it floated so as to be level with the surface.

A negro, a fiend-looking brute, with his
pantaloons above his knees, all covered
with clay in which he had been working,
without hat, without coat or a whole
shirt—but with a hoe and a spade,
mounted the top of the coffin, and
tramped it under the water, and then a
brother-looking being threw the clods on.
—Description of the Catholic Burial
Ground, New Orleans, 1833

We find a great deal of evidence, both folkloric and archaeological, that reflects the return of the body to the surface. As we saw in chapter 9, stones are often used to weigh down the body. Rudolf Grenz, in a valuable article on such finds, observes, "The weighting of [such corpses] with stones can hardly be interpreted otherwise than that people wanted to hinder them from rising up again."[5] This is certainly a reasonable supposition, but note that an *actual* event is being prevented, not a supernatural one; just the explanation is supernatural.[§] Here again we must distinguish between event and explanation. Bodies do return to the surface for a variety of reasons, including simple buoyancy. In New Orleans, where the ground water is high, "Heavy rains or a storm would cast newly buried, half-decomposed cadavers to the surface."[6] (Note how, in the above account, the coffin must be tramped down just to get it below the surface.) And in China, according to Creighton, "The pains taken to secure dry burial-places are especially obvious in those parts of the country, such as the 'reed lands' of the Yang-tsi, which are subject to inundations, annual or occasional."[7] The Chinese did this, presumably, because failure to do so would allow the bodies, during floods, to wash to the surface—not an uncommon occurrence, as a matter of fact. Even in Los Angeles, which has a very dry climate, this has been known to happen. A few years ago, in Verdugo Hills, more than a hundred coffins were washed out of the ground and into city streets (see the epigraph to chapter 16), and in the fall of 1985 the *Los Angeles Times* carried a photograph of a coffin floating in a flooded graveyard in Louisiana.[18] According to the caption, several coffins floated up out of the ground in the floodwaters left by Hurricane Juan. The one in the photograph had been tied to a

---

[§]Sometimes the stone is reinterpreted. I have seen accounts, for example, in which it is represented as being of a weight equivalent to that of the vampire's most likely victim, so that he believes the victim to be present already and has no need to seek him out.

tree in a novel but effective method of preventing the dead from wandering about.

Like bloated bodies, sealed coffins are extremely buoyant. Coffins or caskets are used to protect the body from a variety of nasty fates, but they have their own hazards. Because they trap a considerable amount of air, they are quite buoyant in flooded ground. Some years ago a local casket manufacturer considered manufacturing fiberglass vaults but discovered that, in areas where the water table rose to above their level, these had been known to pop up to the surface to cause a bulge in the earth. His engineers proposed a system of tie-downs—an idea with a long history—but he ended by scrapping the idea.[||]

And here we must digress for a moment to consider terminology: *casket* and *coffin* both derive from the French and refer to a container in which a corpse is buried. If you were to use the word *coffin* in a modern funeral home, however, you would be corrected: the proper word is *casket*. It is difficult to get people in the industry to define the difference between the two words, and *Webster's* (Unabridged, 2d ed.) refers to a casket simply as "a coffin, especially a costly one." I suspect that an inexorable linguistic change is taking place: in time, words of this sort lose their dignity, a commodity of great importance in the burial industry. *Casket* will presumably undergo this process as well, eventually, and we will have to beg another word from the French.

A *vault* (another French word) is in modern terminology a container that looks very much like a casket. The casket is put inside it. The vault may be made of ten- or twelve-gauge steel or of some other strong material, such as concrete. A "liner" is an object that—as you must have anticipated—looks rather like a casket and is put into the vault before the casket.

Together, these containers provide a great deal of support, which is necessary because, with deep burial, they are subjected to an enormous amount of pressure from the earth above them. Indeed, Ranft tells of a gravedigger who, hearing a "knocking" from a grave, dug it up and discovered that the coffin had collapsed from the weight of the earth above.[19] This suggests yet another source of "sounds from the grave" and of slumping of the earth.

Flotation is especially a problem, needless to say, in bog burials. Peat

[||]My source is Robert B. Johnston of S.S. Casket Co., Glendale, California, whom I would like to thank for his kind and patient response to my questions.

bogs fit our "uninhabited land" model and would presumably be as attractive as lakes to anyone with a superfluous corpse, especially one considered dangerous. In modern times, the corpse is usually dangerous because it was murdered—and is evidence of a crime. In the past it was thought dangerous for other reasons as well. Both then and now, however, someone who wished to rid himself of a corpse quickly and also to conceal it was apt to dispose of it in water.

The peat bog burials are evidently a variation of this practice. Peat has been cut for fuel since the Iron Age,[20] and there would presumably have been ready-made cuttings into which a corpse could be laid and covered with the available material—namely peat—so that the body was both removed and hidden as quickly as possible. Evidently, in time it became clear that a rise in the water level was apt to bring bloated, superbuoyant corpses up to the surface, and thus a technology of corpse disposal was born: people learned to pin the body in place with a stake, to lay a latticework of branches or poles over it before covering it up, or to weigh it down with stones. Thus we encounter some of the characteristic finds of the peat bog burials: stakes, brush, and stones. In many cases, indeed, the function of these objects is hardly to be mistaken: P. V. Glob tells of one body—"Queen Gunhild"—that workmen tried to pull out of soft peat, without success. "The reason for the failure was not at first understood, for the body seemed to lie in soft turf. Closer examination, however, revealed that the body was fastened to the underlying peat by wooden crooks, driven down tight over each knee and elbow joint. In addition, strong branches had been fixed like clamps across the chest and lower abdomen, their ends similarly held down by wooden crooks, so that the dead person lay pinned in the bog, the head pointing east and the face towards the setting sun."[21] Then as now, not everyone understood the phenomena of bloating and buoyancy, but the people who pinned "Queen Gunhild" in the bog clearly did. We cannot know, however, how many bodies were simply thrown into bogs, because these are the ones that, remaining at (or returning to) the surface, would be least likely to remain intact.[#]

We now see one reason why it is considered important that the dead

---

[#]It may be that, if thrown into bog water, bodies would not necessarily come to the surface. The specific gravity of a body is slightly greater than that of water, so the body would tend to sink at first, and in winter, if the water were cold enough, it might be preserved by the cold until the antibiotics in the water had a chance to penetrate the corpse and prevent the action of the microorganisms of decay (Christian Fischer, in Cockburn and Cockburn, 177).

undergo the full complement of funerary procedures, many of which are not merely magical in design but are derived from the exigencies of burial. The dead may indeed arise from their graves, aided not by demons but by the physical laws of the universe.

Down to
a Watery Grave

The folkloric reflexes of the buoyancy of the corpse are not limited to the belief that the revenant walks (as we have already seen in the Russian belief that Mother Earth spews forth an unclean corpse). The Grimms report, for example, a similar belief that accounts for bodies coming to the surface in water: a river or lake demands, every year, the sacrifice of an innocent child, but does not tolerate a corpse and sooner or later hurls it onto the bank.[1] Similarly, they recount a medieval story that is worth examining in some detail:

> In the year 1267, in Pforzheim, there was an old woman who, out of greed, sold an innocent seven-year-old girl to the Jews. The Jews stopped up her mouth, so that she could not cry out, cut open her veins, and wrapped her with cloths, to catch up her blood. The poor child soon died from the torture, and they threw her into the Enz with a load of stones on top. After a few days little Margaret stretched her little hand up over the flowing water. The fishermen saw this and were horrified; then the people came running, along with the margrave himself. The fishermen were able to pull the child out, who still lived [!], but after she had cried out revenge over her murderers, she died. Suspicion was on the Jews, who were called together, and when they neared the corpse, the blood

flowed out of the open wounds in streams. The Jews and the old woman admitted their crime and were executed. Near the entrance of the church of the castle at Pforzheim, there where they pull the bell-cord to peal the bells, the coffin of the child stands with an inscription on it.[2]

Faced with such an account, we are apt to throw out the plausible with the implausible. If we resist this urge, however, we are confronted with events that, though they could not have happened this way, could have *appeared* to have done so. We have the following events and pseudoevents to take into account:

1. A body is weighed down to cause it to sink in water. The child died, presumably, either from the gagging or from the wounds (these could have occurred postmortem, from a variety of causes, while the body was in the river).

2. The body returns to the surface after a few days. In Europe, according to Mant, a body will normally return to the surface in the summer in two to three days; in spring or autumn in three to five days; in winter in up to six weeks.[3] Again, there is nothing unusual here, not even that the body brought heavy weights to the surface.

3. The child (said to have died once already) is still alive after all but soon dies. Presumably what is being shown here is not a distinction between life and death at all, but between manipulation and nonmanipulation of the corpse. When the corpse is being moved, it is apt to respond in startling ways, as its limbs, no longer in rigor mortis, move in response to gravity or internal pressures resulting from its being lifted and carried. Once it is left alone, it becomes quite dead. This is also a common phenomenon with the European vampire.

4. The body "cries out revenge." We have no way of knowing exactly what this means. That the body could *literally* cry out is, in certain circumstances, quite possible, but the "revenge" part is evidently an interpretation based on views attributed, by our source, to murdered corpses. There are other possibilities. Where verbal communication fails, signs and portents take over, and it is possible that what is being referred to is based on the appearance of the corpse—for example, open, staring eyes—or on something not expressed in the text.

5. The corpse bleeds in the presence of its murderers. We have already seen (*a*) that corpses can bleed and (*b*) that the suspect may have been expected to manipulate the corpse during this trial. Like so many early trials—trial by torture, for example—this one was designed to find the

guilty party the first time every time. That the Jews confessed is scarcely surprising, since they had already been convicted. A refusal to confess would simply lead to the next step in the trial, namely torture.

The bleeding of the corpse may occur spontaneously under the right circumstances.[4] Brouardel, a French pathologist of the late nineteenth century, gave an account illustrating this:

> A corpse was found in the river Gave at Lourdes; it was carried into a shed; the hour was 11 o'clock a.m., and the weather was very warm. The medical man who examined the body noticed some wounds on the head, which he thought were caused by stones rolled down by the current. The public prosecutor was notified of the case, and the law was put in motion; some hours had passed since the first observations were made.
>
> From each of the wounds of the head there now flowed a little liquid blood, and the physician who accompanied the officers of the court concluded that these wounds were recent. Investigation showed, on the contrary, that the man had thrown himself into the Gave (it turned out to be a case of suicide) the morning before, and that he had been taken out of the water twenty-four hours after death.
>
> The flow of blood was due to the posthumous circulation induced by the formation and accumulation of gas in the abdominal cavity. This development took place only after the removal of the body from the cold waters of the Gave.[5]

We see from this account that once the body warmed up the formation of gases commenced in earnest,* thereby putting pressure on the blood and causing it to flow of its own accord. Dr. Thomas Noguchi has told me of a similar case in which a man fell near a pool, struck his head, fell into the water, and drowned. Photographs of the death scene showed the body lying next to the pool, with a long stream of blood that had flowed, quite spontaneously, from a small head wound. Blood tends to remain fluid, according to Dr. Noguchi, where death is due to drowning, asphyxia, and shock, since the tissues produce enzymes that prevent clotting. In addition, because of its salt content, the body, when immersed in fresh water, tends to soak it up,[6] which increases the pressure in the circulation system; when it is removed from the water, the body then loses its fluids readily.

The events of this story make considerable sense if we remove the

---

*According to Spitz and Fisher, "A body may be submerged for the duration of the winter yet be in excellent preservation when recovered in the spring when the water warms up. However, when brought into a warm environment, such a body is prone to undergo putrefaction at an extremely rapid rate" (p. 23).

explanations of our source. Sad to say, young girls *are* occasionally gagged and murdered, sometimes by sexual deviates, sometimes even by their parents, and the "witch hunt" is a characteristic response, on the part of society, to an atrocity of this sort. The Jews in the Middle Ages were simply the scapegoats-of-choice; it was believed that for their religious rites they required the blood of an innocent child.

This is not to say, however—and this must be stressed—that we are to suppose this account to be truthful merely because these events *could have* been real. The Grimms quite properly treat it as legend: the story may have been told over most of Europe, for all we know, with the location changing according to need, and the details, intended to lend verisimilitude, varying from one version to another. I do not argue that the account is true, only that it could have had its origin in actual events.[†]

The tendency of bodies to return to the surface has generated a great deal of folklore in Europe and elsewhere in the world. The form of such lore is derived, as we have seen, not from the entire process that takes place but from that part of it which is observed, so that we get a series of tableaus crystallized into statements about revenants. Some of these are quite transparent, once we have cracked the code. This is true, for example, of a statement such as "vampires emerge from their graves," which is apparently based on both an observation (dead bodies are found at the surface) and a deduction from an observation (the grave is disturbed: the vampire must be trying to get out). (In chapter 18 we shall consider still another way the vampire escapes from the grave.)

Often, however, we can only speculate on the relationship between the statement and a possible tableau, as with a statement such as "revenants cannot cross water," which is attested for much of Europe.[7] While I will not insist on it, it seems possible that this too is a deduction from an observation: the dead body reaches the surface of water or water-logged earth and is found there, quite lifeless. Now not just its presence but its death must be explained. The explanation tendered is that the revenant tried, and failed, to cross water.[‡]

Such a tableau may also have contributed to the belief that the vampire must return to his grave by daybreak[8]—that is, the vampires found dead

---

[†]Jan Harold Brunvand has written two valuable (and entertaining) analyses of the dissemination of such legends (see Bibliography). In *The Choking Doberman* he deals with the history of the belief that the Jews murdered innocent Christian children for their blood.

[‡]Disembodied spirits cannot cross water either, for somewhat different reasons; see chapter 18.

are the ones that did not succeed in doing so. (I suspect, however, that this belief is largely derived from characteristics of the vampire's non-material form, which we shall discuss later.) And it also seems the simplest explanation for Murgoci's report that "vampires never drown, they always float on top."[9] Dead bodies do in fact become extremely buoyant.

Not only vampires, incidentally, but also witches and sorcerers float. The *iudicium aquae*, or trial by water, became a common test for witches in Europe, the assumption being, according to King James, "that the water shall refuse to receive them in her bosom, that have shaken off them the sacred water of baptism and wilfully refused the benefit thereof."[10] In 1599 in Breslau, an old woman was decapitated by the hangman after having failed to sink in water.[11] Here we have a distinction based on observable events—bodies either sink or float—complete with a mythological explanation: the water chooses not to take them in, much as in Russia Mother Earth rejects the unclean dead.[§]

Vampires and witches have numerous other similarities: both may begin life coifed with a red caul,[12] and both may suck blood, have a white liver, have their origin in nasty people, undergo metamorphosis, have a distinctive mark on their body (for example, Stanacka of *Visum et Repertum* and the Shoemaker of Breslau), and be controlled by the same apotropaics.[13] Finally, both may be dug up, after death, to be killed once again.[14]

That this is altogether too much coincidence should be evident at a glance. We clearly divide up the world of meaning somewhat differently than our informants, many of whom do not distinguish between the two concepts (witch and vampire). In Kashubian, for example, according to Mannhardt, one of the words for the revenant is *stryz*, which he translates as *wizard*, or *sorcerer*, relating it to the Polish word for *witch*.[15] And in much of Eastern Europe the dead, not the witches, are particularly active on the eve of Maundy Thursday.[16] For many of our informants, the Slavs in particular, vampire/revenant and witch tend to merge. Another way of stating this, as we have seen, is that "witches and wizards become vampires after death." That is, those who are under suspicion in life— the witches—remain under suspicion in death and are dug up to be killed.

The exhumation of such corpses happened so often, and in so many areas, that at any given time a large number of such accounts could be expected to be present in local folklore, differing from one another in

---

[§]Like trial by torture, the iudicium aquae has the maddening deficiency that the innocent (those who refuse to confess/those who sink) undergo severe punishment, possibly even death, in demonstrating their innocence.

how far away their place of origin was in both space and time. Thus one might get historical accounts (such as *Visum et Repertum*) that are quite plausible and easily analyzed in addition to legendary accounts in which the events had been so transformed by the process of oral transmission that one could seriously doubt that the story had even a grain of truth (there are a number of vampire *Märchen*, for example).[17] This merging of history and legend causes a characteristic problem: the folklorist, looking at the historical account, is tempted to discount it because of its parallels in legend. That is, we disbelieve "history" if it mimics "legend."

But such an attitude neglects an important consideration: sometimes such accounts occur in both history and legend because they tell of events that happen again and again. In such cases the legendary account might be a historical account that had been transformed, through the ages, by oral transmission, until finally it attained a form so outlandish and implausible that it could only cast doubt on historical accounts of the same phenomenon.

This seems to have been what has happened with the folklore of vampires and revenants. Pathologists, reading accounts such as *Visum et Repertum*, typically respond to them by pointing out that the phenomena described therein are quite normal. They tend to regard my interpretation, moreover, as all but self-evident. That the "vampire" remained such a mystery, therefore, and for so long, would seem to have been because the legendary aspects of the folklore made it impossible for us to take the historical aspects seriously.

An important principle emerges from these considerations: when an event is repeated often, in both "legendary" and "historical" form, we must consider the possibility that what we are seeing is a statement of an anomaly, or apparent anomaly, that is constantly being regenerated, as happened with the "vampires." Rather than discard the historical because of the legendary, we must begin by comparing our best historical accounts with our best information about the actual events concerned. This procedure requires, needless to say, that we learn something about the actual events, even if—as is the case with death and decomposition—it is less than pleasant to do so.

The dead, as we have seen, can quite literally emerge from their graves if the conditions are right, and the right conditions include shallow burial, waterlogged ground, and the presence of predators. These conditions, however, are not always recognized as threats to the corpse: most people do not know, now as in the past, that bodies do not always stay buried.

Consequently, bodies are often buried badly, by people for whom it is important that the job get done quickly. (Dr. Thomas Noguchi has pointed out to me that one reason murder victims are buried poorly is that they are often buried at night, and the murderer has neither light nor tools adequate for the task.) As we shall see in the next chapter, the killing of such bodies, once they have come to the attention of the populace, creates further anomalies that are then incorporated into the folk hypothesis accounting for the vampire.

Killing the Vampire

Down toward the city streets slid rotting
caskets containing more than a hundred
bodies borne on the lip of the mudslide.
Within minutes caskets and corpses
engulfed the area, plunging through
windows into the living rooms of houses,
into stores, and lodging against walls.
One body ended up wedged in the
doorway of a supermarket. . . .
I drove with my staff to Verdugo Hills.
And what I saw there was a scene I'll
never forget. Mud had swept the corpses
everywhere, some of them now standing
grotesquely upright. . . . Most of them,
even some buried for decades, were not
skeletons, as most people would expect.
The skin was gone, but not the muscle
and the tissue. And in a process called
adipocere formation, the fat on the
corpses had changed to a soaplike texture
when the bodies picked up sodium and
moisture underground, and their color
had become a grayish-white. . . .
Whether the citizens of Verdugo Hills
have gotten over the shock of that
invasion of corpses I don't know. Nor, in
all candor, can I be certain that
everybody was correctly identified and
reburied under the right name. But we

did the best we could on that day the
dead rose out of their graves.
—Dr. Thomas Noguchi, *Coroner*

Fra Filippo da Siena tells of parents who
had a sick son, and because they could
not attain his recovery from God, they
sought help from a sorceress, who, in the
name of the parents, gave the child over
to the Devil. At the beginning the boy
seemed to get better, but then he died
after the passage of three months. He
was buried three times and three times
thrown out of the consecrated ground of
the churchyard. That is, consecrated
ground receives the bodies of the damned
only unwillingly. Finally the limbs of the
child, torn apart, were found strewn
about in a small wood in the vicinity of
the churchyard.
—H. F. Feilberg, "Die Sage von dem
Begräbnis König Erik Ejegods von
Dänemark auf Cypern"

As we have seen, there are good reasons for "binding the corpse in place"; otherwise it may be dug up by scavengers, uncovered by erosion, or floated to the surface in storms. These things are seen as action by either another (animate) agency or the corpse itself: things do not just happen; something animate *wills* them to happen. Once the process is seen as possible, it may be conceived of quite differently or be viewed as preventable through magic. Also, since apotropaics can undergo re-interpretation, we cannot always take the word of our informants as to their function. They may not understand the original function, after all. Finally, when cultures protect the body in the grave, it is often impossible to know whether the corpse is being locked in or animals out, or both. In *Die Religion der Jugra-Völker*, K. F. Karjalainen writes, "In the northern area, where the grave is not much deeper than necessary to hold the coffin, it is not filled but just covered over with poles and sheets of birchbark, and so carefully that little odor escapes from the grave."[1] Here the poles and birchbark would seem to be intended to keep animals from the body, creating a barrier both to the odor (which would attract predators) and to the predators themselves. Yet when animals do break in, the same confusion would obtain that we have seen where a "hole in the grave" is regarded as proof that a vampire is seeking to escape. Observers might not know whether something was breaking out or breaking in. Even the presence of wolf or bear tracks might merely convince them that a metamorphosis had taken place rather than a visit by a hungry predator.

Some seeming anomalies make sense if one ascribes them to the exigencies of burial and the need to protect the corpse. For example, while the Yugoslavs consider it appropriate for the corpse to decay quickly, the Russians, according to Mansikka, seek to retard the process. "In order to prevent fast decomposition, the coffin and the boards were singed and the coffin was wrapped with birchbark, smeared with pitch, and sprinkled with lime."[2] Two of these methods (the singeing and the use of pitch) would not, it seems to me, affect decomposition. The wrapping with birchbark might, simply by excluding air, and the use of lime would, by creating a pH in which the microorganisms of decay cannot thrive. But what if Mansikka's sources are correct as to the procedure and incorrect as to the original motive? The methods described make more sense as means of disguising or preventing the *odor* of decomposition. As we have seen, not only is the odor itself viewed as dangerous, but it attracts scavengers that dig up the corpse.

With Christianity we get further reinterpretations of the lore of the revenant, as in Fra Filippo of Siena's tale. There we are told that a sorceress, in the interests of preserving the life of a child, turned the child over to the Devil, who neglected (or was unable?) to keep it alive. The child was buried, but the earth repeatedly spewed up the body. Finally the body was found in a nearby wood, torn limb from limb. Though it is not stated explicitly, it seems safe to assume that it was the Devil who tore the body apart, since this is typical behavior on his part.

As is quite common in such stories (compare the Grimms' account in chapter 15), the narrative begins with a statement of the supposed sin that brought about the course of events. If we ignore that as based on supposition, then we have a story about a child who died and was buried and whose body came to the surface somehow, was dragged off, and was torn to pieces. As we have seen, all this is plausible. That the entire body was removed is not surprising—it was a small body, after all, and children were generally buried much more casually in the past than they are now.* Ac-

---

*Children often receive rather perfunctory burial rites, and often these are different from

cording to Svensson, with dismembered bodies "it is quite normal for the parts of the body to be scattered over a number of places at some distance from one another. The same applies, however, to bodies that have not been dismembered, as various animals and birds can drag the parts for a distance of up to several hundred yards from the original site."[3] (Packs of wolves or dogs do this by pulling the body apart, then escaping with their share.)

Such children, in addition to being torn up by the Devil, may become revenants (Thompson's *Motif-Index*, 425.3: "Revenant as Child"), a distinction that may be based on nothing more than the condition in which the body is found. That is, if the body is just exposed, not completely consumed, it may be viewed as seeking to escape from the grave. If just a hand is exposed, the child may be thought to be reaching out of the grave.

While all three tableaus derive from the same process (a predator attacking a corpse), their explanations differ considerably. Moreover, the first tableau would seem to require no further action, while the second would require that the revenant be killed and that action be taken to prevent such incidents in the future.

As we have seen, people have found many reasons to "kill" or inactivate a corpse. If we keep in mind just what they saw and how they customarily interpreted it, we will note that these methods often aimed quite specifically at preventing certain acts of vampires believed, on the basis of observations of corpses, to be their typical behavior. The tongue protrudes and blood seeps from the open mouth; therefore the vampire must attack his victims with teeth or tongue and suck their blood. Logically enough, the people retaliate by attacking its mouth or head.

Sometimes, as is traditional for the Nachzehrer, the head is cut off; sometimes a spike is driven into the mouth, pinning the head to the ground, or else fixing the tongue in place. (For both of these methods there is abundant archaeological evidence, a good summary of which is in Rudolf Grenz's article on the subject: see Bibliography.) Mouth and tongue are, as we have seen, the target of many apotropaic measures. A thorn may be driven into the tongue so that the vampire cannot use it to draw blood, as the Russian upir is wont to do. A variety of things may be placed in the mouth (dirt, garlic, a coin) to give the revenant something to chew on or to prevent chewing or blood-sucking entirely. The mouth may be propped or tied shut, and food may be provided as a substitute for his diet of blood. Since vampires are put off by strong-smelling sub-

---

those required for adults. In India, for example, "The body of a young child under two years of age must not be burnt, but buried" (Shastri, 3).

stances, incense or garlic may be stuffed into eyes, ears, and nose. The head may be bound with thorns. (Jesus' crown of thorns may have been as much an apotropaic as a punishment: because he was executed, his body would have been seen as a rallying point of evil spirits.) In all cases, however, people's observations and beliefs have clearly suggested the methods they use to kill or forestall a vampire.

The most dramatic treatment of the vampire—driving a sharpened stake into the body—is related to the most striking aspect of his appearance: the bloated corpse. Similar practices are used apotropaically. Sharp objects are buried with the body or even driven into it, so that it will be killed (or deflated) if it should "turn into a vampire." "The view is also widespread," according to Norbert Reiter, "that the vampire has no bones, but is a sack filled with blood and comes into being when the devil pulls the skin off a particular corpse and blows it up. To prevent that, they wound the bodies of such persons of whom it is believed that they might become vampires. (If the skin should inflate, the air would escape.)"[4] Here we seem to see reactions to the fact that the corpse is unrecognizable and vastly bloated, lacks rigor mortis, and, if punctured, loses its air (actually methane) and bleeds.

The practice of puncturing the body may have been reinvented from time to time, when the buoyancy was seen to result from the bloating. The bog bodies may have been transfixed with stakes not only to pin them in place but also to prevent them from becoming buoyant.

According to Cozannet, among the Gypsies the soul is believed to remain in the corpse until decomposition.[5] Certain tribes attempt to hasten its departure by cutting off the head of the corpse and burying it separately—a practice that is attested, as we have seen, for the ancient Celts. Other tribes "pierce the heart of the deceased after a certain time, to permit the departure of the soul."[6] It seems possible—but this is only speculation—that the thwarted soul, which, on its own, cannot leave the body, is part of an interpretation of the bloating of the corpse. Perhaps the bloating is believed to be a result of the soul's attempts to escape, and puncturing the body provides a route.[†] If a decomposing corpse were pierced, it would certainly be evident that *something* was escaping.

[†]Such a relationship between methane and spirit seems to be implied by Finnish *kalma*, which is defined (among other things) as "odour of a corpse; spirit holding sway over a burial-ground" (Collinder, 42).

I have found one eyewitness account (European G[...]
in which the heart is pierced with "a very long pin," t[...]
kill that which remains alive in the body. "If the body [...]
has escaped, the heart itself must remain alive, for at le[...]
human being lives for ever, is immortal. What is it that [...]
knows. This Wise Woman solved the problem, for in s[...]
she killed all the rest. And as a matter of fact, ever since we [...]
this rite, there have been no more apparitions."[7] Some fan[...]   [...]s are
present here: the puncturing as a means of disposing, finally, of a dead body,
and the belief that the body has a kind of second life—a belief based in part
on the colorful and diverse processes of decomposition.

The relationship between the staking and the bloating becomes even
more evident, however, when the corpse is covered before killing it.
Sometimes the corpse is draped with a hide or cloth, sometimes with
dirt, but the rationale is always to prevent the vampire-killers from being
spattered by the vampire's blood. The reader will not be surprised—may
indeed be relieved—to learn that little has been published on the explosive
potential of bloated bodies when they are pierced. I have found one
account, however, from Africa, in which certain natives on elephant hunts
were said to have found a harmless and engaging use for the decomposing
bodies of elephants: they would wait until an acquaintance was near the
body, then thrust a spear at it. The result, according to the author, was
"an immense out-rush of stinking gas and muck," which amused almost
everybody present.[8] Just such an event, apparently, may be averted by
covering the corpse of the vampire. This would seem to be the simplest
explanation for Hauttecoeur's account of a vrykolakas that attacked a
priest, as Summers says, with "vollies of mud and ordure."[9] An eighteenth-century physician also had some experience with this phenomenon. When he was asked to cut into a body and retrieve the herbs that
were supposed to have been fed to the revenant by the Devil, he found
instead—as he remarks drily—"many winds, erupting with force, and
reeking horribly to the point of [causing] unconsciousness."[10]

It is presumably this phenomenon that is described in Romanian folklore, where the blood of the staked vampire is said to spurt high into the
air. There the rationale given is that the vampire has two hearts, and the
second of these, which enables him to live after death, causes the blood
to gush forth.[11] Like the "two souls" theory that we shall consider, this
explains both the "life after death" of the corpse and why the blood seems
still to be under pressure. In reality, of course, the pressure derives from

rcing of a stake into the bloated body, which compresses the body
vities. When killing revenants, people must have learned early on to
cover them with something so as to avoid violently disgorging fluids. One
of our revenants—the Shoemaker of Silesia—is not reported to have bled
on the occasion of his second death, but that is presumably because he
had originally died from loss of blood (he had cut his own throat).

Before leaving this dismal subject, we should note that blood tends to
spurt in any form of death in which the body is compressed violently,
as by beatings, knifings, and certain types of shootings, especially with
large-caliber guns. Typically there is "blood everywhere" in a room where
such a killing has taken place, sometimes even on the ceiling, sprayed
out in a pattern that reflects (and reveals) the direction and force of the
blows. The principal source of blood pressure—the force that causes it
to spray so far—is not the heart, in such cases, but the blow itself.[12]

In relating such information to our vampire-killings, we are limited to
conjecture, but we can safely say that some things would be likely to
happen. In a seventeenth-century French account, we are told that the
vampires "suck the blood of living people and animals in such great
abundance that sometimes it comes out of their mouths, their noses, and
especially their ears, and that sometimes the body swims in its blood
which has spilled out into its coffin."[13] (As a description of a decomposing
body, this is accurate enough, except for the ears: according to pathologists I have spoken to, the blood tends to get to the ear only by flowing
down from the mouth.) When the body is killed, according to the same
seventeenth-century source, "a great quantity of blood" flows—again a
plausible statement, whether the killing is by staking or decapitation.
Staking the body, in fact, would presumably cause blood to well up
noticeably at the mouth and nose, because of pressure from the lungs.
The vampire, therefore, must have acquired all that "fresh" blood from
his victims, since his own blood should be coagulated.

> They found that he was quite complete
> and undecayed, and that fresh blood had
> flowed from his eyes, nose, mouth, and
> ears; that the shirt, the covering, and the
> coffin were completely bloody; that the
> old nails on his hands and feet, along
> with the skin, had fallen off, and that
> new ones had grown; and since they saw
> from this that he was a true vampire,

they drove a stake through his heart,
according to their custom, whereby he
gave an audible groan and bled
copiously.
—Description of Arnod Paole, *Visum et
Repertum*

By now it should be evident that the description of Arnod Paole is an accurate enough account of a dead body exhumed after twenty or thirty days in a grave. The decay of the body has been slowed by burial and is, in fact, most evident from the internal pressure—blood is being forced out of the nose and mouth. The nails have dropped away, revealing the nail bed, which is interpreted as "new nails." Skin slippage has taken place, the epidermis peeling away and revealing the "new" dermis underneath. The redness of the dermis is taken for evidence that the body is that of a vampire: red = blood = vampire.

Some of these events (the nails and skin) seem to have had little influence on the vampire myth, even though they are commonly remarked on as anomalies when vampires are exhumed. Three phenomena, however— the groan of the vampire when staked, the "lack of decomposition," and the presence of blood—have been unusually fertile sources of speculation.

We already understand the "blood at the mouth" phenomenon, and Paole's famous groan need not trouble us at all. Indeed, it would have been odd if his body had *not* let out a sound when a stake was driven into it. When the stake was driven in, the compression of the lungs would force air and gases rather explosively past the glottis, creating a sound similar in both origin and quality to the groan of a living person. This was pointed out in 1732 by the Royal Prussian Society of Science in an analysis of *Visum et Repertum* that explained several of its anomalies. This analysis, however, prosaic as it was, was ignored in the literature of the vampire until a few years ago, when Sturm and Völker included it in their excellent anthology.[14]

The vampire's groan is not always interpreted as such. I have found one account in which it is compared to the squeal of a pig,[15] and Aribert Schroeder quotes an eighteenth-century Serbian account with yet another description of the sound:

The investigation of the doctors determined that the four questionable corpses, which had lain in the earth for twenty days, had remained incorrupt. Out of fear that vampires or snakes[‡] might take them over, the inhabitants of the village

‡The relationship of snakes to vampires, which seems to be a specifically Yugoslavian motif,

beheaded the corpses, drove a stake into the man's heart, whereupon they heard a loud cracking sound, and burned all the corpses.[16]

It is difficult to know what sounds would emanate from a corpse that was first beheaded, then staked. Possibly the sound described could be either that of the swollen body cavity splitting open or of a rib cracking. In any case the "groan" of the vampire appears to be specific to stakings: it does not occur when vampires are dissected (as in *Visum et Repertum*), decapitated, or cremated, presumably because these procedures do not put sudden strong pressure on the chest cavity.

The apparent lack of decomposition has its consequences in folklore, contributing to the need for exhumation and various methods of hastening the process whereby the body becomes inert. Left to its own devices, a body will eventually stabilize or at least reach a point where nothing is happening to it quickly. In the Balkans it is expected to be reduced after a few years to nothing but bones, at which point the remains are dug up for one last ceremony. After this they are disposed of once again, sometimes placed in an ossuary, sometimes reburied.

Bodies that are found not to have decayed completely are a source of great distress to the people who have dug them up. We see an example of this in Loring Danforth's study of exhumation in rural Greece:

> Many women, however, were surprised and puzzled by the poor condition of Eleni's remains. Why after five years had Eleni's hair and clothes not decomposed? Why were the bones not clean and white? Some women attributed this to natural causes. The grave was very deep. It was in a shaded area near the graveyard wall. The clothes were nylon. Other women disagreed. They believed that a person whose body did not fully decompose and whose bones were black[§] and unclean had committed sins that had not been forgiven.[17]

---

may derive from the fact that the snake is a common symbol of regeneration, perhaps because it appears, when shedding its skin, to be transformed from an old, shabby snake to a new shiny one. Perhaps "vampires" are associated with snakes because they too are supposed to be regenerated (and do in fact shed their skin). According to Frazer ([1913], 59 *passim*) in many cultures snakes are viewed as immortal and appear in myths to explain the origin of human mortality: the Creator's messenger got confused and mistakenly announced that it was the snake, not man, who was to acquire the habit of shedding his skin and thereby become immortal.

§According to Svensson, "The color of bones can vary from light grayish white to dark brownish black, depending on the age of the find, kind and properties of the soil, whether the parts are or were enclosed or covered in some way, or the measures that may have been taken with the body before burial, e.g., more or less complete burning" (p. 399).

Here we see, side by side, naturalistic and mythological explanations for the same phenomena.ǁ The latter derives the body's condition not from ideologically neutral physical laws but from purposeful moral ones.

We may understand the distress of the Greek villagers if we recall several aspects of a corpse's "life after death" and its implications for the living. First is the shock of encountering the loathsomeness of a corpse that does not just quietly disintegrate but turns ugly and emits an appalling stench.# Another is confusion over the great variety of behavior of corpses resulting from the differing effects of decomposition. People can simply never get used to everything that a corpse can do. In Greece this is reflected in a variety of terms for the vrykolakas, the etymologies of which clearly relate to normal events associated with decomposition.**

A third cause of distress is fear of contagion, though it may not be expressed in ways familiar to us. In Karelia it is said that the dead "fired projectiles which transmitted diseases."[18] And we must not forget that murder, too, tends to be contagious: if one person is murdered, others tend to be as well, in retaliation. If the murderers are known, the events may be described as a feud. But if they are not, it may be believed that the deceased has returned from the dead to gain revenge. Thus we are told that "murder victims become revenants."[19]

We must try to understand the attempts to kill the revenant against

---

ǁWilke suggests that the colors of the revenant are related to colors of dead bodies: "Since the corpse looks pale at first [this is not necessarily true], ghosts usually look white. On the other hand the progressive coloration of the corpse, with the development of decomposition, leads to red or black ghosts" (*Reallexikon*, 7:259).

Some of the different possible colors of the body may be reflected in Thompson's *Motif-Index*, which lists the following motifs: 422.2.1 Revenant red [in color]; 422.2.2 Revenant green; and 422.2.3 Revenant gray. Revenants (and corpses) can also be dark blue, as was Glam in *Grettir's Saga*, and black (Maundrel, 201).

Greta Grober-Glück (1983), following Geiger and Ranke, has objected to the common term *lebender Leichnam* (living corpse) because such revenants, although occurring in a quite material and corporeal condition, "only seldom have such characteristics of the corpse as paleness, odor, immobility, and skeleton" (p. 150). Aside from the fact that it seems unfair to criticize an oxymoron for containing a contradiction, this observation simply reveals that the scholar, like our informants, has expectations of the corpse not in accordance with what people find when they exhume bodies.

#While we are dwelling on the unutterably loathsome, I might point out that sometimes a corpse can appear to be intact on the top, yet be disintegrated underneath, owing to the presence there of maggots, which require darkness and moisture. One wonders if this condition may have contributed to the memento mori motif of the woman who is beautiful in front but crawling with worms behind.

**An analysis of these may be found in my article in the *Journal of Folklore Research*: see Bibliography.

this background. Sometimes the vampire's own weapons are attacked, as we have seen (the mouth, the tongue, the head), and sometimes he is staked in order to "kill" or release whatever is inside him. In all cases, however, the need to deal with him has great influence on funerary and body-disposal methods, many of which must be understood as attempts to neutralize the revenant.

Typical methods of body-disposal follow:

Burial, with or without later exhumation
Depositing the body in a cave or crevice
Covering the body with rocks
Covering the body with brush
Disposal in water
Cremation
Excarnation (allowing scavengers—birds, wolves, dogs, crocodiles, and so forth—to eat away flesh of body)
Exposing the body on a platform or in a tree
Mummification by chemical means
Mummification by burial in hot sand or exposure to hot air
Embalming
Drying the body with fire

These methods, which seem at first glance to be so diverse, usually do only one of two things: they either hold the body in one place, so that it lives out its second life where it cannot harm its friends and relatives, as in the first list, or else they render the body inert, incapable of undergoing further changes, as in the second list. In either case the body is expected ultimately to be brought into a state of equilibrium. Cremation and mummification, therefore, actually have the same function: both cause the body to stop its development, which is seen as a cause, by analogy, of deaths and disorders that take place after the original death.

According to Van Gennep, "As for the destruction of the corpse itself (by cremation, premature putrefaction, etc.), its purpose is to separate the components, the various bodies and souls. Only very seldom do the remains (bones, ashes) constitute the new body of the deceased in the afterlife."[20] At issue is the need to end the second, and destructive, life of the deceased. For this to happen, the body must be prevented from changing.

It may seem curious that decomposition is itself one of these processes that end the second life of the corpse (for example, when the corpse is buried long enough to be reduced to bones). The very process that frightens the people, convincing them that they are looking at a monster, is also the process that renders the monster inert. But it is we, not they, who see the two phenomena—the ugliness of the corpse and its resolution into inert bones—as aspects of the same process. For our informants two events take place: a monster is created out of a bad corpse (early stages of decomposition) or else a good corpse decays into harmless bones (late stages of decomposition).

Our informants look for causes just as we do. They find them, however, not in impersonal laws of the universe but in benevolent or malevolent wills. The body does not bloat; something inflates it. In addition, two other important cognitive biases affect their reasoning. First, if two events occur one after the other, the first must cause the second: *post hoc, ergo propter hoc*. Second, they do not require a series of events to deduce a pattern: one event is enough.

As a consequence of these habits of mind, a European peasant, on finding a corpse, was likely to conclude that it was "doing" something rather than that things were happening to it. Moreover, he would relate these doings of the corpse to anything untoward happening in his community. From there it was only a small step to checking on the corpse in its grave, when further deaths took place.

In time, such corpses were habitually killed in advance, even if they were not yet undergoing the processes that so upset the people observing them. Stakes were driven into murder victims (or witches, or outlaws) before burial, or they were cremated. Thus Jirecek says that, on the Black Sea, the people of certain isolated Bulgarian villages "burned all the dead . . . so that they would not become vampires."[21] In other words, funerary and burial procedures evolved out of the need to dispose of the dangerous corpse both quickly and efficiently. In the next chapter we shall consider some of these procedures and ponder their relationship to the exigencies of burial.

Body Disposal and
Its Problems

Some bones make best skeletons, some
bodies quick and speediest ashes: Who
would expect a quick flame from
Hydropsicall *Heraclitus?* The poysoned
Souldier when his Belly brake, put out
two pyres in *Plutarch.*
—Sir Thomas Browne, *Hydriotaphia*

He looks like he's asleep.
It's a shame that he won't keep,
But it's summer and we're runnin' out of
ice . . .
—"Pore Jud is Daid," *Oklahoma!*

The fear of the corpse, which Sir James Frazer saw as virtually universal,[1] has some important implications for body disposal. We may expect the following exigencies to be among those determining how methods are chosen:

1. Disposal should be quick, taking place before the corpse has a chance to "act."
2. The corpse should be rendered inert as quickly as possible.
3. The corpse should require as little handling as possible.

In times of epidemic, the first and third exigencies may override the second. In a study of the customs of the Chamars of India, Briggs says,

"When a person dies of smallpox, plague or cholera, the body is disposed of as soon as possible. Sometimes it is buried. Usually the body is not burned, but cast into a stream without any ceremony."[2]

Some old arguments acquire a new look when considered from this perspective. Though cremation and embalming seem to imply radically different philosophies (since the one method destroys the body while the other preserves it), in a sense they actually do the same thing: both render the body inert, preventing its transformation into a monster. When von Negelein says that mummification can only have the purpose of "preserving the life to be found in the corpse as long as possible,"[3] he would seem to ignore the fact that precisely what mummification does *not* do is to maintain life—of any kind—in the corpse.

True, the body is often maintained in order to ensure continued life, but the life involved is apparently not that of the body. Generally the body's *double* is maintained by the body's preservation. This double—in Egypt it is the *ka*—is evidently derived from reflections, shadows, and dream images, which are not clearly differentiated from one another and may even be seen as a single significant, purposeful phenomenon, which apes the body during consciousness, has its own life during sleep, and then lives on after death (and note that the dead do "live on" in our dreams and memories). Since this double is altered when its original is (one can verify this by making a face at a mirror), it is apparently assumed that, to prevent it from being transformed into a monster as the corpse undergoes change, and then returning to haunt us, the corpse must be maintained in its original condition. And since the double is altered only by a change in the outward appearance of the body, cultures that mummify often focus all their attention on how the body appears. They try to preserve not the body but the body's appearance. With some exceptions, the entrails are commonly thrown away. And because it is only appearance that is important, often a statue is thought to function just as well as the body as a means of retaining the image of the double in its original form.*

As Emily Vermeule has pointed out, we look for more meaning than is probably to be found in the choice of different forms of body disposal: "Students of Greek culture have long tried to detect differences in how the different generations understood the *psyche* or the *soma* according to whether the prevailing fashion was to bury or burn. It does not seem to matter."[4] What matters, I would suggest, is that the body be stabilized, whether by decomposition, cremation, or mummification.

---

*This is a brief statement of a complicated problem. I hope to deal with the problem in detail in a later publication. For more on the various kinds of doubles, see chapter 18.

Before mummification was introduced in Egypt, bodies were dismembered before burial, much as they have been in Europe, where this was evidently done to prevent "life after death."[5] They then underwent secondary burial, remaining in the ground until the flesh had disintegrated, after which the bones were dug up, cleaned, and reburied—the same process, in other words, that we have seen in the Balkans and many other parts of the world. Wiedemann saw this, in Egypt, as a means of preventing the return of the dead. Like mummification, this procedure could have been seen as a method of controlling the actual body or its double, or both, since the double depends on the body for its own form.

We may gain considerable insight into the phenomenon of the vampire by viewing body-disposal methods as procedures derived, in large part, from the fear of the corpse and the desire to bring about its neutralization. Such methods all have their own advantages and disadvantages.

Cremation

Cremation fulfills our first condition, quick disposal, rather badly, for it takes hours to cremate a body on a wood fire, even using accelerants, and someone must tend the fire. It is in fulfilling the second condition that cremation is most successful, for it may render the body completely inert and even reduce it to inorganic ash, so that it no longer "does" anything at all. That this is its objective, in Northern India at least, is suggested by Crooke's observation that it was important for a body to be cremated soon after death, since otherwise the soul might return (presumably animating the body in the ways we have discussed earlier).[6] And as I have mentioned, certain Bulgarian villages along the Black Sea at one time routinely burned their dead "so that they would not become vampires."[7] It has been observed that cultures that cremate tend not to have revenants in corporeal form,[8] but since India has abundant revenants in its folklore, we might suggest that such cultures cremate in order *not* to have revenants.

Burial

Disposal by burial is also rather slow because of the need to dig a grave, with considerable labor, especially in rocky soil. But the labor is unskilled, therefore cheap, and in Europe a grave was often dug by family or friends.

Burial renders the body inert slowly, but it is both pinned in place and hidden from view while this process is taking place, so that it will normally not come to the attention of the populace unless someone digs it up. As we have seen, its influence on local events does not necessarily depend on its escape: many revenants exert their influence from the grave. In general, though, shallow burial causes, deep burial discourages vampirism, presumably because bodies buried deep tend to stay put and not be noticed.[9]

With burial the handling of the body may be minimal. Usually the corpse is washed, often by a person who specializes in this function, and the water, washcloth, and soap are disposed of as potentially dangerous.

Burial does have some other disadvantages: because it is fairly labor-intensive, it may prove impractical during epidemics. "During the great yellow-fever epidemic of 1853 [in New Orleans] there was even a serious shortage of gravediggers and men were offered five dollars an hour to perform this task."[10] At such times, as we have seen, mass graves come into fashion. Other problems with burial are that the buried body may not stay put or that it may undergo saponification or mummification and remain intact for many years.[†]

Secondary burial has similar problems, in addition to requiring much more handling of the body and much more work. It ensures, however, that the body is finally neutralized. In a study of a tribe from Borneo, Peter Metcalf has given a succinct analysis of what the problem looks like from the point of view of the people disposing of the body: "As the body rots away to leave dry bones, so the soul is transformed slowly into spirit form. As the corpse is formless and repulsive until putrefaction is completed, so the soul is homeless. It lurks miserably on the fringes of human habitation and, in its discomfort, may affect the living with illness."[11] It is clear from this that body and soul are related after death as well as before. Their relationship ends when the body is finally inert, which suggests that the Berawan view its changes as a kind of animation. It is not surprising, then, that they were dismayed by Metcalf's account of American burial practices, which do not separate the inert bones from the active flesh: "For the Berawan, America is a land carpeted with potential zombies."[12]

Often crevices, caves, or other already-existing holes are used for body disposal, because this obviates the need to dig a hole, thereby saving both time and effort. Livingstone, for example, mentions the unseemly haste with which a South African tribe got rid of their dead, often depositing them in an anteater's hole in order to save digging a grave.[13]

[†]This phenomenon may be reflected in the following bit of folklore from Illinois: "Another reason against burial in a low-lying ground is the belief that water seeping into the grave may petrify the body" (UCLA folklore encyclopedia collection; see also Saxon, 345).

Covering Body With Rocks or Brush

This disposes of the body very quickly, since a grave need not be dug and little handling of the body is necessary. Moreover, because the body is exposed to air, moderate temperatures, and insects, it would be rendered inert quickly. These considerations would make the method attractive, especially for high-risk bodies (murder victims, for example). On the other hand, it is extremely difficult, using this method, to protect the body from large and determined predators—a problem that may be reflected in the old tradition of throwing a rock or twig onto such a site. Perhaps this habit was inspired by the discovery that such bodies tended not to rest easy and had to be covered up again from time to time. And if the body was disturbed, it would appear to emerge from the grave in a rather horrid state of decomposition.

Disposal in Water (fresh running; fresh standing; brackish standing)

In any type of disposal in water the body is hidden from view, as in burial, but very quickly, and it requires a minimum of handling. On the other hand, it is rendered inert much more slowly than a body that is cremated or embalmed. It may, in fact, undergo saponification and be preserved indefinitely.

Sometimes the body is simply thrown into running water, on the theory that it will be removed permanently in this manner. Since, however, it becomes quite buoyant with decomposition, it may fetch up on shore a short distance away in a dreadful state of decay. To prevent its reemergence, it is often heavily weighted down. Bodies are also thrown into the ocean and into lakes in this way.

The major problem here, as we have seen, is that it takes a great deal of weight to keep a body submerged. And if sufficient weight is used, one has to transport not just a heavy body but a heavy weight as well. Just dumping these into the water—and it must be fairly deep water, since the body floats as high as it can—presents a considerable problem.

Disposal in peat bogs has advantages over disposal in water, since one can use a cutting already in existence in which to put the body. The Grauballe man, for example, "was deposited in a small peat-cutting which was not fresh at the time but overgrown."[4] This would limit the necessary work and with it both exposure to the corpse and the time necessary for disposal. Such bodies tend to be preserved, however, especially when deposited during cold weather, which would encourage the belief that they are really not dead at all.[‡] And as we have seen, if they bloat (as

---

[‡]The best-known bog bodies were evidently killed in winter or early spring (to go by the

they would in warm weather) they must be pinned in place to keep them from popping to the surface when the water level rises.

Excarnation

Considered only from the point of view of efficiency, excarnation would seem one of the more effective methods of body disposal. The body could be disposed of quickly—and rendered inert quickly—merely by setting it out where animals can get at it. In practice, however, the sheer messiness of the procedure encourages the use of a special caste, which adds to its cost. In Tibet the process is particularly gruesome: the flesh is separated from the bones of the body by workers with knives rather than by the birds that consume the flesh.[15] Sir Charles Bell has suggested that the practice derives from the difficulty in Tibet of relying on other methods: "This method has much to recommend it in a country like Tibet. Burial is difficult, for the ground is frozen hard during the winter. Cremation is difficult, for there is no coal, and but little firewood. Casting into rivers pollutes the drinking supply."[16] Here we see what an eternal embarrassment corpses can be; they are simply not easy to get rid of. If the birds do not consume the entire body, incidentally, the event is given a folkloric interpretation: "Only the bodies of the condemned, it is believed, are shunned by the birds."[17]

The practice of cutting the flesh from the bones, which Lawson reports observing in Greece at an exhumation,[18] should make us cautious about the conclusions we may draw from the presence of cut marks on human remains. Last year, I noted in my morning paper (Los Angeles Times, 19 April 1987) that a group of British archaeologists, excavating at Somerset, have uncovered late Paleolithic skeletons with "cut marks made by stone tools which may relate to cannibalism." Since cannibalism is uncommon, whereas excarnation is not, the latter would seem to be a more logical (if less newsworthy) choice to explain this phenomenon.

In his book The Man-Eating Myth, W. Arens has pointed out the "hearsay" quality of the evidence for cannibalism. I wonder if excarnation is sometimes interpreted as cannibalism. In other words, perhaps the neigh-

---

stomach contents), leading to the hypothesis that they might have been killed as sacrifices during the winter solstice (Glob, 27; Fischer, in Cockburn, 177). This sounds plausible, but it could be that selective preservation has contributed to this view. Fischer argues, "If the body had been deposited in warm weather, one can assume that the presence of anaerobic bacteria in the intestinal system would have had a destructive effect on the interior of the corpse before the liquid of the bog could penetrate the body" (Glob, 27; Fischer, in Cockburn, 191). If this is so, then we would know of the stomach contents only of those bodies deposited during cold weather, weighting our evidence toward the winter solstice theory.

Figure 3. Reconstruction of Çatal Hüyük shrine decorated with wall-paintings of vultures pecking at human bodies. Drawing by Mark C. Stone, after illustration by Grace Huxtable in James Mellaart, *Earliest Civilizations of the Near East* (New York: McGraw-Hill, 1965).

bors of the supposed cannibals are making the same assumption as the British archaeologists: if people are cutting the meat off the bones of their dead enemies, it must be because they are eating the meat! Arens has found no persuasive evidence of cannibalism among the people from whose name the word *cannibal* is derived, the Caribs, who, we are told, believed that the dead did not go to the land of souls until they were without flesh.[19] Perhaps, like the Greeks and the Tibetans, they stripped the flesh from the body to ensure the passage of the soul. This explanation would account for the fact that reports of cannibalism tend to implicate *neighboring* tribes, rather than that of the informant himself. The supposed cannibals always deny the practice and frequently accuse yet another culture. The phenomenon is not unlike that of the "foaf," or "friend of a friend" of urban legend, who has so many bizarre, outlandish, and— alas!—completely unverifiable adventures.

We have early evidence of excarnation: at Çatal Hüyük, in Anatolia (ca. 6,000 B.C.), wall paintings depict vultures attacking headless corpses. Some of these representations from Çatal Hüyük show the vultures with what seem to be human legs (they bend the wrong way), and it has been suggested that perhaps a funerary ritual (excarnation?) is being performed by priestesses done up to represent vultures (fig. 3).[20] Moreover, on one wall a human figure toward whom vultures are flying is shown with something like a sling, which Schüz and Künig have interpreted as a means of calling the vultures. They cite a modern example in which a whip is used in this way.[21]

Scavenging birds are apparently no longer used for this purpose in Turkey, but a nineteenth-century report from the Anatolian side of the Black Sea illustrates how vultures may be fitted into the human ecosystem:

> One of the most disagreeable and yet striking sights frequent in this town is presented by the number and the horrid tameness of the large white vultures, which perform with alacrity and zeal the disgusting office of street-sweepers and scavengers. Roosting at night in the clefts and fastnesses of the mountains which surround the town [Amasya], they pass the day either perched on the low roofs of the houses, watching for garbage, or, careering aloft in large and beautiful gyrations, soar for hours on their expanded wings, ready to pounce upon their meals. The Turks never molest them, but, appreciating their useful qualities, accustom them to approach their dwellings by throwing to them from time to time heads of fresh killed fowls and pieces of refuse meat.[22]

One wonders if, in the vultures of Çatal Hüyük, we are looking at a source of the harpies (snatchers) of Greek mythology, which are represented on the Harpy Tomb from Xanthos in Lydia (also in Anatolia), as birds with the face of women. This representation on a tomb recalls their typical association with death.[§]

This interpretation has the advantage that it makes sense out of a diverse group of reported views concerning the harpies: they are associated with winds in Homer (*Odyssey* 2.66)—which would not be unusual for vultures—but distinguished from the winds in Hesiod;[‖] and in the *Argonautica*, blind Phineas, on the Anatolian coast of the Black Sea, is tormented by harpies that swoop down to snatch the food left for him and leave a loathsome stench behind. Rose suggests that these harpies "seem to be modelled on carrion-feeding birds."[23] Perhaps they got their half-woman, half-bird form, in mythology from the rituals associated with excarnation and carried out—as Mellaart's reconstruction suggests—partly by women disguised as vultures and partly (or originally) by actual vultures.[#]

[§]Their association with death is well attested. See Vermeule, 145–177, and Weicker, 5 *passim*.
[‖]They "follow together with the blowings of the winds and with the birds" *Theogony*, l.268). Their names are given in various sources as Aello, Okypete, and Kelaino, all of which have transparent etymologies that Rose translates respectively as "Stormwind," "Swiftwing," and "Dark" (p. 28).
[#]Certain conditions seem to bring into existence body-disposal castes, especially a technology that requires considerable expertise and much handling of the body in its intermediate condition (no longer intact, not yet inert, and thoroughly messy). Cremation, excarnation, and (especially) embalming are usually left to experts; burial is often done by the family. In the United States we use the Egyptian method: first we embalm the body, then we bury it. *Plus ça change . . .*

I received unexpected support for this view of the harpies when, in connection with some remarks in chapter 10, concerning the place of scavenging birds in folklore, I wrote to the learned archaeologist Marija Gimbutas to request some bibliographical references. She sent an extensive study of the folklore of birds that she had just presented at the World Archaeological Congress (Southampton/London), in which, approaching the subject from a different perspective, she had concluded that the harpies "must have descended from the Old European/Anatolian Vulture Goddess," or some other figure of this sort.[24]

Embalming and Mummification

When bodies are embalmed, they are rapidly rendered inert, but embalming is an extremely messy and time-consuming project, requiring that the intestinal flora be removed or neutralized and the blood removed, which is generally done by specialists. Consequently, the practice is least satisfactory when it is most needed. During epidemics, for example, the embalmers may be overwhelmed by the number of bodies in need of treatment or may prove unwilling to handle them at all. And because, like cremation, it is quite expensive, it is often reserved for those bodies whose relatives can pay for it.

In the nineteenth century a traveler observed that the Swedish Lapps had an odd way of burying those who died in the summer. "They carefully remove the entrails from the body, smoke it and then hang it in the sun for then it is easier to carry and transport, so they say."[25] This is a classic case of mummification: the entrails are removed to eliminate the source of decay, and the body is dried to render it inert. It is also made lighter in weight, but this was probably a secondary consideration: we are told that they dried the body only in summer, most likely because only in the summer would the body decay and bloat. In the winter cold temperatures would render it inert. In such cultures, in fact, bodies were often simply frozen during the winter, then disposed of when the weather turned warm. Only then did they become a problem, since freezing kept them from "doing" anything. For that matter, bodies are still "kept on ice."

High temperatures, combined with a lack of moisture and a good air supply, will also cause a body to mummify, as when it is buried in loose desert sand. Because sand is an inherently unstable environment, however, such bodies may return to the surface and give a scare to those who find them. The stabilization of the body, while desirable from one point of view, is from another point of view quite scary. Indeed, if the vampires tell us anything, it is that bodies are frightening when they undergo the process of decomposition, whereas when they don't—then they are frightening, too.

Exhumation and Staking or Beheading

This is a special case, because it deals with the corpse after its initial disposal, as it is decomposing and in the condition of "vampirism." Special conditions obtain: handling the body is both scary and messy. Consequently, the body is usually "killed" in ways that allow a minimum of handling and that direct the attack at the body's "weapons" (that is, its head and mouth), that seek to kill the heart that supposedly animates it (staking the chest), or that release the spirit, devil, soul, and/or "air" from its body (staking the abdomen). So that it need not be handled, the body is usually left in situ, although there are many exceptions. Where the body is exhumed by order of a public authority, rather than clandestinely, public interest may cause it to go on display for a time, as the shoemaker of Breslau did for twenty days.** In some cases the body is not even dug up: "In the region of Voks [Yugoslavia]," according to Vukanovic, "when it becomes known that somebody has turned into a vampire, the Moslem Gypsies go to the cemetery and thrust a sharp juniper stick through the centre of the grave into the stomach of the deceased to prevent his rising again."[26] Such a procedure would allow the killing with an absolute minimum of handling. It also implies that the body is not buried very deep—a characteristic of vampires.

Decapitation requires little handling. It was usually accomplished by means of a sexton's spade, which would be already at hand and would allow one to conduct the operation without nearing the body. Meyer quotes an informant (from the area of Danzig) who stated that the revenant's blood on one's skin would be lethal, for which reason a spade with a long handle was used for the decapitation.[27] The head, however, then had to be moved to where it could not be reached by the body: in *Grettir's Saga*, Glam's head was placed behind his buttocks. Since the

---

**Exhumed bodies often go on display thus. Bartsch, 366, cites such an example from Mecklenburg, and I have seen a mummified body on display in the Saint Thomas Church in Strasbourg, in a glass coffin (see also Lee, 132, for a Greek example). Gerschke says that in 1916, in Jakobsdorf, he saw the body (and head!) of the famous "vampire" Wollschläger, whose corpse was decapitated around 1750. When Gerschke went back in 1940 to photograph the body, he found that it had been buried two weeks previously (pp. 90–91). Also, a friend of mine recalls as one of his most distinctive childhood memories the mummified body of Saint Vibiana in the church of that name in Los Angeles, also under glass. He tells me that such bodies (on display, that is) are not uncommon in churches in Mexico. See Ariès, 385–88, for other examples.

head was generally reburied in the same grave (to save digging another?), the object would seem to be to hide it from the revenant so that he would neither put it back on his shoulders nor carry it about, like the Headless Horseman. A layer of dirt was generally put between the head and body, presumably so that the revenant would not become aware that his head was nearby. As we have seen, we have much evidence that skulls were sometimes buried separately or at a different depth from the rest of the body.[28]

Valvasor's account of a seventeenth-century vampire probably gives an accurate view of events. A group of men were sent off to kill the vampire, Giure Grando by name, but fled when they unearthed him: "The dead body being uncovered, they found its face quite red, and it smiled at them and opened its mouth." Forced to return, they tried to drive a sharpened hawthorn stake through its stomach, but the stake always rebounded. One of the men then "began, from a distance, to chop off the head with a hoe," but because he was too tentative and fearful, another man took over and chopped the head away, whereupon "the deceased let out a cry and twisted no differently than if he had been alive, and also bled all over the grave."[††] Here we see that the participants fear touching the corpse or having blood spurt on them. When one method (the staking) does not work, they simply kill the corpse by another means. If this had not worked (the apparitions were said to have stopped afterwards), they would presumably have dug up the corpse and cremated it at the cost of further handling of something both odious and scary.

We have seen that some of the typical goods that we find with the body have an apotropaic intent. Sometimes physical restraint is involved, such as a net or a sharp object that is expected to puncture the corpse if it bloats.[‡‡] Such objects, once established as appropriate grave goods, often have a long history, even after they have been reinterpreted or have lost their function. Thus the net is eventually interpreted as giving the revenant something harmless to do—untying one knot a year—and the sharp objects are included even in urns that contain the remains of cre-

---

[††]That the mouth of the corpse was open and the face was red would be quite normal. The stake would presumably rebound because of the elasticity of the (bloated) body cavity. Also, it should not surprise us, by now, that a body moves when it is struck and bleeds when it is cut. I would guess that Giure Grando's cry resulted from the manipulation of the corpse but can really not say much about the matter, since I almost never have occasion to decapitate a corpse with a shovel.

[‡‡]Nets get into graves in yet another way as well: they may be used to lower the body (Talbot, 221).

mated bodies.[29] It would seem as if, in such urn burials, the belief has progressed to the point that the spirits are considered to have an abiding phobia of sharp objects and that their original function has been forgotten.

Often the objects themselves are considered dangerous, usually because of close association with the dead person, and are therefore put in the grave. I suspect that such habits come about in part because the culture is aware of but has little understanding of contagion: the deceased, along with his utensils, may in fact be dangerous if he died from a communicable disease. But the populace regards death itself as communicable. In support of this view is Crooke's report from the central provinces of India:

> Provision is also made for the wants of the dead by burying or burning with the dead certain implements or other articles which the spirit may need in the other world, but this motive is often supplemented by the feeling that it is unlucky for the survivors to use them. It is denied that the custom is connected with the resurrection of the body or the reincarnation of the soul, or that the dead could derive benefit from such gifts. They are unwilling, they say, to derive any benefit from the death of a relative, and so they commit to the flames the dead man's personal effects—clothing, vessels, weapons, and money in his possession—*but this does not apply to his belongings which have never been used* [my emphasis].[30]

Such a distinction would seem to imply that what renders the objects unusable is not ownership but the actual handling of the objects by the deceased.

Often such objects are found to have been smashed or rendered unusable in some way,[31] and we are given a variety of explanations for this. Weapons may be damaged so that the deceased will not use them against relatives. In one of the Finno-Ugric tribes such objects are broken "because otherwise the deceased would not receive them":[32] in short, they too must be killed so that they can follow their owner into the realm of death. Such weapons might also be damaged simply so that no one will dig them up again. The practice of smoothing over the grave so that it could not be found—reported in the thirteenth century for the Tatars[33]— could have a similar function. Moreover, practices of this sort may be provided with a whole series of justifications, one after the other, because a practice is not necessarily discontinued when its function has been forgotten: it may simply be provided with a different explanation.

The Soul after Death

Now I lay me down to sleep,
I pray the Lord my soul to keep;
If I should die before I wake,
I pray the Lord my soul to take.
—Child's prayer

We have seen that bodies continue to "act" after death. Such functioning is deduced not just from the alterations in the body but from events that may follow the death. As we have seen, our informants believe that death itself is passed around, not viruses and bacteria. Because they live in a world governed by personal relationships, not impersonal laws, contagion tends to be seen as meaningful and deliberate and its patterns based on values and vendettas, not on genetic predisposition or the domestic accommodations of the rat flea.

In recent history, the closest parallel to this situation may be seen in the AIDS epidemic, which has caused a great deal of fear, even panic, among people who, for the time being at least, can know little about the nature of the disease. In California recently there was an attempt to pass a law requiring the quarantine of AIDS victims. Doubtless the fear will die down if we gain control over the disease—but what would it be like to live in a civilization in which *all* diseases were mysterious? Presumably one would learn—as was done in Europe in past centuries—to shun the dead, as potential bearers of death.

Since a body can also become completely inert, as when it is cremated, there must be a clear distinction between its life after death and its second death. The latter occurs either as a gradual, "natural" death, after the body lies buried for a period of years, or may be induced by such chemical and physical means as cremation or embalming.

Now a live body may be distinguished from a dead one by its possession of an animating principle, or what we call a soul. This is frequently identified with the breath (for example, in the Latin *anima*), presumably because, when a body dies, its most immediate and obvious change is that it stops breathing.* Similarly, the soul may be identified with fire or warmth because the body grows cold after death.¹ (One of the names for death among the Saxons of Transylvania is *Der Kaltmacher*, the one who makes [one] cold.²) A body undergoing its second life, after what we call death, must contain such an animating principle as well to account for its being alive. A wide variety of these exist. In trying to understand such souls, we would do well to ask ourselves, as usual, what our informants were observing.

Homer provides a good (and in many ways typical) starting point for our discussion. After death, a Homeric *psyche* may manifest itself to the living, as Patroclos does to Achilles,³ and Elpenor to Odysseus.⁴ Such a soul, as Walter Otto points out, is a shadowlike and insubstantial, but otherwise complete (and life-size), representation of the living person.⁵

We do not have to look very far, in nature, for life-size, insubstantial representations of our bodies, all of which, in one culture or another, have been seen as essential aspects of the human being, capable of surviving after death.

THE MIRROR IMAGE

According to Alfred Métraux, "In a considerable number of South American tribes, the soul is identified with the shadow or the reflection in water or in a mirror. Sometimes the idea of soul, heart, and pulsation is expressed by the same word."⁶ Here we see shadow and image perceived as an essential part of the person, rather than mere optical phenomena, and, as with anima, the soul, or vital principle, is identified with what ends at death (in this case, pulsation).

We get similar conceptions in European folklore. Note, however, that the folklorist, in asking his informants about the soul, is likely to encounter

---

*This explains why animals also are believed to have souls (Leach, 1050; see also Paulson, 84, and Caland, 494). Animals too breathe (until they die), have reflections and shadows, and can appear in dreams. The breath-as-vital-principle notion may be seen in the tradition that any interruption of breathing—yawning, hiccuping, or sneezing—is viewed with great concern.

what I think of as the Multiple Aspects Principle: the soul does not necessarily have just one guise but presents us with a variety of possibilities. Moreover, such conceptions will differ from one community to the next, even within a given culture. Thus, among the Transylvanian Saxons, we are told of about a dozen conceptions of the soul.[7] The soul is an invisible spirit, or a white, incorporeal (and formless) being, or a spirit hung with linen (presumably after death: the shroud), or a form similar to the body it inhabits, or a mere breath, or a shadow, or a light or torch (birthday candles have been viewed as remnants of this belief),[8] or a white dove, or a bee, or a gnat. If it originates in an evil person, it may be obliged to take the form of a small black dog to wander about the earth, but if it is that of an innocent child, it may become an angel.

Popular belief has it that it is bad luck to break a mirror, an idea that apparently originates in the belief that the mirror can contain one's soul in the form of a reflection. The Blums, for example, quote a Greek informant who says, "Some people think that it is bad luck if a mirror breaks because it can have your soul and then, when it breaks, you will die."[9] With the advent of photography, the soul took on yet another aspect. The same informant says, "I have known people who have been afraid to be photographed. Farmers in the north of Greece are like that; they think you can capture their soul if you take their picture."[†] Von Negelein gives numerous examples of this belief.[10]

In Europe, a number of vestiges of this view remain, the most common of which is the practice of turning mirrors to the wall when someone dies. Von Negelein demonstrated how widespread this belief was.[11] Usually it is explained as a means of preventing the dead from returning or preventing another death from occurring. We have seen that in some areas it is considered important to pour out any standing water, as in Bulgaria.[12] Perhaps this custom, too, may have derived from the need to remove anything that can reflect an image, in the belief that the soul, on removing itself from its body, might consider the (reflecting) water a convenient soul receptacle and so remain in the vicinity. This interpretation is made more plausible by the fact that it is sufficient just to cover the water rather than dispose of it and by Vakarelski's report that the soul is sometimes believed to have bathed in the water.[13]

Cabej reports that in Romania containers of water are to be covered,

---

[†]Considering this question caused me to wonder if our version of the story of Narcissus is a reinterpretation and if the story originally had to do with losing one's soul by scrutinizing one's reflection. I then found that Frazer had proposed this hypothesis in 1922 (p. 223).

"since otherwise the soul, which is decidedly hydrotropic, might fall into a container filled with water and drown in it.''[14] Possibly the soul is viewed as hydrotropic because it is associated with the reflection, which is known to leap into any available standing water. This could also explain the practice, reported from Macedonia, of leaving a container full of water in the empty grave after exhumation.[15] Perhaps the water is intended to capture the soul, keeping it in the grave if it should still be present and show a disposition to follow the bones (which are now in the church). In Bulgaria a jar of water is left at the grave. "Such containers, leaning against the cross, are an everyday sight in Bulgarian graveyards.''[16] Similarly, in Hungary, where we are told that evil souls creep into the corpse and cause it to bloat and acquire an odor, we are also told that this can be prevented by putting a container of water under the bier,[17] a practice reported for eastern Prussia as well, as we saw in chapter 7. Perhaps in each case the water was intended to capture souls.

This may be a corollary of the belief that spirits cannot cross water: if you consider your reflection to be your soul, after all, you might consider it significant that it instantly appears in any body of water that you gaze into. One common consequence of this belief in European folk customs is the practice of pouring water between the corpse and the location where the person died. As I mentioned earlier, in some areas, such as eastern Prussia, the *Leichenwasser*—the water used to wash the corpse—was poured out between the coffin and the house as the funeral procession set out to provide a barrier to death, and then its container was broken, perhaps against the possibility of the soul having remained in it.[18] Similarly, the Wends in Lausitz are said to return from a burial through water, which is a barrier for the soul of the dead person.[19] Yet another consequence of the belief that spirits cannot cross water may be found in the practice of burying the dead—especially the restless dead—on islands, which have other advantages as well: they are isolated and may offer protection from the depredations of animals.[20]

This view of the reflection-as-soul receives some support from Schnee-weis's observation that in Serbo-Croatia the graves of those who died young may be decorated with a variety of things, including mirrors.[21] Within the house, he tells us, mirrors must be covered, and water must be poured out;[22] yet mirrors are specifically mentioned as grave goods for those who died prematurely. As we know, these are the dead who are potentially dangerous. It may be that the mirror functions here exactly as it does in the house—that is, it captures the soul. The difference is that you do not want the soul to remain in the house. If it must linger, then let it be at the grave, where it belongs. Similar reasoning may be behind the practice in Serbo-Croatia[23] of providing the grave with a picture of the deceased.[‡]

Just as mirrors are covered or turned to the wall, so are the eyes of the deceased closed or covered, perhaps because they too reflect an image and thus have the potential to capture the soul. If one were to look into them, one would see a tiny version of one's self, and this image would be the only thing on the corpse that moved at all. It becomes extremely important, in these circumstances, to avoid the gaze of the dead man— so much so that in one of the Icelandic sagas a man is described going behind his dead father, who is in a seated position, and covering his head with a cloth so that his gaze cannot fall on anyone.[24] In funerary practice, this belief shows up in the custom of closing the eyes of the deceased or covering them with something (sometimes coins, sometimes a piece of cloth or a stone).[25] Some methods are quite extreme, as when the eyelids are sealed shut with wax or pinned shut with needles. As Grober-Glück observes, such methods imply the critical importance of the procedure.[26]

Finally, the reflection may be responsible for one of the odder beliefs about the world to come: according to Stora, "Many Siberian peoples considered 'the other world' quite literally a mirror reflection of this world. Everything was upside down when compared with this life."[27] This belief makes a certain kind of sense since spirits are manifested to us, reflected in water, in mirror-image, and this is the world that they go to after death. Imagine, for example, how a mountain looks when it is reflected in a lake: the image appears to be (1) less substantial than the actual mountain (as the Homeric shades are when compared to actual people), (2) below it, and (3) upside down. The world of the beyond is "down," in this case, not just because bodies go downward when they are buried, as Needham has pointed out,[28] but because the image of the mountain appears to extend just as far below the level of the earth as the actual mountain extends above it. It may be a corollary of this view that, in so

---

[‡]If water is indeed significant because of its reflectivity, then it might be useful to consider the history of grave goods from this point of view. The Bronze Age Cycladic "frying pans," for example, which have been interpreted as primitive, water-filled mirrors, may turn up in graves because they have the potential to keep the soul of the deceased in place. One account (from Ohio) seems to express two common functions of water—purification and banning of the dead: "After the burial, the Greeks fill an earthenware crock with water and break it on the steps of the home of the deceased. This serves the dual purpose of keeping the soul of the dead pure and of keeping the household free from death" (Puckett [1981], 2:1141). The place of mirrors in graves deserves further study. Hayes (1:301) describes a copper mirror found in front of the face of an Egyptian mummy, and Li (295 *passim*) discusses in detail the many bronze mirrors found in graves in China.

many cultures, the dead are obliged to cross water to get to the world of the spirits.

Other beliefs also seem to derive from the observation of the mirror-image condition of the spirit world. The spirit world is reached, as we know, by means of movement contrary to the "normal" (widdershins): the Black Mass is read backwards. Perhaps because the visible manifestation of the world of the spirits is exactly opposite to the world we live in, it is seen by analogy as accessible only through movement contrary to the normal. It could also be that this idea contributed to the notion that the dangerous dead—the ones disinclined to enter the hereafter— might be persuaded to rest in peace by being placed face-down in the grave (that is, opposite to the normal). A report mentioned earlier (that vampires are visible to twins wearing their clothes inside out) makes a certain kind of sense: like the spirit world, such twins are doubled and reversed.

DREAM IMAGES

In many cultures the soul is only rather casually attached to its body, as is demonstrated by its habit, during sleep or unconsciousness as well as death, of leaving the body entirely. The changes that occur during such conditions—the lack of responsiveness, the cessation or slowing of breathing and pulse—are attributed to the soul's departure, either temporary or permanent. When the soul is identified with the image of the body, then it is seen to make periodic forays into the minds of others when they dream.

Thus, among the reasons why the dead are believed to live on is that their image can appear in one's dreams and memory even after death. Their image is seen not as an incidental quality but as an essential one. The image is the essence of the person, and its presence in the mind of another is evidence that body and soul are separated. For this reason it is considered unwise, in some cultures, to awaken someone suddenly: he may be dreaming, and his soul may not have a chance to return before he awakens, in which case he will die.[§]

[§]This belief may have come into being because people sometimes die in their sleep. Their souls did not reenter the body, either because they were awakened suddenly (as is sometimes reported) because their body position was changed. This belief can be put to practical use: in Trier a witch could be killed by changing her position while she was asleep, because her soul would not find it way back into her body, through her mouth (Kyll [1964], 179). In the United States this belief still occurs in modified form: "Never wake a sleepwalker up quickly, or he will

In India, "the spirits of the dead reveal themselves in dreams," according to Crooke.[29] We have seen how this happens in Homer as well, where the dead Patroclos appears to Achilles after he has fallen asleep. Often in Greek literature the dead person appears as an *eidolon*, or image. And in *Visum et Repertum*, Stanacka is said to have awakened to report that she had been attacked by a man who had died nine weeks earlier. That is, the events took place in her sleep, presumably while she was dreaming. Similarly, in our account of the Shoemaker of Silesia, we are told, "The ones most bothered [by the ghost] were those who wanted to rest after heavy work; often it came to their bed, often it actually lay down on it and was like to smother the people."[‖] In short, the ghost appeared most often to people who were sleeping, or trying to sleep. Moreover, it awakened people with noises, which again suggests the association of the events with sleep and dreams. For that matter, we may see a similar phenomenon in the account of Arnod Paole, who "bothered" a number of people after his death. Peter Plogojowitz, too, "had come to [his victims] in their sleep." When we are told that he also visited his wife, demanding his opanki, we may perhaps assume that he did so on the same astral plane on which he made his visits to his other victims. Since the dream image of a person is regarded as a kind of soul, it is not too daring, perhaps, to conclude that people dreamed about the dead Peter Plogojowitz and that they related their illness to what he did in their dreams.[#]

In European folklore it is evident that the dream was viewed as a visit from the person dreamed about. How otherwise, for example, can we interpret the following account from Posen?

---

die" (Puckett [1981], 2:1141). See also Sell, 58, for similar Indonesian beliefs. The notion that sleep can be dangerous—because it is akin to death and the soul is at risk—seems also to be implied by the children's prayer quoted above, which, in its earliest known version, dates from the twelfth century.

[‖]This sounds less like a nightmare per se than the Old Hag experience analyzed by David J. Hufford in his book, *The Terror that Comes in the Night*. During this experience, one "awakens," senses something approaching, and feels an oppressive weight while being unable to move or cry out. The experience often happens to people who are extremely tired, and the victim invariably believes that he has been awake during the experience. A scientist of my acquaintance has suggested that the phenomena could derive from the different parts of our brain waking up one after the other, rather than simultaneously, which would explain the victim's belief that he is awake, while he has no motor functions.

[#]In Podrima, Yugoslavia, we are told that a person has two souls, and that when he sleeps, one soul wanders about (Vukanovic [1958], 24). This seems to be a way of accounting for the fact that, during sleep, people may be visited by the images of other people—that is, dream about them—yet these other people may survive the temporary loss of their soul.

Once the wife of a poor shoemaker in Jaraczewo died. On the day of the funeral, he wanted to be awakened early in the morning, at four o'clock, by his apprentice, in order to run some errands for the funeral. The apprentice, however, overslept the time. Then the dead wife arrived, exactly at four o'clock, and boxed him on the ear four times with her ice-cold hand of death. Frightened, *he awakened* [my emphasis] and jumped out of the bed.[30]

Although the specter appeared while the apprentice was asleep, the event is viewed as something actual rather than as a dream. Nothing is more common, in European folklore, than tales in which every event is clearly plausible except for the visit by a dead person. More often than not, in such accounts, the victim was visited at night during sleep. Frequently the victim is described as awakening in the morning, having lost consciousness; one has to be attentive to find evidence that the events occur during sleep. Veckenstedt tells a story of a woman whose husband died and was buried: "The deceased, however, gave his wife no peace but came every night and tortured her."[31] The wife went to the pastor for a remedy, and he recommended sprinkling red ribbons with holy water. "Of these ribbons she should tie one around her neck, *when she lay down to sleep* [my emphasis]." The specter, in other words, appears during sleep, but since it is nonetheless quite real to the narrator, he does not find it necessary to point this out. Veckenstedt also tells of a dead woman who appeared "next to the bed" of her husband, which seems to imply that the events took place when he was asleep.[32] And he recounts a story in which a gravedigger deals casually with old bones in a graveyard: "In the evening of the same day, *when the gravedigger went to bed* [my emphasis], the dead person appeared and begged the gravedigger to put the bone back into the grave again, since he would otherwise find no peace."[33] Similarly, a woman comes back to haunt her son: "Henceforth the deceased came every night, laid herself down *on her sleeping son* [my emphasis], and sucked his blood out, whereupon she disappeared again."[34] In each case, the events seem to take place in a dream. As often happens in such stories, incidentally, the son is advised to resort to a magical remedy and thus recovers from the effects of his mother's visits. Or, to state the matter differently, he gets well and the dreams end.

Although we are often obliged to figure out for ourselves that such events were actually nightmares, we are sometimes told outright that the revenant appeared in a dream. The Blums cite a story in which a man died and then became a revenant. "When he died, he became a vrikolax and presented himself to his fiancée and his three brothers." Here nothing is said of the manner of his appearance. After this, however, the vrykolakas appeared to the informant herself: "That night when I went to sleep I saw a dream. In the dream the vrikolax came to me."[35] The events are presented as real, but they occur in a dream: clearly the dream events are perceived as real.

In some stories it is obvious that the informant could not have witnessed the events. Usually these stories appear to have been modified to provide a rationale, which is usually moralistic in nature. Thus we are told of a coachman who, failing to care for his (deceased) master's horse after having promised to do so, is throttled by the dead man, who appears to him during the night.[36] The specter in the night, already made suspect by his victim's tendency to see him only while asleep, becomes problematic indeed in such stories. Here, for example, one wonders how the information got to the informant, for no other witnesses are mentioned, and the coachman did not survive the experience!

Such stories seem designed to make sense out of something that, on the face of it, does not make sense. A sudden death, for example, if it happens after the person in question has done something frivolous, criminal, or selfish, is typically thought to result from that action.** In the case of the coachman, the master's specter may have been supplied to account for his otherwise inexplicable death. The alternative is to speculate that some catastrophes may be completely random, quite unrelated to the quality of one's morals—and this philosophy has not had great currency throughout history. In Christianity, for example, this view might be difficult to reconcile with the notion of a nurturing deity.

Finally, the function of the dream as the milieu of specters becomes most evident in accounts of the Slavic mora. According to Jan Machal,

> It is a general Slavic belief that souls may pass into a Mora, a living being, either man or woman, whose soul goes out of the body at night-time, leaving it as if dead. Sometimes two souls are believed to be in such a body, one of which leaves it when asleep.... The Mora, assuming various shapes, approaches the dwellings of men at night and tries to suffocate them.... First she sends re-

** I must stress again that in preliterate societies events do not just "happen," they are willfully caused. The Blums cite a striking example of this: "A little later, as he was riding his donkey over some steep rocks, a divine power pushed him off the animal so that he fell down and was badly hurt" (p. 78). It is not the steepness of the rocks that caused the accident, but a previous act of the man (he had refused to let his sister become a nun). Nowhere is this tendency so evident as in matters having to do with death. The accidental death is a foreign concept in many societies: if someone dies, it is because someone else killed him (cf. Lévy-Bruhl, 361; Sell, 2).

freshing slumber to men and then, when they are asleep, she frightens them
with terrible dreams, chokes them, and sucks their blood.[37]

That we are seeing here a personification of the nightmare/old hag experience, combined with apnea (the "choking"), can scarcely be dis-
puted.[38] Etymologically, in fact, *mora* is cognate with the *mare* of
nightmare, with German *Mahr*, and with French *cauchemar*. Again the
nightmare is viewed not as a psychological phenomenon, contained within
the sleeping person's psyche, but as an outside agency. As always, the
dreams are purposeful, not random; they are related to the evil intentions
of another being, not to what you ate last night before you went to bed
or how tired or anxious you felt. Moreover, the nightmare is held responsible for the choking (which we might view as the cause of the
nightmare) and blood-sucking. As we have already seen with the vampires, the blood-sucking is an interpretation of the effects of disease, the
reasoning being, apparently, that since losing one's blood causes one to
die, then the person who died must have lost his blood. I have the
impression that the notions of choking and blood-sucking show a distinction between sudden and slow deaths—strokes and heart attacks on
the one hand, wasting diseases on the other. The choking seems to be
an interpretation based on fact: knowing that some people awaken and
report that they were choked or smothered (which is a common dream-
phenomenon associated with apnea), they assume that, if a person dies
suddenly during sleep, the choking must not have been interrupted in
time.

THE SHADOW

According to Raymond Jameson, "The belief that life essence, frequently
referred to by observers as 'soul,' is implicit in shadows has been reported
from all parts of the world: Tasmania, Africa, North and South America,
Asia, and Europe."[39] Thus, in an account of the beliefs of a Nigerian
tribe, Talbot reports that "the shadow cast by a live man is really the
shape of the soul which is within him, though compressed, for the time,
into a small space."[40] Both Greek (*skia*) and Latin (*umbra*) show this relationship of the soul to the shadow.[††] Ovid refers to Pluto as *umbrarum*

[††]I use the word *soul* as a generic term for an animating principle or, as Jameson says, a "life
essence." It is true, of course, that our "soul" is not their "soul." Lévy-Bruhl, 358, illustrates
the dilemma when he suggests that it is unwise to use the term soul (âme), then, a few pages

rex, or king of the shades.[41] And in New Kingdom Egypt, "the defunct soul is distinctly identified with the shadow, which is symbolized by the silhouette of the body or by the hieroglyph of a parasol."[42]

In Romanian folklore the shadow of a person may be secured to ensure that a building will be durable (see chapter 5), with the result that, after death, that person becomes a vampire. Similarly, in Yugoslavia, certain Moslem gypsies are said to believe that a vampire is a dead person's shadow.[43]

In many cultures, especially in some of the northern Eurasian cultures, the shadow and the mirror image are both unmistakably associated with the soul. This is most clear in the Tungusic language family, where the same word is often used for "soul," "shadow," and "reflection."[44] According to Harva, among the Mordvins the same word is used to designate "soul" (or spirit), "form," and "photograph."[45] Again, shadow and image are part of the person, not just optical phenomena. There may be no distinction made between the different types of image: among the Kiwai Papuans of New Guinea we are told, "For soul the Kiwais use the word *urío*, which also means shadow, reflection in the water and any kind of picture or drawing."[46] When these phenomena are endowed with significance, there are important implications for the experience of death.

---

later, does so anyway, observing that "j'emploie ce mot, faut d'un meilleur" (p. 363). I too use the word for lack of a better. Ankermann, 129, also draws attention to this dilemma.

Keeping Body
and Soul Apart

We have seen that to account for death people hypothesize an animating principle that is generally associated with a variety of natural phenomena. The presence or absence of breath, the temperature of the body, the existence of images in dreams, reflections, and shadows—any of these may be interpreted as a kind of servomechanism that operates the body and ceases to function or departs at death. The reader may protest that neither reflection nor shadow can be demonstrated to depart at death, but here the facts of optics and those of folklore simply do not jibe: it is widely believed that, like Peter Schlemihl, you may lose your shadow (after all, you can see it diminish at midday).[1] Thus Benet tells us that in Poland the soul is "pictured as the breath or, in a more condensed form, as a puff of fog; or it is imagined as a ghost or spirit. It is also identified with the shadow, and murderers who have no soul may be detected by their lack of a shadow."[2] Moreover, our various "doubles" are generally not distinguished clearly from one another in preliterate cultures, but are seen as different manifestations of the spirit world. In the Andaman Islands the visible form of the soul is the reflection, and the soul leaves the body at night when one dreams.[3] Here (and this is common) the dream image is not only conflated with the reflection but is seen as an invader from outside rather than a phenomenon contained in one's psyche. Such a conflation may also be seen in the Russian injunction against children looking into mirrors, since otherwise they may not sleep peacefully.[4] Similarly, in Hungarian folk-belief, looking into a mirror will cause one to have bad dreams.[5] It should be remembered that in a preindustrial culture, where high-quality mirrors are unavailable, the reflected image is not stable but deformed and ever-changing, as in water. Thus, it has more in common with the dream image than one might at first think.

Often the multiple souls (see below) are seen to account for the corpse retaining these aspects (shadow and image) of its being. Among one group of Lapps, at death the "breath soul" leaves, while another soul, which Stora calls the "free shadow soul," remains behind for a time, animating the body in some sense.[6] This explains not only the supposed animation of the body after death but also why the body retains its shadow at death.

Just as life *before* death is explained by postulating a soul, then, so is this done with life *after* death. If the body returns to life, then this must occur as the result of the action of a soul of some kind. There is a great variety of such souls in European folklore, and I do not intend to catalog them, but certain tendencies may be noted.

Often just one soul is involved, which leaves at the death of the body but then decides to return. It reanimates the body, creating a revenant. For this reason people often take steps to ensure that the soul is successful in leaving the place of death: doors and windows are opened, and anything that might capture the soul (for example, any reflecting surface) is covered. Sometimes the house is swept out, against the possibility that the soul has hidden in a corner somewhere.[7] According to Vakarelski, in Bulgaria it is believed that the soul wanders on earth for forty days and tries to get back into its corpse, but seeing it in a condition of decay, flies off.[8] When the body has not decayed, presumably, this is proof that the soul has returned to it prematurely. Similarly, in Northern India, according to Crooke, it was important to cremate the body early, since otherwise the soul might return.[9] This would seem to suggest, as I have mentioned elsewhere, that the rationale behind cremation is to prevent the body from becoming reanimated—in short, to render it inert. As Wiedemann remarks in a discussion of Egyptian cremation, "with the ashes of the deceased the soul climbs up to the heavens."[10] And Hellwald accounts for the practice in Hertzgovina of burning the vampire, by saying that "If the flame has consumed the body down to the bones, then the soul has also been burned out of it and finally finds peace."¹¹ These body-disposal methods are intended to neutralize or release the animating principle of the body. It must then stop functioning.

It is extremely common, worldwide, for postmortem functioning to be explained as the action of a second "soul." One soul departs at death, but another remains in the corpse, animating it for a time, until it too departs or simply dies. "These [vampires] have two souls," according to a Silesian source, "of which only the one dies and the second remains in the corpse."¹² This soul, whether it is viewed as the original soul returned after death or as a second soul, typically departs when the body has completely decayed. When the body is no longer functioning—no longer changing shape and color or emitting an odor—it is assumed that its animating principle has departed and can no longer do unkind things to the living. Sometimes, as we have seen in Romanian folklore, it is a second heart rather than a second soul that animates the body. Sometimes an outside agency, not the body itself, brings the corpse to life. In Hungary, evil souls may creep in; in Slavic folklore, the vampire may be created by the Devil.

Whatever the operating mechanism, decomposition is seen as one of the keys to pacification of the corpse. Among the Slavs, as von Negelein points out, the soul's traffic with the living was terminated only with complete decomposition.¹³ In an account of the beliefs of the Mordvins, Harva says that the spirit of the deceased remains in the closest association to the body itself, "which, even after death, still continues its mysterious life, as long as the corpse endures."¹⁴ That is, the "life" of the corpse ends when it becomes inert. Harva also remarks that a hole is left in the grave, for which two explanations are given: the deceased can see through the hole, or the soul has an escape route.¹⁵ The latter interpretation suggests that the soul does not leave immediately after death but after the body is in the grave—presumably when stabilized.

Because the flesh, rather than the skeleton, continues to change, often it is simply removed from the skeleton, as in excarnation. At that point the deceased is viewed as truly and completely dead. Thus Lafitau observes that the Caribs "are convinced [that the dead] do not go to the land of souls until they are without flesh."¹⁶ Similarly, Schneeweis observes that the practice of exhumation has its origin "in the belief that the soul can attain the beyond only after complete decomposition of the corpse."¹⁷ And the Blums say that "upon dying [in Greece] the soul does not leave the earth immediately but rather hovers around the house for the forty-day period, until, hopefully, the body is 'dissolved', at which time the spirit is free to leave the earth."[18] As we have seen, such an expectation virtually ensures that some bodies will "live after death," for when they are buried, they are apt to take much longer than forty days to decay completely.

As important as it is, then, for the corpse to decompose (otherwise it comes back to haunt one) it is not surprising that methods have been devised to determine its condition without resorting to digging it up. From Switzerland there are reports that the cloth the deceased was washed with might be hung in a tree and observed: its decay was believed to correspond to that of the corpse.[19] Similarly, in German Bohemia it was believed that as the *Leichenstroh* disintegrated—the straw on which the corpse lay—so did the corpse disintegrate in the grave.[20] Such straw might be burned to speed up the process whereby the dead "attained peace."[21] Ranke cites many other examples of this belief,[22] and Stora relates the breaking of grave goods to it: "The process of breaking the different articles led also to their rotting away more quickly."[23] Such a belief may account in part for the custom of sacrificing an animal as part of the funerary ritual: as its flesh is stripped away, so is that of the deceased. Among the Burjats, if scavengers ate the flesh of a sacrificial horse it was considered a good sign,[24] perhaps because this process paralleled the disintegration of the corpse, which was not at peace until it was consumed by the grave. The relationship between the two processes is implied by the requirement that it be not just any horse but the one owned by the deceased.

Similarly, among the Skolt Lapps, there was a custom of naming a reindeer after the deceased, then slaughtering it and eating it "at a commemorative feast held in conjunction with the burial."[25] Such reindeer were chosen to correspond to the sex and status of the deceased: "a castrated buck in the case of married men[!], an uncastrated buck for unmarried men, a young doe for unmarried women and a doe that had calved in the case of married women."[26] Here again we see the reindeer first associated with the deceased, both by the naming and by the choice of animals, and then consumed, as though to further, by sympathetic magic, the all-important disintegration of the body of the deceased.*

> On first considering funeral ceremonies,
> one expects rites of separation to be their
> most prominent component, in contrast

---

*The reindeer may have been intended also to accompany the dead into the world of the spirits. In Lapp belief, a new reindeer could be created from the bones of the old.

> to rites of transition and rites of
> incorporation, which should be only
> slightly elaborated. A study of the data,
> however, reveals that the rites of
> separation are few in number and very
> simple, while the transition rites have a
> duration and complexity sometimes so
> great that they must be granted a sort of
> autonomy. Furthermore, those funeral
> rites which incorporate the deceased into
> the world of the dead are most
> extensively elaborated and assigned the
> greatest importance.
> —Arnold van Gennep, *The Rites of Passage*

Van Gennep's observation, certainly, is accurate enough, nor is it even surprising when one considers what is at stake. After all, however tragic your death may be, it would be far more tragic if you were to take me with you. The rites of transition and incorporation are intended to prevent this from happening.

The practice of mourning would appear to have some correspondence to the period during which the corpse is thought to be dangerous.[27] Thus Danforth describes a Greek woman who wore black for five years, after which her daughter's remains were exhumed.[28] He points out, "The word *kimitiri* [ossuary] means literally a place for sleeping and is derived from the verb *kimame*, to sleep. What is significant here is that the positive connotation of death as a peaceful sleep is associated with the bones in the ossuary rather than with the undecomposed remains in the grave."[29] While the body is still changing, still decomposing, it is still involved with the world, still a potential source of trouble. For that to end, the corpse must be rendered inert, and unless this process is sped up by chemicals or by fire, it is not completed until the flesh has decayed from the bones.

Here we might consider briefly the function of mourning. While we see it as an expression of sorrow and respect for the dead, it is in many cultures viewed as a necessity, not a courtesy; it is organized rather than spontaneous. Often professional mourners are hired.[30] In Europe, during mourning, one changed to different-colored clothing (either white or black, depending on the area and the era), a practice that, in the United States, has now been reduced to the symbolic (for example, professional athletes in team sports often wear a black armband when someone in the organization has died). As Schneeweis argues, however, this tradition presumably had a different function originally: "The mourning-clothing and the changing of the hair-style originally had the purpose of rendering unrecognizable those who remained behind."[31] That is, when the dead considered returning, whether as nightmare or epidemic, they would fail to recognize their putative victims, who had changed their appearance. Köhler describes mourning women (in the Voigtland) "scratching their thickly made-up faces and tearing the false hair they had put on."[32] Since the dead are most dangerous, as a rule, to those closest to them in life (and clearly what is at issue is proximity rather than relatedness, as Ranft pointed out in 1734[33]), it was these particular mourners who were obliged to mourn for the longest period. In Potamia, Greece, for example, "The length of time a woman wears black is determined primarily by her relationship to the deceased. A widow should wear black for the rest of her life or until she remarries, something she should not do prior to the exhumation of her husband."[34] It is no mere coincidence, certainly, that in Potamia the period of mourning coincides with the duration of the original burial of the deceased before exhumation (also five years). After the remains are exhumed and found to be inert—the flesh completely gone—the need for a change in appearance no longer exists. It is also no coincidence, surely, that in this same village, "The mourning period is likely to be longer than usual in the case of someone who dies at a very young age or in a particularly tragic manner."[35] Such people are, as we know, the most dangerous of the dead, presumably because many of the ways they die tend to communicate themselves to others (epidemic disease and murder, for example). If, on being exhumed, the body is found to be partly decomposed, "it is simply reburied and the liminal period extended until the body has decomposed completely."[36] That is, the wearing of black continues until the body is thoroughly and incontrovertibly dead, whereupon the threat ends and life returns to normal.

Conclusion

Requiescat in pace
—Roman tomb inscription

Most folklore is not presented to us as a simple account of experience but is put through a series of cognitive filters, so that a narrated event, however "real," may end up in later retellings with little or no resemblance to what we think of as reality. A variety of processes shape the event. Events may be seen, for one thing, as the outcome of animate forces rather than impersonal laws. The particular events associated with the discovery of dead bodies are especially subject to reinterpretation, because they are likely to be experienced incompletely. Thus, a process may be experienced as a tableau: a body is uncovered, but the people who discover it see only one stage of the process—a hand sticking out of the earth, or a body emerging from the earth, or animals eating the body—and this is then presented as a supernatural event. The hand belongs to a sinner; the body is emerging to attack the living; and the animals are killing a vampire. One event gives rise to multiple folkloric forms, which, when reformatted by the observer—made coherent by being provided with motives, then told as a process—take on forms that we may not even recognize as the original event. The evidence, in other words, is first interpreted, then the interpretation is used to eke out the evidence.

It is thus, evidently, that the European vampire came into being. Dead bodies do bloat and bleed at the mouth—as our informants tell us—but these functions are seen not as evidence of decomposition but as a consequence of their having sucked blood from the living. When such re-formatting is done by people from different cultures, the events are placed into different frameworks, so that the folklorist may not think of the dead bodies as "vampires," though the source of the account may be the same as that of the vampires. Among the Galela of Indonesia, for example, in the kingdom of death, certain dead people—those who died suddenly—are differentiated from the other dead by their practice of drinking blood.[1] This seems to be a de facto distinction between different forms of death. It takes into account that some dead bodies—those injured in certain ways, for example, and those left undiscovered for a time—prove to have blood at their lips and are thus believed to practice blood-drinking.* The hankering of the dead for blood is common throughout the world, contributing, perhaps, to the practice of providing them with sacrifices of blood or even with an apparent blood-substitute such as red ochre.

Besides its corporeal form, however, the vampire or revenant may take other forms, apparently because death does not extinguish various aspects of a person, notably one's image, which when it appears in dreams is taken for a visit by the deceased. Various forms of one's image—shadow, reflection, memory—have their place in the lore of the dead. Because the image of the dead in memory is subject, unlike dreams, to the will of the living, it shows less dramatic reflexes in folklore, but they are nonetheless there: among the Voguls, for example, "The destiny of the common man is to die, to go to the realm of the dead and, then, die a 'second death'. When the memory of the dead has faded among the living, the departed 'dies' the final death."[2] And, according to Emily Vermeule, "The Greeks made a clear distinction between body and soul, between the flesh that decayed and must be buried, and the wind-breath psyche that left the carcass and went elsewhere into a pool of personalities which could be activated by memory."[3] According to Meuli, there is a "widespread, perhaps even universal division between the recently deceased and those who have been dead a long time."[4] The former tend to be dangerous, the latter not.† When the body has stabilized, when the image has receded,

---

*This explains why, as Pettersson has pointed out in a discussion of Lappish beliefs, "As a rule it is not ethical values that decide the fate of the departed but the manner of his death" (p. 146). The "fate of the departed" can be observed, after all (for example, by whether he is sucking blood), and what is observed is determined not by whether he was a good or a bad man, but by how he died.

†In general the most powerful people—great leaders, for example—tend to have the greatest potential for mischief after their death. Presumably this is both by analogy (as before death, so after) and because they linger in the communal memory more than other people.

the deceased is no longer dangerous, and the remains may be handled with the utmost casualness.[5]

By a far-reaching analogy, the dead are blamed for sickness and death: death comes, in other words, from the dead, who, through jealousy, anger, or longing, seek to bring the living into their realm. And to prevent this, the living attempt to neutralize or propitiate the dead—by proper funerary and burial rites, by "killing" the corpse a second time, or by sacrifice—until the dead have become powerless. This is a condition which, worldwide, tends to correspond not just to when they stop entering one's dreams but also to when their bodies stop undergoing change and are reduced to inert bones. The bare skeleton—in our culture the very symbol of the terror of death—is in other cultures evidence that the dead body is finally safe and that the living are out of harm's way.

Notes

INTRODUCTION

1. China: Willoughby-Meade, 245; Indochina: Sell, 43; the Philippines: Ramos (1969), 238.

CHAPTER 1: PETER PLOGOJOWITZ

1. Görres, 275; Filipovic, 64.
2. Quoted in Grenz, 263–65. His source is the 1728 edition of Ranft's *De masticatione mortuorum*.
3. Yovanovich, 311.
4. Horst, 1:253.
5. Calmet, 31–32.
6. Ernest Jones in Frayling, 326; Gottfried, 112.
7. Gottfried, 114.
8. Vukanovic (1959), 111–12.

CHAPTER 2: THE SHOEMAKER OF SILESIA

1. Grässe, 2:176–79.
2. Klapper (1909), 86.

CHAPTER 3: *VISUM ET REPERTUM*

1. Glaister and Rentoul, 121.

CHAPTER 4: DE TOURNEFORT'S *VRYKOLAKAS*

1. Lee, 127.
2. Trigg, 150.
3. See, e.g., Father Richard's account, quoted in Summers (1968), 231.
4. Chapter 9 contains an example from a court case in 1913. There have also been stakings in this century. For an example from Serbia (1923) see Cajkanovic.
5. Stetson, 9.
6. Schneeweis (1961), 10. Presumably wine is used because of its religious significance.
7. Singer, 3:636.
8. See, e.g., Kittredge, 178; Puckett, (1981), 2:1228.

CHAPTER 5: HOW REVENANTS COME INTO EXISTENCE

1. Löwenstimm, 102.
2. Köhler, 258, citing Hahn, *Geschichte von Gera*, 2:882.
3. Cremene, 85.
4. Burkhart, 216.
5. Burkhart, 216.
6. Cremene, 38.
7. Bargheer, 88.
8. Cremene, 38.
9. W. Hertz, 123.
10. Cremene, 38; Senn, 61.
11. Mackenzie, 92–94.
12. W. Hertz, 123; Burkhart, 238. See also Vildomec (Polish folklore), 78; Drechsler (Silesian), 319.
13. Jaworskij, 331.
14. Cremene, 89.
15. Burkhart, 225.
16. Mannhardt, 260; Cremene, 37.
17. Perkowski (1972), 26.
18. Cremene, 37.
19. Mannhardt, 260, 263. Weals on the neck are also said to predispose toward vampirism: Tetzner (Kashubes), 461–62.
20. Mannhardt, 261; "Die alte Welmsche," 262. See Perkowski (1972), 22, for a similar report for the Canadian Kashubes. Wilhelm Hertz, 127, gives a similar report for Iceland.
21. Lemke, 1:57.
22. Cremene, 38.
23. Cremene, 101; Haase, 296.
24. Mannhardt, 260. The Schotts, 298, say that "people do not at all view the sign of the vampire-bite on the neck as an essential sign." This is the only source I've found so far, in folklore, that suggests that the vampire may bite the neck.
25. Löwenstimm, 96.
26. Mannhardt, 264.
27. Mannhardt, 270.
28. Cremene, 100.
29. Sturm and Völker, 525; Leatherdale, 33.
30. Vukanovic (1958), 21.
31. Bartsch, 2:89.
32. Blum and Blum, 78.
33. Vakarelski, 312. A friend from Peking happened to mention this belief to me in conversation. See de Groot, 1:43.
34. Weigand, 122. Cremene, 84, says that a dog or cat may cause vampirism by going between the wheels of the hearse while the body is being transported to the cemetery.
35. Cremene, 84.
36. Blum and Blum, 73.
37. Ralston, 412.
38. Cremene, 31, 82. For a similar account from Bulgaria, see Andree, 84.
39. Haase, 328.
40. Zelenin, 329.
41. Cajkanovic, 266. See also Mackensen, 9.
42. Vakarelski, 304.
43. Vakarelski, 306–7.

44. Löwenstimm, 98–100.
45. Danforth, 39, 42, 52.
46. Jaworskij, 335.
47. Blum and Blum, 75; Lawson, 370–75.
48. Weigand, 122.
49. Cremene, 85.
50. Vukanovic (1958), 25.
51. Senn, 66, citing Schneeweis (1961).
52. Bargheer, 88. In Gypsy belief, a child that is born dead may become a mulo, but in Prussia such children become will-o'-the-wisps instead: Cozannet, 209; Lemke, 3:50.
53. Blum and Blum, 71.
54. Lee, 127.
55. Burkhart, 245.
56. Vukanovic (1958), 24; Honko, *Wörterbuch*, 352; see also Perkowski (1972), 29.
57. Strackerjan, 154.
58. Dömötör, 107. Hungarian revenants also occur in cemeteries, old castles, and ruins.
59. Schneeweis (1931), 100; Löwenstimm, 95; Vakarelski, 308.
60. Sturm and Völker, 524.
61. Cremene, 84, citing Gorovei.
62. Knoop (1885), 167.
63. Bargheer, 77.

CHAPTER 6: THE APPEARANCE OF THE VAMPIRE

1. Tallar, 63, 71–72. Tallar was an eighteenth-century German physician who observed the opening of graves on five occasions. The term used for *vampire* here is *Blutsauger*, or *bloodsucker*.
2. Leo Allatius, quoted in Lawson, 366–67.
3. Burkhart, 217.
4. Vukanovic (1958), 23.
5. *Grettir's Saga*, 72.
6. Sanders (1962), 273.
7. Bächtold-Stäubli, 813.
8. Senn, 66.
9. Another famous vampire (from the year 1336) was described as "blown up like an ox": Andree, 82–83, n. 4.
10. Andree, 88.
11. Folklore Archives, UC Berkeley.
12. Reiter, 200.
13. Perkowski (1972), 22.
14. Wuttke, 222.
15. Creighton, 1:122; Hecker, 25.
16. Burkhart, 219.
17. Cremene, 85.
18. Bächtold-Stäubli, 814.
19. Burkhart, 238; Wlislocki (Sachsen), 190.
20. *Oxford English Dictionary*, S. V. "white-livered."
21. Summers (1960), 201.
22. See Knoop (1906), 96.
23. Zelenin, 394.
24. Mannhardt, 270.

CHAPTER 7: APOTROPAICS I

1. Vildomec, 78.
2. Lawson, 405–6.
3. Mannhardt, 260–61.
4. Knoop (1885), 164.
5. Perkowski (1972), 22.
6. Kurtz and Boardman, 212.
7. Cremene, 90.
8. Perkowski (1982), 313.
9. Knoop (1885), 164.
10. Vakarelski, 302.
11. Cajkanovic, 263.
12. Cremene, 88.
13. Vakarelski, 305.
14. Maspero, 107.
15. Bernd and Bernd, 410.
16. Cozannet, 209.
17. See also Vreeland, in Cockburn, 135.
18. Schneeweis (1931), 112.
19. Perkowski (1972), 29.
20. Beitl (1933), 187.
21. Abbott, 219.
22. Abbott, 220.
23. Bartsch, 2:96.
24. B. Meyer, 164.
25. Perkowski (1972), 23.
26. Kmietowicz, 161; Faivre, 83.
27. Wuttke, 222.
28. Löwenstimm, 96.
29. Mannhardt, 260.
30. Reiter, in Haussig, 201.
31. Drechsler, 319.
32. Spindler, 191.
33. Schullerus, 125; Wlislocki (*Sachsen*), 194. See also Schneeweis (1961), 88.
34. Dömötör, 251–52.
35. Tilney, 221.
36. Cremene, 84.
37. Reiter, in Haussig, 201. Gerschke (92) cites a skeleton that was found in Prussia with a scythe over the neck.
38. Perkowski (1982), 313.
39. Vakarelski, 305.
40. Balassa and Ortutay, 673–74.
41. Wlislocki, *Sachsen*, 187.
42. Haase, 301.
43. Eisel, 375.
44. Eisel, 375.
45. Westermarck, 2:451.
46. Westermarck, 2:491.
47. Haase, 298–99.
48. Lemke, 1:57; See also Sanders (1962), 271, for a similar practice in Greece.
49. Cremene, 89.

50. Wlislocki, *Magyaren*, 134.
51. Reiter, in Haussig, 201.
52. Grenz, 260–62.
53. Cremene, 89.
54. Schneeweis (1961), 88.
55. Krauss (1908), 127.
56. Trigg, 156.
57. Karoly, 99–100.
58. Honko, in Haussig, 352.
59. Vakarelski, 306.
60. Haase, 309.
61. Cremene, 84.
62. Wlislocki, *Sachsen*, 195–96.
63. Vakarelski, 303.
64. Trigg, 153.
65. Andree, cited in Pauli (1975), 174; see also Gimbutas, 126.
66. See Dieck, 50–126, for examples; see Drechsler, 317, for an example of a body with its hands tied in back.
67. P. Geiger, 163.
68. P. Geiger, 163.
69. Grimm, 1:298.
70. W. Geiger (1960), 53.
71. P. Geiger, 156; Löwenstimm, 101.

CHAPTER 8: APOTROPAICS II

1. Cajkanovic, 265.
2. Bartsch, 2:100.
3. Vakarelski, 312; Hock, 27. Jellinek (p. 323) points out that other cultures remove the corpse headfirst, for the same reason.
4. Drechsler, 320.
5. Cremene, 84.
6. Lemke, 2:280.
7. Vakarelski, 302.
8. Cremene, 86.
9. Danforth, 37.
10. Cremene, 86.
11. Cremene, 87; Senn, 71.
12. Pauli (1975), 147, 149; (1978), 55.
13. Schneeweis (1961), 103.
14. Sinitsyn, 153.
15. Blum and Blum, 319.
16. Schneeweis (1961), 9.
17. W. Hertz, 127.
18. Cremene, 89.
19. Lauri Honko, in Haussig, 352.
20. E.g., Rohde, refuted by Childe, 14.
21. Childe, 14.
22. Vakarelski, 305, 307; see also Schneeweis (1961), 9, 87.
23. Schneeweis (1961), 88.
24. Hock, 127; Burkhart, 250; W. Hertz, 126.
25. Lawson, 364. As I point out in a later chapter, India is another exception to this rule.

26. Childe, 14; Kurtz and Boardman, 177.
27. Lawson, 364.
28. Masters, 74.
29. Danforth (1982), 53.
30. Vakarelski, 305.
31. Schneeweis (1961), 10. See also Baroti, 220, for a similar account.
32. Petrovic, 17.
33. Anonymous informant, cited in typescript by Jacquelynne Garner, Folklore Archives, UC Berkeley.
34. Burkhart, 234.
35. Andree, 84.
36. Andree, 84, n. 3; Jaworskij, 332–33.
37. Perkowski (1972), 23, 25.
38. Bargheer, 78.
39. Lemke, 1:57.
40. Knoop (1885), 166.
41. Schneeweis (1931), 103.
42. Reiter, in Haussig, 201.
43. Folklore Archives, UC Berkeley.
44. Westermarck, 1:307.
45. Summers (1960), 179; Vukanovic (1960), 47; Lawson, 367.
46. Krauss (1908), 129. See also Reiter, 201; Vukanovic (1960), 49; Trigg, 153.

CHAPTER 9: SEARCH AND DESTROY

1. Vukanovic (1958), 30.
2. Schneeweis (1961), 9.
3. Reiter, in Haussig, 201; Krauss (1908), 130; Hellwald, 367.
4. Lambertz, 489.
5. Stetson, 7; Hellwald, 369.
6. Krauss (1908), 130; Ralston, 413.
7. Stetson, 7.
8. Reiter, 201.
9. Vakarelski, 239 (Bulgaria); Bohnenberger, 220 (Württemberg).
10. W. Hertz, 124.
11. Krauss (1908), 130.
12. Vukanovic (1958), 30.
13. Vukanovic (1959), 114.
14. Burkhart, 224.
15. Frayling, 220.
16. Vukanovic (1958), 30.
17. *Grettir's Saga*, 36.
18. Maurer, cited in W. Hertz, 19; see also Mogk (1897), 266.
19. Leach, 253.
20. Barber, 22.
21. Veckenstedt, 355.
22. Alseikaite-Gimbutiene, 128.
23. Klapper (1909), 75.
24. Vukanovic (1959), 117.
25. Cajkanovic: intro. by Sjoberg, 260.
26. Cajkanovic, 260.

27. Reiter, 201.
28. Vukanovic (1959), 117.
29. Cozannet, 203.
30. Cozannet, 203; see also Vakarelski, 310, and Lauri Honko, 352, in Haussig.
31. Filipovic, 65 (stomach); Löwenstimm, 99, Bächtold-Stäubli, 815 (mouth).
32. Mannhardt, 260.
33. Perkowski (1972), 23.
34. Knoop (1893), 139.
35. Vukanovic (1959), 117; (1960), 45; see also Burkhart, 222, and Trigg, 156.
36. Bargheer, 37.
37. Stetson, 9.
38. Zelenin, 329; Haase, 329–30.
39. Löwenstimm, 102–3.
40. Haase, 302.
41. Cabej, 224.
42. Vakarelski, 303.
43. Vakarelski, 309.
44. Lemke, 1:56.
45. Lemke, 3:51.
46. *Grettir's Saga*, 72.
47. Vakarelski, 307; see Brown, 35, for other examples.
48. Mannhardt, 262.
49. Löwenstimm, 97.
50. Tallar, 54.
51. Vakarelski, 239.
52. Freudenthal, 101.
53. Evans, 83.
54. Polson, 115.
55. Polson, 119.
56. Evans, 86.
57. Polson, 84.
58. Shastri, 21.
59. Shastri, 24.
60. Klapper (1909), 75–76.
61. Klapper (1909), 77, 78, 80.
62. Lauterbach, 27; see also Swieten, 22, for another account of a revenant that proved difficult to burn.
63. Polson, 84.
64. Filipovic, 69.
65. Rau, 245.
66. Rau, 245.
67. Meaney, 16.
68. Jewitt, 140.
69. Kurtz and Boardman, 73.
70. Wuttke, 222. This is just one of various popular explanations of plague, of course.
71. Hecker, 48.
72. Pauli (1975), 174; (1978), 6off.
73. Pauli (1975), 177; (1978), 61; see also Levy, 66, 69, for Paleolithic deposits of skulls severed after death.
74. Ashbee, 83.
75. Leca, 1.

76. Leca, 2. Burkhart, 250, cites Wiedemann, who says that decapitation in ancient Egypt "offers a complete parallel to the treatment of the body in the countries in which the belief in vampires has remained."
77. Meaney, 20.
78. Bartsch, 98; see also Wirth, 160, Mansikka, 20.
79. Hertz, 125.
80. Karjalainen, 193.
81. Hellwald, 370.
82. Cited in Garland, 6.
83. Grenz, 256–58; Pauli (1975), 179; Dieck, 47ff.
84. Blum and Blum, 71.
85. Blum and Blum, 73. see also Christiansen, 36, for an example from Norway.
86. Vakarelski, 307.
87. Fischer (in Cockburn), 183.

CHAPTER 10: THE VAMPIRE'S ACTIVITY

1. W. Hertz, 127.
2. See also Mogk (1919), 108.
3. Trigg, 150. Note, however, that according to Trigg, the Gypsy vampires do "cause loud noises," just like the Icelandic revenants.
4. Mannhardt, 264, 268; Bächtold-Stäubli, 818–19.
5. Zedler, 46:478.
6. Hock, 31–32.
7. Lilek (Bosnia, Hertzgovina), 209, 211.
8. Lambertz, 489.
9. Mech, 186.
10. Van Lawick-Goodall, 138.
11. Schaller, 269.
12. Hammerstein, plates 93, 94, 128, 133, 136, 139, 222, 230a.
13. Vaillant, 1.
14. Andree, 84; Hellwald, 369.
15. Creighton, 2:171.
16. Creighton, 2:165.
17. Stora, 130; see also 106, 108. Schüz ([1966] 738) cites an eighteenth-century account in which half-wild dogs are described following an army to feed on the bodies of the dead. And Grünhagen ([1884] 253) cites a similar situation in Silesia in the eighteenth century, when, because of an epidemic, bodies were left about and eaten by dogs.
18. Tilney, 223. Smith and Dawson give an early account from Egypt: "As the door [of a tomb] was left wide open, the well-preserved bodies had suffered from wolves, which had partly devoured them" (p. 69).
19. Eisel, 376.
20. W. Hertz, 88.
21. Weitershagen, 29.
22. Robbins, 560.
23. W. Hertz, 63; also Vukanovic (1960), 49, and Strauss, 189.
24. Trigg, 155.
25. Vukanovic (1957), 129.
26. Schneeweis (1961), 8–9; see also Dömötör, 127, for a similar belief from Romania.
27. Karjalainen, 192.
28. Veckenstedt (1880), 354.
29. Polson, 6.

30. Van Lawick-Goodall, 120.
31. Rose, 135.
32. W. Hertz, 41.
33. W. Hertz, 41.
34. Leach, 1180.
35. Leach, 928.
36. Mansikka, 105.
37. Crooke (1926), 234.
38. See Mellaart, 86, 88, 90, 101.
39. Beitl (1933), 187.
40. Lilek, 211.
41. Vukanovic (1960), 52.

CHAPTER 11: SOME THEORIES OF THE VAMPIRE

1. H. Meyer, 166, has pointed out the implausibility of the "buried alive" theory. See also Masters, 25.
2. Hartmann, 47; see also 4, 9, 10, 45, 46.
3. Illis, 23–26. Illis's article contains several pictures of porphyria victims.
4. Leatherdale, 41.
5. Dolphin, 2.
6. Dolphin, 2.
7. Tallar, 13; Fritsch, 32.
8. Jirecek, 100; Vukanovic (1960), 46, 55.
9. Jiracek, 100.
10. Meuli, 311.
11. Meuli, 312.
12. Fritsch, 56–59.
13. Fritsch, 72.
14. Tallar, 68.

CHAPTER 12: THE BODY AFTER DEATH

1. Ponsold, 291. Note that I do not attempt to cite all the possible reasons for a change in the coloration of the skin after death. A few examples must suffice.
2. Glaister and Rentoul, 117.
3. Evans, 56.
4. Evans, 54.
5. Glaister, 117.
6. Ponsold, 296.
7. Cockburn and Cockburn, 1.
8. Mant, 152; see also Parikh, 167, and Gaute, 351–52.
9. Cockburn and Cockburn, 177.
10. Evans, 40–41.
11. Evans, 40.
12. Evans, 57.
13. See, e.g., Andree, 84, n. 3.
14. Vukanovic (1958), 25.
15. Schmidt, 162.
16. Fisher, in Spitz and Fisher, 20.
17. Quoted in Sturm and Völker, 459.
18. Smith, 88; Quibell, 70.

19. B. Meyer, 165, cites two such accounts.
20. Glaister and Rentoul, 121.
21. Glaister, 120.
22. Summers (1960), 118.
23. Summers (1960), 120.
24. Summers (1960), 6.
25. Sell, 29 (Indonesian).
26. Quoted in Summers (1968), 200, 201.
27. Habenstein and Lamers, 406.
28. Trigg, 157,
29. Klapper (1909), 85, 86.
30. See also Summers (1968), 237.
31. Glaister, 115–16.
32. Ponsold, 292.
33. Mant, 139.
34. Summers (1968) quotes Phillip Rohr on the bleeding corpse and cites Bacon and King James: pp. 192, 213, n. 69. See also Le Braz, 1:48.
35. Ponsold, 292.
36. Mant, 147.
37. Bartsch, 2:93.
38. Paul Geiger, 161; Ernest Jones, in Frayling, 319; Hertz, 125.
39. Pausanias, 533.
40. Page, cited by Garland, 76.
41. Stein, 36; see also Bahr and König, 112.
42. Klapper (1909), 86; Toeppen, 106.
43. Glaister, 114.
44. Parikh, 155.
45. Buchholz, 28.
46. De Groot, cited by Willoughby-Meade, 245–46.
47. Ponsold, 294.
48. Parikh, 156.

CHAPTER 13: ACTIONS AND REACTIONS

1. Dobeneck, 2:103–6. He says that the account had been sent from Wertheim to Tübingen but gives no date. He gives his source (rather confusingly) as follows: "Besold (Thes. pr. p. 83 und Schottel de singular. Germ. jurib. C. III. vom Bahrrechte, #22.) beim Worte 'Bahrrecht' eingerückt." Harsdörffer included this account in "Der grosse Schau-Platz" in 1644 (pp. 190–96).
2. Hellwald, 370.
3. Mant, 152.
4. Strackerjan, 154. See also Puckett (1981), 2:1240: "If a person is buried in a shallow grave, his soul will not go to heaven" (Bohemian informant, Ohio); Grober-Glück (1981), 439 (deep grave as apotropaic); and Schoetensack, 526.
5. Hecker, 49.
6. Blum and Blum, 52.
7. Swieten, 20.
8. Habenstein and Lamers, 252; Tilney, 223.
9. Habenstein and Lamers, 207.
10. Quoted in Klapper (1909), 86.
11. Sturm and Völker, 526.
12. Brouardel, 86. See also Ariès, 476.

13. Gottfried, 9.
14. Dr. Terence Allen.
15. Ponsold, 290.
16. Dr. Terence Allen.
17. Ramos (1969), 245.
18. Quoted from *Mississippi State Guide*, p. 29, UCLA folklore encyclopedia collection.
19. *Portland Oregonian*, 5 June 1986.
20. Gottfried, 112.
21. Quoted in Robbins, 524.
22. Turi, 90.
23. Lewy, 35.
24. Grober-Glück (1983), 154.
25. Tilney, 219.

CHAPTER 14: HANDS EMERGING FROM THE EARTH

1. Hartmann, 7.
2. UCLA folklore encyclopedia collection, unpublished.
3. Parikh, 159.
4. Von Haller, 109.
5. Masters, 79.
6. Schlenther, 37, 41, 42, 71, 120, 121.
7. See *Grettir's Saga*, 72, for rocks; Zelenin, 327, for brush. Both motifs are extremely common world-wide.
8. Quoted in Creighton, 2:167.
9. Özgüç, 78ff.; see also Pettersson, 176.
10. Cited in Ebert (1921), p. 4: Servius ad Aen., 6:154.
11. Mellaart, 86–87.
12. Von Negelein (1935), 2:124. See also Machal, 231; Zelenin, 328; and Paul Geiger, 158.
13. Söderman, 283.
14. Brouardel, 87; see Parikh, 165, for a similar account.
15. Grenz, 258; see also Haase, 310–11.
16. Saxon, 337.
17. Creighton, 1:161.
18. *Los Angeles Times*, 1 November 1985.
19. Ranft, 50.
20. Christian Fischer, in Cockburn and Cockburn, 178.
21. Glob, 45.

CHAPTER 15: DOWN TO A WATERY GRAVE

1. Grimm, 1:87.
2. Grimm, 1:357.
3. Mant, 151.
4. Parikh, 159.
5. Brouardel, 85.
6. Parikh, 165; Spitz and Fisher, 361.
7. Schneeweis (1961), 9; Vukanovic (1958), 23; Schmidt, 168; Trigg, 154; Hock, 27; Burkhart, 221; Lawson, 368.
8. Burkhart, 219, 238; McNally and Florescu, 150.
9. Murgoçi, 332; see also Weslowski, 209.
10. Quoted in Robbins, 492.

11. Drechsler, 317–18.
12. Burkhart, 225.
13. Burkhart, 239.
14. Löwenstimm, 93–106; Klapper (1909), 74–75.
15. Mannhardt, 259.
16. Holmberg, 37.
17. See, for example, Uhlik, 42.

CHAPTER 16: KILLING THE VAMPIRE

1. Karjalainen, 115.
2. Mansikka, 23.
3. Svensson, 401; see also 396.
4. Reiter, in Haussig, 201.
5. Cozannet, 202; see also Trigg, 123.
6. Cozannet, 203.
7. Maximoff, 65.
8. Taylor, facing p. 342. See also Hallet, 91.
9. Cited in Summers (1968), 269–70.
10. Tallar, 69.
11. Cremene, 89.
12. See Gaute and Odell, 69–73, for a more detailed analysis of the problem.
13. *Mercure galant*, quoted in Hock, 33–34.
14. Sturm and Völker, 457; see also Ranft, 185–86.
15. Wuttke, 222.
16. Schroeder, 45–46.
17. Danforth, 22.
18. Stora, citing Honko, 202.
19. Strackerjan, 1:154; Vakarelski, 30.
20. Van Gennep, 164.
21. Jirecek, 101.

CHAPTER 17: BODY DISPOSAL AND ITS PROBLEMS

1. Frazer (1933). See also Wiedemann (1917), 24–25, and Steinmetz, cited by Meuli, 306.
2. Briggs, 106.
3. Von Negelein (1901), 28.
4. Vermeule, 2.
5. Leca, 1–2. Wiedemann (1917) analyzes the Egyptian "vampires" in detail. See also Wainwright, 11–15.
6. Crooke (1926), 185.
7. Jirecek, 101.
8. Hock, 1; Burkhart, 250; W. Hertz, 126; Andree, 81.
9. Wilke, in Ebert, 7:260.
10. Saxon, 339.
11. Metcalf, in Lehmann and Myers, 313.
12. Metcalf, in Lehmann and Myers, 313.
13. Quoted in Lévy-Bruhl, 363.
14. Glob, 20.
15. Habenstein and Lamers, 83.
16. Bell, 84.
17. Habenstein and Lamers, 83. See also Robert, 1:69.

18. Lawson, 540–41.
19. Lafitau, quoted in van Gennep, 148.
20. Mellaart, 101.
21. Schüz and König (1973), 197.
22. Hamilton, 372. The vultures here could be the Egyptian, or scavenger, vulture (*neophron percnopterus*), for whom such behavior is cited by Robert Grubh in Wilbur, 109.
23. Rose, 29.
24. Gimbutas (1986), 7.
25. Hogguér, cited in Stora, 106.
26. Vukanovic (1959), 118.
27. H. Meyer, 165.
28. Pauli (1978), 146–47.
29. Haase, 298.
30. Crooke (1926), 232.
31. Wirth, 156; Karjalainen, 147.
32. Holmberg, 34.
33. Harva (1938), 317.

CHAPTER 18: THE SOUL AFTER DEATH

1. Haase, 332; Kahle, 9.
2. Wlislocki (1893), 198.
3. Iliad 23.l.65.
4. Odyssey 11.l.51.
5. Otto, 21ff.
6. Alfred Métraux, in Leach (1972), 1051.
7. Wlislocki (1893), 193–94.
8. Kahle, 24.
9. Blum and Blum, 78.
10. Von Negelein (1902), 10.
11. Von Negelein (1902), 22–24. For U.S. examples, see Puckett (1981), 2:1219.
12. Vakarelski, 303, 312.
13. Vakarelski, 303.
14. Cabej, 224.
15. Schneeweis (1961), 103.
16. Vakarelski, 309.
17. Csiszár, 200.
18. Schnippel, 394–98.
19. Samter, *Geburt, Hochzeit, Tod*, 85–86: cited in UCLA folklore encyclopedia collection files.
20. Stora, 128–29 (Lapps); Schmidt, 168 (Greeks); Lawson, 368 (Greeks).
21. Schneeweis (1961), 104. For mirrors as grave offerings in Madagascar, see Attenborough, 209.
22. Schneeweis (1961), 89.
23. Schneeweis (1961), 104.
24. Cited in Mogk (1919), 108.
25. Stora, 218–20.
26. Grober-Glück (1981), 442.
27. Stora, 197, 199.
28. Needham, 79.
29. Crooke (1926), 187.
30. Knoop (1893), "Wiedererscheinende Tote," no. 13.
31. Veckenstedt (1883), 264.

32. Veckenstedt (1883), 264.
33. Veckenstedt (1883), 266. Often we are told that it is inadvisable to be disrespectful toward bones found in graveyards (Strackerjan, 154).
34. Veckenstedt (1883), 268.
35. Blum and Blum, 75.
36. Veckenstedt (1883), 264.
37. Machal, 228.
38. See Seyfarth, 22–23, for a brief discussion of the vampire as nightmare.
39. Raymond Jameson, in Leach (1972), 1001.
40. Talbot, 231.
41. *Metamorphoses* 7.l.249.
42. Müller, 174.
43. Vukanovic (1958), 23.
44. Paulson (1960), 97, 87ff.; see also Harva (1938), 252–53.
45. Harva (1952), 20–21.
46. Landtman, 269.

CHAPTER 19: KEEPING BODY AND SOUL APART

1. Jameson, in Leach (1972), 1000; see also Negelein (1902), 18.
2. Benet, 242.
3. Camerling, 28–29.
4. Ralston, cited in Roheim, 7.
5. Roheim, 173 *passim*.
6. Stora, 217.
7. Köhler, 254; Benet, 244.
8. Vakarelski, 310.
9. Crooke (1926), 185.
10. Wiedemann (1900), 16.
11. Hellwald, 371.
12. Kühnau (1910), 170.
13. Von Negelein (1901), 20; see also Ebert, 279, and Karjalainen citing Castrén, 196.
14. Harva (1952), 24.
15. Harva (1952), 47.
16. Quoted in Van Gennep, 148.
17. Schneeweis (1961), 103.
18. Blum and Blum, 314.
19. Ranke, 346.
20. Ranke, 347.
21. John, 170; see also Csiszàr, 199 (Hungary).
22. Ranke, 347.
23. Stora, 183.
24. Harva (1938), 299.
25. Stora, 247.
26. Stora, 247.
27. Ranke, 87.
28. Danforth, 14.
29. Danforth, 61.
30. Köhler, 255.
31. Schneeweis (1961), 106. See Meuli, 334, for a summary of interpretations of mourning.
32. Köhler, 255.
33. Ranft, 82.

34. Danforth, 54.
35. Danforth, 54.
36. Danforth, 53.

CONCLUSION

1. Theo Körner, cited by Sell, 57; see also Sell, 72, 274.
2. Pettersson, 140.
3. Vermeule, 7.
4. Meuli, 321.
5. For a modern example (from Madagascar) of such casual handling of the (inert) body, see Attenborough, 214, 216.

Bibliography

Abbott, G. *Macedonian Folklore*. Cambridge, 1903.

Afanas'ev, Aleksandr. "Poetic Views of the Slavs Regarding Nature." In Perkowski, *Vampires of the Slavs*, 160–79.

Ahern, Emily. *The Cult of the Dead in a Chinese Village*. Stanford: Stanford University Press, 1973.

Aikens, C. Melvin, and Takayasu Higuchi. *Prehistory of Japan*. New York: Academic Press, 1982.

Airth, R. L., and G. E. Foerster. "Some Aspects of Fungal Bioluminescence." *Journal of Cellular and Comparative Physiology* 56 (1960): 173–82.

Alseikaite-Gimbutiene, Marija [Marija Gimbutas]. *Die Bestattung in Litauen in der vorgeschichtlichen Zeit*. Tübingen, 1946.

Amtliches Material zum Massenmord von Katyn. Berlin, 1943. [forensic analysis of mass burial in Poland.]

Andree, Richard. *Ethnographische Parallelen und Vergleiche*. Stuttgart, 1878.

Ankermann, Bernhard. "Totenkult und Seelenglaube bei afrikanischen Völkern." *Zeitschrift für Ethnologie* 50 (1918): 89–153.

Arens, W. *The Man-Eating Myth*. Oxford: 1979.

D'Argens, Boyer. *Lettres juives*. Haye, 1764.

Argenti, Philip P., and H. J. Rose. *The Folk-Lore of Chios*. Cambridge, 1949.

Ariès, Philippe. *The Hour of Our Death*. Trans. Helen Weaver. New York: Alfred A. Knopf, 1981. [Orig. pub. *L'Homme devant la mort*. Paris: Editions du Seuil, 1977.]

Armstrong, Edward A. *The Folklore of Birds*. London: Collins, 1958.

Ashbee, Paul. *The Earthen Long Barrow in Britain*. London: J. M. Dent & Sons, 1970.

Attenborough, David. *Journeys to the Past: Travels in New Guinea, Madagascar, and the Northern Territory of Australia*. Guildford, Surrey: Lutterworth Press, 1981.

Bächtold-Stäubli, Hanns. *Handwörterbuch des deutschen Aberglaubens*. Berlin, 1934–35. Vol. V: "Leiche," etc., by Paul Geiger. Vol. VI: "Nachzehrer," also by Geiger. Vol. IX, "Sense," "Sichel," by Haberlandt.

Bahr, Ernst, and Kurt König. *Niederschlesien unter polnischer Verwaltung*. Frankfurt and Berlin: Alfred Metzner Verlag, 1967.

Balassa, Ivan, and Gyula Ortutay. *Ungarische Volkskunde*. Budapest: Corvina Kiadó; and Munich: Verlag C. H. Beck, 1982.

Balys, Jonas. *Dvasios ir zmones: Ghosts and Men: Lithuanian Folk Legends about the Dead.* Bloomington: Indiana University Press, 1951.

Barber, Paul. "Forensic Pathology and the European Vampire." *Journal of Folklore Research* 24:1 (1987): 1–32.

Bargheer, Ernst. *Eingeweide: Lebens- und Seelenkräfte des Leibesinneren im deutschen Glauben und Brauch.* Leipzig, 1931.

Baroti, L. "Beiträge zur Geschichte des Vampyrismus in Südungarn." *Ethnologische Beiträge aus Ungarn* 3 (1893): 219–21.

Bartels, Max. "Was können die Toten?" *Zeitschrift des Vereins für Volkskunde* 10 (1900): 117–42.

Bartsch, Karl. *Sagen, Märchen und Gebräuche aus Meklenburg.* Vienna, 1879.

Beitl, Richard. *Deutsches Volkstum der Gegenwart.* Berlin, 1933.

————. *Deutsche Volkskunde.* Berlin, 1933.

Bell, Sir Charles. *The People of Tibet.* Oxford, 1928.

Belovic, J. *Die Sitten der Südslaven.* Dresden, 1927.

Benet, Sula. *Song, Dance, and Customs of Peasant Poland.* London, 1951.

Berndt, Ronald and Catherine. *The World of the First Australians.* Chicago: University of Chicago Press, 1965.

Blum, Richard and Eva. *The Dangerous Hour: The Lore of Crisis and Mystery in Rural Greece.* New York: Charles Scribner's Sons, 1970.

Boase, T. S. R. *Death in the Middle Ages.* London: Thames and Hudson, 1972.

Bohnenberger, Karl, ed. *Volkstümliche Überlieferungen in Württemberg.* 1904; reprint, Stuttgart: Kommissionsverlag Müller & Gräff, 1980.

Bosi, Roberto. *The Lapps.* Trans. James Cadell. London: Thames and Hudson, 1960. Revised version of *I Lapponi.* Milan, 1959.

Bradley, G. P. "Burial Customs formerly Observed in the Naval Service." *Journal of American Folklore* 7 (1894): 67–69.

Braus, H. "Leichenbestattung in Unteritalien." *Archiv für Religionswissenschaft* 9 (1906): 385–96.

Briggs, G. W. *The Chamars.* Calcutta, 1920.

Brixius, Lothar. *Erscheinungsformen des Volksglaubens.* Halle, Saale: Max Niemeyer Verlag, 1939.

Brouardel, P. *Death and Sudden Death.* London, 1897.

Brown, Theo. *The Fate of the Dead: A Study in Folk-Eschatology in the West Country after the Reformation.* Ipswich: D. A. Brewer, and Totowa, N.J.: Rowman and Littlefield, 1979.

Browne, Sir Thomas. *The Prose of Sir Thomas Browne.* Ed. J. Endicott. New York: Anchor Books, 1967.

Brückner, A. "Beiträge zur älteren Geschichte der Slaven und Litauer." *Archiv für slavische Philologie* 23 (1901): 215.

Brunner, Karl. *Ostdeutsche Volkskunde.* Leipzig, 1925.

Brunvand, Jan Harold. *The Choking Doberman and other "New" Urban Legends.* New York and London: W. W. Norton & Company, 1984.

————. *The Vanishing Hitchhiker: American Urban Legends and Their Meanings.* New York and London: W. W. Norton & Company, 1981.

Buchholz, Gustav. *Neuvorpommersches Leben im 18. Jahrhundert: Nach dem Tagebuch des Stralsunder Predigers Joh. Chr. Müller, 1720–72.* Greifswald, 1910.

Burkhart, Dagmar. "Vampirglaube und Vampirsage auf dem Balkan." In *Beiträge zur Südosteuropa-Forschung.* Munich, 1966.

Cabej, E. "Sitten und Gebräuche der Albaner." *Revue internationale des études balkaniques* 1 (1934–35): 218–34.

Cajkanovic, Veselin. "The Killing of a Vampire." *Folklore Forum* 7:4 (1974): 260–71. Trans. Marilyn Sjoberg. [Article originally appeared in the *Serbian Literary Herald* (Belgrade, 1923).]

Caland, W. "Die vorchristlichen baltischen Totengebräuche." *Archiv für Religionswissenschaft* 17 (1914): 476–512.

Calmet, Augustine. *The Phantom World.* Ed. Henry Christmas. Vol. 2. London, 1850. [Translation of *Dissertations sur les apparitions des anges, des démons et des esprits* (1746).]

Camerling, I. *Über Ahnenkult in Hinterindien und auf den grossen Sunda Inseln.* Rotterdam, 1928.

Cammann, Alfred. *Märchenwelt des Preussenlandes.* Schloss Bleckede, Elbe: Otto Meissners Verlag, 1973.

Camps, Francis E., ed. *Gradwohl's Legal Medicine.* 3d ed. Bristol: John Wright and Sons, 1976.

Carey, George Gibson. *A Faraway Time and Place.* New York: Arno Press, 1977.

Chernetsov, V. N., and W. Moszynska. *Prehistory of Western Siberia.* Montreal and London: McGill-Queen's University Press, 1974.

Childe, Gordon. "Directional Changes in Funerary Practices during 50,000 Years." *Man* 45 (1945): 13–19.

Chotjewitz, Peter O. "Der Vampir: Theorie und Kritik einer Mythe." *Merkur* 8 (1968): 708–19.

Christiansen, Reidar Thorwald, ed. *Folktales of Norway.* Trans. Pat Shaw Iversen. Chicago: University of Chicago Press, 1964.

Cockburn, Aidan and Eve. *Mummies, Disease and Ancient Cultures.* Cambridge: Cambridge University Press, 1983.

Collinder, Björn. *Fenno-Ugric Vocabulary.* Hamburg, 1977.

Corliss, William R. *Handbook of Unusual Natural Phenomena.* Glen Arm, Md.: The Sourcebook Project, 1977.

Cozannet, Françoise. *Mythes et coutumes religieuses des tsiganes.* Paris, 1973.

Creighton, Charles. *A History of Epidemics in Britain.* Vol. 1. Cambridge, 1891.

Cremene, Adrien. *La mythologie du vampire en Roumanie.* Monaco: Editions du Rocher, 1981.

Crooke, W. "The Burning of the Property of a Gypsy at Death." *Folk-Lore* 20 (1909): 353.

Crooke, William. *Religion and Folklore of Northern India.* Oxford: Oxford University Press, 1926.

Crusius, Martinus. *Turcograeciae.* Basel, 17th c. (date illegible).

Csiszár, Árpád. "A hazajáró lélek." *A nyíregyházi Jósa András Múzeum Évkönyue* 8–9 (1965–66): 159–96; summary in German: 199–201.

Dähnhardt, Oskar. *Natursagen.* Vol. 1. Leipzig and Berlin: B. G. Teubner Verlag, 1907.

Dale-Green, Patricia. *Dog.* London: Rupert Hart-Davis, 1966.

Danforth, Loring. *The Death Rituals of Rural Greece*. Princeton, N.J.: Princeton University Press, 1982.

Delitzsch, Friedrich. *Das Land ohne Heimkehr*. Stuttgart: Deutsche Verlags-Anstalt, 1911.

Deubner, Ludwig. "Russische Volkskunde." *Archiv für Religionswissenschaft* 9 (1906): 445–63.

Dieck, Alfred. *Die europäischen Moorleichenfunde*. Neumünster: Karl Wacholtz Verlag, 1965.

Diederichs, Ulf, and Christa Hinze. *Hessische Sagen*. Düsseldorf and Cologne: Eugen Diederichs Verlag, 1978.

Dioszegi, V., ed. *Glaubenswelt und Folklore der sibirischen Völker*. Budapest, 1963.

Dobeneck, Friedrich Ludwig Ferdinand von. *Des deutschen Mittelalters Volksglauben und Heroensagen*. Berlin, 1815; reprint, Hildesheim and New York: Georg Olms Verlag, 1974.

Dölger, F. "Die mittelalterliche Kultur auf dem Balkan." *Revue internationale des études balkaniques* 1:2 (1935): 108–21.

Dömötör, Tekla. *Volksglaube und Aberglaube der Ungarn*. Budapest: Corvina Kiadó, 1981.

Dörpfeld, W. "Über Verbrennung und Bestattung der Toten im alten Griechenland." *Zeitschrift für Ethnologie* 36 (1905): 538–41.

Dolphin, David. "Werewolves and Vampires." Abstract of paper presented at annual meeting of American Association for the Advancement of Science, 1985.

Drechsler, Paul. *Sitte, Brauch und Aberglaube in Schlesien*. Leipzig, 1903.

Duffy, John. *Sword of Pestilence: The New Orleans Yellow Fever Epidemic of 1853*. Baton Rouge: Louisiana State University Press, 1966.

Durey, Michael. *The Return of the Plague: British Society and the Cholera, 1831–2*. Dublin: Gill and MacMillan Humanities Press, 1979.

Durham, Edith. "Of Magic, Witches and Vampires in the Balkans." *Man* 23 (1923): 189–92.

Ebert, Max. "Die Anfänge des europäischen Totenkultes." *Prähistorische Zeitschrift* 13–14 (1921–22): 1–19.

Ebert, Max, ed. *Reallexikon der Vorgeschichte*. Vols. 7, 13. Berlin, 1926, 1929.

Eisel, Robert. *Sagenbuch des Voigtlandes*. Gera, 1871.

Eschker, Wolfgang, ed. *Mazedonische Volksmärchen*. Düsseldorf: Eugen Diederichs Verlag, 1972.

Evans, W. E. D. *The Chemistry of Death*. Springfield, Ill.: Charles C. Thomas, 1963.

Eylmann, Erhard. *Die Eingeborenen der Kolonie Südaustralien*. Berlin, 1908.

Faivre, Tony. *Les vampires*. Paris, 1962.

Fatteh, Abdullah. *Handbook of Forensic Pathology*. Philadelphia and Toronto: J. B. Lippincott Co., 1973.

Faye, Andreas. *Norske Folke-Sagn*. Oslo, 1948.

Fehrle, Eugen. *Feste und Volksbräuche*. Kassel, 1955.

Feilberg, H. F. "Die Sage von dem Begräbnis König Erik Ejegods von Dänemark auf Cypern." *Zeitschrift des Vereins für Volkskunde* 5 (1895): 239–46.

———."Der Vampyr." *Am Ur-Quell* 3 (1892): 331–35.

Feist, Sigmund. *Kultur, Ausbreitung und Herkunft der Indogermanen*. Berlin, 1913; reprint, Hildesheim: Georg Olms Verlag, 1964.

Filipovic, Milenko. "Die Leichenverbrennung bei den Südslaven." *Wiener völkerkundliche Mitteilungen* 10 (1962): 61- 71.

Fischer, Adam, and Tadeusz Lehr-Splawinski. *The Cassubian Civilization.* London, 1935.

Fischer, Helmut. *Erzählgut der Gegenwart: Mündliche Texte aus dem Siegraum.* Cologne: Rheinland-Verlag, 1978.

Fortis, Alberto. *Viaggio in Dalmazia.* 1774; reprint, Munich: Verlag Otto Sagner, 1974.

Fox, Denton, and Hermann Pálsson. *Grettir's Saga.* Toronto: University of Toronto Press, 1974.

Folklore Archives, UC Berkeley. Material under headings of "Superstition, Romanian"; "Superstition, Serbo-Croatian"; "Superstition, Polish"; "Superstition, German."

Frankfort, H. and H. A. *Before Philosophy.* Harmondsworth, Middlesex: Penguin Books, 1963. [Orig. pub. Chicago: University of Chicago Press, 1946.]

Frazer, J. G. *The Belief in Immortality and the Worship of the Dead.* 3 vols. London, 1913.

———. *The Fear of the Dead in Primitive Religion.* London: Macmillan and Co., 1933.

———. *The Golden Bough.* 1922; reprint, New York: Macmillan Company, 1963.

Freistedt, Emil. *Altchristliche Totengedächtnistage und ihre Beziehung zum Jenseitsglauben und Totenkultus der Antike.* 1928; reprint, Münster: Aschendorffsche Verlagsbuchhandlung, 1971.

Freudenthal, Herbert. *Das Feuer im deutschen Glauben und Brauch.* Berlin and Leipzig: de Gruyter Verlag, 1931.

Fritsch, Johann Christian. *Eines Weimarischen Medici muthmassliche Gedancken von denen Vampyren, oder sogenannten Blut-Saugern.* Leipzig, 1732.

Gábor, Szinte. "Speerhölzer oder Kopfhölzer (Grabstelen) im Szeklerlande." *Anzeiger der ethnographischen Abteilung des ungarischen National-Museums* 3:2 (1905): 87–98.

Gaidoz, H., et. al. "Cadavres percés de clous." *Revue des études anciennes: Annales de la Faculté des Lettres de Bordeaux* 4 (1902): 300–301.

Garland, Robert. *The Greek Way of Death.* Ithaca: Cornell University Press, 1985.

Gaute, J. H. H., and Robin Odel. *Murder 'Whatdunit'.* London and Sydney: Pan Books, 1982.

Gavazzi, Milovan. "The Dug-out Coffin in Central Bosnia." *Man* 53:202 (1953): 129–30.

Geiger, Paul. "Die Behandlung der Selbstmörder im deutschen Brauch." *Archiv für Volkskunde* 26 (1926): 145–70.

Geiger, Werner. *Totenbrauch im Odenwald.* Lindenfels, 1960.

Gencev, Stojan. "Gemeinsame Elemente im Brauchsystem von Bulgaren und Russen: Das rituelle Wärmen der Toten mit Feuer." *Ethnologia Slavica* 8–9 (1976–77): 227–34.

Gerschke, Leo. "Vom Vampirglauben im alten Westpreussen." *Westpreussen-Jahrbuch* 12 (1962): 89–94.

Gimbutas, Marija. "Birds, Animals, Amphibians and Insects of the Old European Goddess of Death and Regeneration." Paper delivered at the World Archaeological Congress, Southampton and London, 1–7 Sept. 1986.

Glaister, John, and Edgar Rentoul. *Medical Jurisprudence and Toxicology.* 12th ed. Edinburgh and London: E. & M. S. Livingstone, 1966.

Glob, P. V. *The Bog People. Iron-Age Man Preserved.* Trans. Rupert Bruce-Mitford. New York: Ballantine Books, 1969.

Görres, Joseph von. *Die christliche Mystik.* Regensburg, 1840.

Gottfried, Robert S. *The Black Death: Natural and Human Disaster in Medieval Europe.* New York: Free Press, 1983.

Grässe, J. *Sagenbuch des preussischen Staats.* Glogau, 1868.

Grenz, Rudolf. "Archäologische Vampirbefunde aus dem westslawischen Siedlungsgebiet." *Zeitschrift zur Ostforschung* 16:2 (1967): 255–65.

Grimm, Jakob and Wilhelm. *Deutsche Sagen.* 2 vols. 1816; reprint, Frankfurt: Insel Verlag, 1981.

Grinsell, L. V. "Early Funerary Superstitions in Britain." *Folk-Lore* 64 (1953): 271–81.

———. "The Breaking of Objects as a Funerary Rite." *Folklore* 84 (1973): 111–14.

Grober-Glück, Gerda. "Der Verstorbene als Nachzehrer." In Zender, *Atlas* (1981): 427–56.

———. "Volksglaubensvorstellungen über die scheidende Seele." *Jahrbuch für Volkskunde* 6 (1983): 149–81.

De Groot, J. J. M. *The Religious System of China.* The Hague, 1892–1910.

Grünhagen, C. *Geschichte Schlesiens.* Gotha, 1884.

———. *Schlesien unter Friedrich dem Grossen.* Vol. 2. Breslau, 1892.

Guiart, Jean, ed. *Les hommes et la mort: Rituels funéraires à travers le monde.* Paris: Muséum national d'histoire naturelle, 1979.

———. *Rites de la mort: Exposition du Laboratoire d'Ethnologie du Muséum d'Histoire Naturelle.* Paris, 1979.

Györffy, Stefan. "Gross-Kumanische Kopfhölzer." *Anzeiger der ethnographischen Abteilung des ungarischen National-Museums* 6 (1907): 88–99.

Haase, Felix. *Volksglaube und Brauchtum der Ostslaven.* 1939; reprint, Hildesheim and New York: Georg Olms Verlag, 1980.

Habenstein, Robert W., and William M. Lamers. *Funeral Customs the World Over.* Milwaukee: National Funeral Directors Association of the United States, 1963.

Haller, Albrecht von. *De partium corporis humani praecipuarum fabrica et functionibus.* Bern and Lausanne, 1768.

Hallet, Jean-Pierre, with Alex Pelle. *Animal Kitabu.* New York: Random House, 1967.

Hamilton, William J. *Researches in Asia Minor, Pontus and Armenia.* London, 1842; reprint, 2 vols. Hildesheim: Georg Olms Verlag, 1984.

Hammerstein, Reinhold. *Tanz und Musik des Todes.* Bern and Munich: Francke Verlag, 1980.

Hand, Wayland D., ed. *The Frank C. Brown Collection of North Carolina Folklore,* vol. 7. Durham, N.C.: Duke University Press, 1964.

Hansen, Jens P. Hart, Jørgen Meldgaard and Jørgen Nordqvist. "The Mummies of Qilakitsoq." *National Geographic* 167 (February 1985): 190–207.

Hanus, J. J. "Die Wer-Wölfe oder Vlko-dlaci." *Zeitschrift für deutsche Mythologie und Sittenkunde* 4 (1859): 193–201.

Harrington, M. Raymond. "An Abenaki 'Witch-Story.'" *Journal of American Folklore* 14 (1901): 160.

Harsdörfer, Georg Philipp. *Der grosse Schau-Platz lust- und lehrreicher Geschichte.* Frankfurt, 1664.

Hartmann, Franz. *Premature Burial.* London, 1896.

Harva, Uno. *Die Religion der Tscheremissen.* Porvoo, 1926.

———. *Die religiösen Vorstellungen der altaischen Völker.* F. F. Communications no. 125. Helsinki, 1938. [Orig. pub. in Finnish in 1933.]

———. *Die religiösen Vorstellungen der Mordwinen.* F.F. Communications no. 142. Helsinki, 1952.

Hastings, James, ed. *Encyclopedia of Religion and Ethics.* Vol. 4: *Death and Disposal of the Dead.* Edinburgh, 1911.

Haupt, Karl. *Sagenbuch der Lausitz.* Leipzig, 1862.

Haussig, Hans Wilhelm, ed. *Wörterbuch der Mythologie.* Vol. 2. Stuttgart, 1973. Slavic Mythology: Norbert Reiter. Finnish: Lauri Honko. Baltic: Jonas Balys and Harolds Biezais. Albanian: Maximilian Lambertz.

Havekost, Ernst. *Die Vampirsage in England.* Halle, 1914.

Hayes, Wm. *The Scepter of Egypt.* Vol. 1. New York, 1953.

Hecker, J. F. C. *Die grossen Volkskrankheiten des Mittelalters.* 1865; facsimile reprint, Hildesheim: Georg Olms Verlagsbuchhandlung, 1964.

Hedin, Sven. *My Life as an Explorer.* Trans. Alfhild Huebsch. New York, 1925.

Hellwald, Fr. *Die Welt der Slawen.* Berlin, 1890.

Henne am Rhyn, Otto. *Die deutsche Volkssage.* Vienna, Pest, and Leipzig, 1879.

Herrmann, Joachim, ed. *Die Slawen in Deutschland.* Berlin: Akademie-Verlag, 1970.

Hertz, Robert. *Death and the Right Hand.* Trans. Rodney and Claudia Needham, intro. by E. E. Evans-Pritchard. Glencoe, Ill.: Free Press, 1960. [Essays orig. pub. in French, 1907, 1909.]

Hertz, Wilhelm. *Der Werwolf.* Stuttgart, 1862.

Hesiod. *The Homeric Hymns and Homerica.* Ed. and trans. Hugh G. Evelyn-White. Cambridge, Mass., and London: Loeb Classical Library, 1914; reprint, Cambrige, Mass., and London: Leob Classical Library, 1977.

Hess, J. J. *Von den Beduinen des innern Arabiens.* Zürich and Leipzig: Max Niehans Verlag, 1938.

Hock, Stefan. *Die Vampyrsagen und ihre Verwertung in der deutschen Litteratur.* Berlin, 1900.

Hösch, Edgar. *Orthodoxie und Häresie im alten Russland.* Wiesbaden: Otto Harrassowitz, 1975.

Holmberg, Uno. See Harva, Uno.

Homer. *The Iliad.* Vols. 1 and 2. Ed. and trans. A. T. Murray. Cambridge, Mass., and London: Loeb Classical Library, 1925.

———. *The Odyssey.* Vols. 1 and 2. Ed. and trans. A.T. Murray. Cambridge, Mass., and London: Loeb Classical Library, 1919.

Horst, Georg Conrad. *Zauber-Bibliothek.* Vols. 1, 4, and 5. Mainz, 1821, 1823, 1825.

Hugger, Paul. "Die Beerdigung der Selbstmörder im Kanton St. Gallen." *Schweizer Volkskunde* 51 (1961): 41–48.

Humphreys, S. C., and Helen King, eds. *Man and Immortality: The Anthropology and Archaeology of Death.* London: Academic Press, 1981.

Illis, L. "On Porphyria and the Aetiology of Werwolves." *Proceedings of the Royal Society of Medicine* 57 (Jan. 1964): 23–26.

Izikowitz, Karl Gustav. *Fastening the Soul.* Göteborg, 1941.

Jakobson, Roman. *Selected Writings.* Vol. 4: *Slavic Epic Studies.* The Hague and Paris: Mouton & Co., 1966.

Jansen, Hans Helmut, ed. *Der Tod in Dichtung, Philosophie und Kunst.* Darmstadt: Steinkopff, 1978.

Jaworskij, Juljan. "Südrussische Vampyre." *Zeitschrift des Vereins für Volkskunde* 8 (1898): 331–36.

Jenny, Urs. "Auf der Vampir-Welle." *Merkur* 8 (1968): 762–64.

Jensen, Adolf. *Mythos und Kult bei Naturvölkern.* Wiesbaden: Franz Steiner Verlag, 1951.

Jewitt, Llewellynn. *Grave-Mounds and Their Contents: A Manual of Archaeology.* London, 1870.

Jirecek, Constantin. *Das Fürstenthum Bulgarien.* Vienna, 1891.

John, Alois. *Sitte, Brauch und Volksglaube im deutschen Westböhmen.* Prague, 1905.

Jungbauer, Gustav. *Deutsche Volksmedizin.* Berlin and Leipzig: de Gruyter Verlag, 1934.

Kahle, B. "Seele und Kerze." *Hessische Blätter für Volkskunde* 6:1 (1907): 9–24.

Kampffmeyer, G. "Ein alter Bericht über litauische Totengebräuche." *Globus* 69 (1896): 375.

Kanitz, F. *La Bulgarie Danubienne et le Balkan.* Paris, 1882.

Karjalainen, K. F. *Die Religion der Jugra-Völker.* F. F. Communications no. 41. Helsinki, 1921.

Károly, Sebestyén. "Speerhölzer und Kreuze auf dem Széklerboden." *Anzeiger der ethnographischen Abteilung des ungarischen National-Museums* 3:2 (1905): 98–102.

Kiej'e, Nikolas. *Japanese Grotesqueries.* Rutland, Vt., and Tokyo: Charles E. Tuttle Company, 1973.

Kittredge, G. L. *Witchcraft in Old and New England.* 1929; reprint, New York: Atheneum, 1972.

Klapper, Joseph. "Die schlesischen Geschichten von den schädigenden Toten." *Mitteilungen der schlesischen Gesellschaft für Volkskunde* 11 (1909): 58–93.

———. *Schlesische Volkskunde auf kulturgeschichtlicher Grundlage.* Breslau, 1925.

Kleinpaul, Rudolf. *Die Lebendigen und die Toten in Volksglauben, Religion und Sage.* Leipzig, 1898.

Klimkeit, Hans-Joachim, ed. *Tod und Jenseits im Glauben der Völker.* Wiesbaden: Otto Harrassowitz, 1983.

Kmietowicz, Frank. *Slavic Mythical Beliefs.* Windsor, Ontario: F. Kmietowicz, 1982.

Knoop, Otto, "Sagen aus Kujawien." *Zeitschrift des Vereins für Volkskunde* 16 (1906): 96–97: "Vampyrsagen."

———. *Sagen und Erzählungen aus der Provinz Posen.* Posen, 1893.

———. *Volkssagen, Erzählungen, Aberglauben, Gebräuche und Märchen aus dem östlichen Hinterpommern.* Posen, 1885.

Koch, William E. *Folklore from Kansas.* Lawrence, Kans.: Regents' Press, 1980.

Köhbach, Markus. "Ein Fall von Vampirismus bei den Osmanen." *Balkan Studies* 20 (1979): 83–90.

Köhler, J. A. E. *Volksbrauch, Aberglauben, Sagen und andere alte Überlieferungen im Voigtland*. Leipzig, 1867.

Köröshazy, Ferenz. *Die Vampyrbraut*. Trans. from Hungarian. Weimar, 1849.

Krauss, Friedrich. *Slavische Volksforschungen*. Leipzig, 1908.

———. "Vampyre im südslawischen Volksglauben." *Globus* 61 (1892): 325–28.

Kühnau, Richard. *Schlesische Sagen*. Vols. 1 and 2. Berlin, 1910–11.

———. "Über Weisse Frauen und die symbolische Bedeutung der weissen und schwarzen Farbe." *Mitteilungen der hessischen Gesellschaft für Volkskunde* 15 (1913): 186–207.

Kuhn, Adelbert. *Sagen, Gebräuche und Märchen aus Westfalen*. Leipzig, 1859.

Kunt, Ernö. *Volkskunst ungarischer Dorffriedhöfe*. Budapest: Corvina Kiadó, 1983.

Kurtz, Donna C., and John Boardman. *Greek Burial Customs*. Ithaca: Cornell University Press, 1971.

Kyll, Nikolaus. "Die Bestattung der Toten mit dem Gesicht nach unten." *Trierer Zeitschrift für Geschichte* . . . 27 (1964): 168–83.

———. *Tod, Grab, Begräbnisplatz, Totenfeier*. Bonn: Ludwig Röhrscheid Verlag, 1972.

Landtman, Gunnar. *The Kiwai Papuans of British New Guinea*. London, New York: Johnson Reprint Corporation, 1970. [Orig. pub. London: Macmillan and Co., 1927.]

Lange, Erwin Rudolf. *Sterben und Begräbnis im Volksglauben zwischen Weichsel und Memel*. Würzburg: Holzner-Verlag, 1955.

Lauterbach, Samuel Friedrich. *Kleine Fraustädtische Pest-Chronica*. Leipzig, 1701.

Lawson, John Cuthbert. *Modern Greek Folklore and Ancient Greek Religion*. Cambridge, 1910.

Leach, Maria, ed. *Standard Dictionary of Folklore, Mythology and Legend*. New York: Funk & Wagnalls, 1972.

Leake, W. M. *Travels in Northern Greece*. Vol. 4. London, 1935; reprint, Amsterdam, 1967.

Leatherdale, Clive. *Dracula: The Novel and the Legend*. Wellingborough, Northamptonshire: Aquarian Press, 1985.

Le Braz, Anatole. *La légende de la mort*. 2 vols. Paris: Honoré Champion, 1945.

Leca, Ange-Pierre. *The Egyptian Way of Death (Les Momies)*. Trans. by Louise Asmal. New York: Doubleday & Company, 1981.

Lee, B. Demetracopoulou. "Greek Accounts of the Vrykolakas." *Journal of American Folklore* 55 (1942): 126–32.

Lehmann, Arthur C., and James E. Myers, eds. *Magic, Witchcraft, and Religion*. Palo Alto and London: Mayfield Publishing Company, 1985.

Lemke, G. *Volksthümliches in Ostpreussen*. Mohrungen, 1884.

Lentz, W. "Sitten, Gebräuche und Anschauungen, besonders im Lumdatal." *Hessische Blätter für Volkskunde* 6:2 (1907): 97–121.

Le Roux, C. C. F. M. *De Bergpapoea's van Nieuw-Guinea en hun woongebied*. Vol. 2. Leiden, 1950.

Levy, G. Rachel. *Religious Conceptions of the Stone Age and Their Influence Upon European Thought*. New York and Evanston: Harper and Row, 1963. [Orig. pub. as *The Gate of Horn* (London: Faber & Faber Limited, 1948).]

Lévy-Bruhl, Lucien. *Les fonctions mentales dans les sociétés inférieures.* 1910; reprint, Paris, 1951.

Lewis, Waller. "On the Chemical and General Effects of the Practice of Interment in Vaults and Catacombs." *Lancet* (1851): 125–26.

Lewy, H. "Morgenländischer Aberglaube in der römischen Kaiserzeit." *Zeitschrift des Vereins für Volkskunde* 3 (1893): 23–40.

Li, Xueqin. *Eastern Zhou and Qin Civilizations.* Trans. K. C. Chang. New Haven and London: Yale University Press, 1985.

Liebrecht, Felix. *Zur Volkskunde.* Heilbronn, 1879.

Lilek, Emilian. "Familien- und Volksleben in Bosnien und in der Herzegowina." *Zeitschrift für österreichische Volkskunde* 6 (1900): 202–25.

Littlejohn, Harvey. *Forensic Medicine.* London, 1925.

Loorits, Oskar. "Eine Beschreibung der livischen Beerdigungsbräuche." *Zeitschrift für Volkskunde* 51 (1955): 252–58.

———. *Estnische Volksdichtung und Mythologie.* Tartu, 1932.

Löwenstimm, Aug. *Aberglaube und Strafrecht.* Berlin, 1897.

Lucas, A. *Ancient Egyptian Materials and Industries.* 2d ed. London: Edward Arnold and Co., 1934.

Lyncker, Karl. *Deutsche Sagen und Sitten.* Cassel, 1854.

Machal, Jan. *Slavic Mythology.* Boston, 1918.

Mackensen, Lutz. *Geister, Hexen und Zauber in Texten des 17. und 18. Jahrhunderts.* Dresden, 1938.

Mackenzie, Andrew. *Dracula Country: Travels and Folk Beliefs in Romania.* London: Arthur Barker Limited, 1977.

Malinowski, Bronislaw. *Magic, Science and Religion and Other Essays.* Glencoe, Ill.: Free Press, 1948.

Mannhardt, W. "Über Vampyrismus." *Zeitschrift für deutsche Mythologie und Sittenkunde* 4 (1859): 259–82.

Mansikka, V. J. *Die Religion der Ostslaven.* Helsinki, 1922.

Mant, A. Keith, ed. *Taylor's Principles and Practice of Medical Jurisprudence.* 13th ed. Edinburgh, London, Melbourne, and New York: Churchill Livingstone, 1984.

Maspero, Henri. *China in Antiquity.* Trans. from the French by Frank A. Kierman, Jr. 1965; reprint, Amherst: University of Massachusetts Press, 1978.

Masters, Anthony. *The Natural History of the Vampire.* New York: G. P. Putnam's Sons, 1972.

Maundrell, Henry. *A Journey from Aleppo to Jerusalem in 1697.* 1703; Beirut, 1963: reprint of 1810 ed.

Maximoff, Matéo. "The Tribe of the Miyeyesti." *Journal of the Gypsy Lore Society* 28 (1949): 61–65.

Meaney, Audrey. *A Gazetteer of Early Anglo-Saxon Burial Sites.* London: George Allen and Unwin, 1964.

Mech, David L. *The Wolf: Ecology and Behavior of an Endangered Species.* Garden City, N.Y.: Natural History Press, 1970.

Menghin, Wilfried. *Kelten, Römer und Germanen.* Munich: Prestel-Verlag, 1980.

Metcalf, Peter. *A Borneo Journey into Death.* Philadelphia: University of Pennsylvania Press, 1982.

Meuli, Karl. *Gesammelte Schriften.* Vol. 1. Basel and Stuttgart: Schwabe & Co., 1975.

Meyer, Carl. *Der Aberglaube des Mittelalters und der nächstfolgenden Jahrhunderte.* Basel, 1884.

Meyer, Elard Hugo. *Mythologie der Germanen.* Strasbourg, 1903.

Meyer, Hans B. *Das Danziger Volksleben.* Würzburg: Holzner-Verlag, 1956.

Mogk, Eugen. "Altgermanische Spukgeschichten." *Neue Jahrbücher für das klassische Altertum, Geschichte und deutsche Literatur* 22 (1919): 103–17.

———. "Gestalten des Seelenglaubens; Gespenster." In *Grundriss der germanischen Philologie,* pp. 264–67. Strasbourg, 1897.

Morley, John. *Death, Heaven, and the Victorians.* Pittsburgh: University of Pittsburgh Press, 1971.

Morris, R. J. *Cholera 1832. The Social Response to an Epidemic.* London: Croom Helm, 1976.

Moszynski, Kazimierz. "Slavic Folk Culture." Trans. Jan Perkowski. [Orig. pub. Cracow, 1938.] In Perkowski, *Vampires of the Slavs.*

Müller, W. Max. *Egyptian Mythology: The Mythology of All Races.* 1918; reprint, New York: Cooper Square Publishers, Inc., 1964.

Murgoçi, Agnes. "The Vampire in Roumania." *Folklore* 37 (1926): 320–49.

Nandris, Grigore. "The Historical Dracula: The Theme of His Legend in the Western and in the Eastern Literatures of Europe." *Comparative Literature Studies* 3:4 (1966): 367–96.

Naumann, Hans. *Primitive Gemeinschaftskultur.* Jena, 1921.

Needham, Joseph. *Science and Civilization in China.* Vol. 5. Cambridge: Cambridge University Press, 1974.

Negelein, Julius. "Bild, Spiegel und Schatten im Volksglauben." *Zeitschrift des Vereins für Volkskunde* 5 (1902): 1–37.

———. "Die Reise der Seele ins Jenseits." *Zeitschrift des Vereins für Volkskunde* 11 (1901): 16–28; 149–58.

———. *Weltgeschichte des Aberglaubens.* Vol. 2: *Haupttypen des Aberglaubens.* Berlin and Leipzig: de Gruyter Verlag, 1935.

Nield, Ted. "An Iron Age Murder Mystery." *Sciences* (May-June 1986): 4–5.

Nilsson, Martin P. *Geschichte der griechischen Religion.* Munich: C. H. Beck Verlag, 1955.

———. *Greek Popular Religion.* New York: Columbia University Press, 1940.

Ninck, Martin. *Die Bedeutung des Wassers im Kult und Leben der Alten.* Leipzig, 1921.

Nodier, Charles. *Infernaliana.* 1822; reprint, Paris, 1966.

Noguchi, Thomas T., with Joseph DiMona. *Coroner.* New York: Simon and Schuster, 1984.

———. *Coroner at Large.* New York: Simon and Schuster, 1985.

Oinas, Felix. *Essays on Russian Folklore and Mythology.* Columbus, Ohio: Slavica Publishers, 1984.

Olsen, Jack. *The Man with the Candy: The Story of the Houston Mass Murders.* New York: Simon and Schuster, 1974.

Opler, Morris E. "Myth and Practice in Jicarilla Apache Eschatology." *Journal of American Folklore* 73 (Apr.–June 1960): 133–53.

Otto, Walter. *Die Manen.* 3d ed. Darmstadt: Wissenschaftliche Buchgesellschaft, 1962.

Ovid. *Metamorphoses.* Cambridge, Mass., and London: Loeb Classical Library, 1960.

Özgüç, Tahsin. *Die Bestattungsbräuche im vorgeschichtlichen Anatolien.* Ankara, 1948.

Page, D. L. *Greek Literary Papyri.* Vol. 3. Cambridge, Mass., and London: Loeb Classical Library, 1941.

Panofsky, Erwin. "Father Time." In *Studies in Iconology.* New York: Harper Torchbooks, 1962 [Orig. publ. Oxford: Oxford University Press, 1939.]

Parikh, C. K. *Parikh Text Book of Medical Jurisprudence and Toxicology.* 3d ed. Bombay: Medical Publications, 1979.

Pashley, Robert. *Travels in Crete.* Vol. 2. London, 1837.

Pauli, Ludwig. *Der Dürrnberg bei Hallein III: Auswertung der Grabfunde.* Munich: C. H. Beck Verlag, 1978.

———. *Keltischer Volksglaube.* Munich: C. H. Beck Verlag, 1975.

Paulson, Ivar, Ake Hultkrantz, and Karl Jettmar. *Die Religionen Nordeurasiens und der amerikanischen Arktis.* Stuttgart: W. Kohlhammer Verlag, 1962.

———. "Seelenvorstellungen und Totenglaube bei nordeurasischen Völkern." *Ethnos* 25 (1960): 84–118.

Pausanias. *Description of Greece.* Vol. 4. Cambridge, Mass., and London: Loeb Classical Library, 1975.

Perkowski, Jan Louis. "The Romanian Folkloric Vampire." *East European Quarterly* 16:3 (Sept. 1982): 311–22.

———. "Vampires, Dwarves, and Witches among the Ontario Kashubs." Ottawa: Canadian Centre for Folk Culture Studies, 1972.

———. *Vampires of the Slavs.* Cambridge, Mass.: Slavica Publishers, 1976.

Pettersson, Olof. *Jabmek and Jabmeaimo: A Comparative Study of the Dead and the Realm of the Dead in Lappish Religion.* Lund: C. W. K. Gleerup, 1957.

Petrovic, Alexander. "Contributions to the Study of the Serbian Gypsies, #9." *Journal of the Gypsy Lore Society* 16:1, 2 (1937): 9–26.

Petzoldt, Leander. *Deutsche Volkssagen.* Munich: C. H. Beck Verlag, 1970.

Petzoldt, Leander, ed. *Schwäbische Sagen.* Düsseldorf: Eugen Diederichs Verlag, 1975.

Philippson, Ernst. *Germanisches Heidentum bei den Angelsachsen.* Leipzig, 1929.

Pohl, Erich. *Die Volkssagen Ostpreussens.* 1943; reprint, Hildesheim: Georg Olms Verlag, 1975.

Polivka, G. "Über das Wort 'Vampyr.'" *Zeitschrift für österreichische Volkskunde* 7 (1901): 185.

Polson, C. J. *The Scientific Aspects of Forensic Medicine.* Edinburgh: Oliver & Boyd, 1969.

Polson C. J., R. P. Brittain, and T. K. Marshall. *The Disposal of the Dead.* New York: Philosophical Library, 1953.

Ponsold, Albert. *Lehrbuch der gerichtlichen Medizin.* 2d ed. Stuttgart: Georg Thieme Verlag, 1957.

Prokop, O. *Lehrbuch der gerichtlichen Medizin.* Berlin: VEB Verlag, 1960.

Puckett, Newbell Niles. *Folk Beliefs of the Southern Negro.* 1926; reprint, Montclair, N.J.: Patterson Smith, 1968.

———. *Popular Beliefs and Superstitions.* Ed. Wayland D. Hand, Anna Casetta, and Sondra B. Thiederman. Boston: G. K. Hall and Company, 1981.

Putoneus [Johann Christoph Meinig]. *Besondere Nachricht, von denen Vampyren oder so genannten Blut-Saugern.* Leipzig, 1732.

Quibell, M. J. E. *Tomb of Yuaa and Thuiu.* Cairo, 1908.

Ralston, W. R. S. *The Songs of the Russian People*. London, 1872.

Ramos, Maximo. "Belief in Ghouls in Contemporary Philippine Society." *Western Folklore* 28:3 (1968): 184–90.

———. "The *Aswang* Syncrasy in Philippine Folklore." *Western Folklore* 28:4 (1969): 238–48.

———. *The Creatures of Midnight*. Quezon City, Philippines: Island Publishers, 1967.

Ranft, M. Michael. *Tractat von dem Kauen und Schmatzen der Todten in Gräbern*. Leipzig, 1734.

Ranke, Kurt. *Indogermanische Totenverehrung*. F. F. Communications no. 140. Helsinki, 1951.

Rau, Santha Rama. "Banares, India's City of Light." *National Geographic* 169 (1986): 214–51.

Redfield, R. *The Primitive World and Its Transformations*. Ithaca: Cornell University Press, 1953.

Reinsberg-Düringsfeld, ———. "Aberglauben der Küsten- und Inselbewohner Dalmatiens." *Globus* 17 (1870): 380–82.

Reuschel, Karl. Review of Hock's *Vampyrsagen*. *Euphorion* 8 (1901): 734–38.

Robert, Cyprien. *Les slaves de Turquie*. Vol. 1. Paris, 1844.

Rodd, Rennell. *The Customs and Lore of Modern Greece*. London, 1892.

Rohr, Philip. *De masticatione mortuorum*. Leipzig, 1679.

Rose, H. J. *A Handbook of Greek Mythology*. New York: E. P. Dutton, 1959.

Sanders, Irwin T. *Balkan Village*. Lexington: University of Kentucky Press, 1949.

———. *Rainbow in the Rock*. Cambridge: Harvard University Press, 1962.

Sanderson, Stewart F. "Gypsy Funeral Customs." *Folklore* 80 (Autumn 1969): 181–87.

Sartori, Paul. "Das Wasser im Totengebrauche." *Zeitschrift des Vereins für Volkskunde* 18 (1908): 352–78.

———. "Feuer und Licht im Totengebrauche." *Zeitschrift des Vereins für Volkskunde* 17 (1908): 360–86.

Saxon, Lyle, et al. *Gumbo Ya-Ya: A Collection of Louisiana Folk Tales*. Boston: Houghton Mifflin Company, 1945.

Schell, O. "Reste des Vampyrglaubens im Bergischen." *Zeitschrift des Vereins für rheinische und westfälische Volkskunde* 18 (1921): 21–29.

Schlenther, Ursula. *Brandbestattung und Seelenglauben*. Berlin: Deutscher Verlag der Wissenschaften, 1960.

Schmidt, Bernhard. *Das Volksleben der Neugriechen und das hellenische Alterthum*. Vol. 1. Leipzig, 1871.

Schneeweis, Edmund. *Feste und Volksbräuche der Lausitzer Wenden*. Leipzig, 1931; reprint, Nendeln, Lichtenstein: Kraus Reprint, 1968.

———. "Fremde Beeinflussungen im Brauchtum der Serbokroaten." *Revue Internationale des études balkaniques* 1 (1934–35): 173–79.

———. *Serbokroatische Volkskunde*. Berlin: de Gruyter Verlag, 1961.

Schnippel, Emil. "Leichenwasser und Geisterglaube in Ostpreussen." *Zeitschrift des Vereins für Volkskunde* 20 (1910): 394–98.

Schoetensack, Otto. "Über die Bedeutung der 'Hocker'-Bestattung." *Zeitschrift für Ethnologie* 33 (1901): 522–27.

Schott, Arthur and Albert. *Walachische Mährchen*. Stuttgart and Tübingen, 1845.

Schreuer, Hans. *Das Recht der Toten*. Stuttgart, 1916.

Schroeder, Aribert. *Vampirismus*. Frankfurt am Main: Akademische Verlagsgesell-schaft, 1973.

Schüz, Ernst. "Berichte über Geier als Aasfresser in Abessinien aus dem 18. und 19. Jahrhundert." *Anzeiger der ornithologischen Gesellschaft in Bayern* 7 (1966): 736–38.

Schüz, Ernst, and Claus König. "Geier und Mensch, mit Deutung archäologischer Funde in Kleinasien." *Bonner zoologische Beiträge* 24 (1973): 192–203.

——. "Old World Vultures and Man." In *Vulture Biology and Management*. Ed. Sanford R. Wilbur and Jerome A. Jackson. Berkeley and Los Angeles: University of California Press, 1983.

Schulenburg, Wilibald von. *Wendisches Volksthum*. Berlin, 1882.

Schullerus, Adolf. *Siebenbürgisch-sächsische Volkskunde im Umriss*. Leipzig, 1926.

Schwebe, Joachim. *Volksglaube und Volksbrauch im Hannoverschen Wendland*. Cologne and Graz: Böhlau Verlag, 1960.

Schwebel, Oskar. *Tod und ewiges Leben im deutschen Volksglauben*. Winden, Westphalia, 1887.

Searight, Sarah. *New Orleans*. New York: Stein and Day, 1973.

Seifart, Karl. "Hingerichtete Thiere und Gespenster." *Zeitschrift fur Deutsche Kultur-geschichte* (1856): 424–32.

Seligmann, S. *Der böse Blick und Verwandtes*. Berlin, 1910.

Sell, Hans Joachim. *Der schlimme Tod bei den Völkern Indonesiens*. 'S-Gravenhage: Mou-ton & Co., 1955.

Senn, Harry A. *Were-Wolf and Vampire in Romania: East European Monographs*. Boulder, 1982.

Seyfarth, Carly. *Aberglaube und Zauberei in der Volksmedizin Sachsens*. Leipzig, 1913.

Shastri, Dakshina Ranjan. *Origin and Development of the Rituals of Ancestor Worship in India*. Calcutta, Allahbad, and Patna: Bookland Private Limited, 1963.

Shrewsbury, J. F. D. *A History of Bubonic Plague in the British Isles*. Cambridge: Cambridge University Press, 1970.

Singer, Charles, et al. *A History of Technology*. 4 vols. New York and London: Oxford University Press, 1954–58.

Singh, Purushottam. *Burial Practices in Ancient India*. India: Prithivi Prakashan, 1970.

Sinitsyn, I. V. "Finds of the Pre-Scythian Era in the Steppes of the Lower Volga." *Sovetskaya Arkheologija* 10 (1948): 148–60.

Smith, G. Elliot, and Warren R. Dawson. *Egyptian Mummies*. London: George Allen & Unwin, 1924.

Söderman, Harry. *Modern Criminal Investigation*. 4th ed. New York: Funk & Wagnalls, 1952.

Soldan, W. G., and H. Heppe. *Geschichte der Hexenprozesse*. Revised by Max Bauer. Hanau: Müller and Kiepenheuer, 1968.

Spindler, Konrad. *Die frühen Kelten*. Stuttgart: Reclam Verlag, 1983.

Spitz, Werner U. and Russell S. Fisher, eds. *Medicolegal Investigation of Death*. 2d ed. Springfield, Ill.: Charles C. Thomas, 1980.

Stein, Barthel. *Descripcio tocius Silesie et civitatis regie vratislaviensis*. Breslau, 1902. [This is a modern printing of a sixteenth-century account of Silesia that was lost, then rediscovered and published in 1722.]

Stetson, George, "The Animistic Vampire in New England." *American Anthropologist* 9:1 (1896): 1–13.

Stoker, Bram. *Dracula*. Oxford and New York: Oxford University Press, 1983.

Stora, Nils. *Burial Customs of the Skolt Lapps*. F. F. Communications no. 210. Helsinki, 1971.

Stout, Earl J. *Folklore from Iowa*. New York: American Folklore Society, 1936.

Strackerjan, L. *Aberglaube und Sagen aus dem Herzogthum Oldenburg*. Vol. 1. Oldenburg, 1867.

Strauss, Adolf. *Die Bulgaren*. Leipzig, 1898.

Stuhlman, C. W. "Die Bauern in Mecklenburg." *Globus* 13 (1868): 212–14.

Sturm, Dieter, and Klaus Völker. *Von denen Vampiren oder Menschensaugern*. Munich: Carl Hanser Verlag, 1968.

Summers, Montague. *The Vampire: His Kith and Kin*. New York: University Books, 1960.

———. *The Vampire in Europe*. New York: University Books, 1968.

Svensson, Arne, Otto Wendel, and Barry A. J. Fisher. *Techniques of Crime Scene Investigation*. New York and Oxford: Elsevier, 1981.

Swieten, Gerhard van. *Vampyrismus*. In Mayer, Andreas Ulrich, *Abhandlung des Daseyns der Gespenster*. Augsburg, 1768.

Talbot, P. Amaury. *In the Shadow of the Bush*. London, 1912.

Tallar, Georg. *Visum Repertum Anatomico- Chirurgicum oder gründlicher Bericht von den sogenannten Blutsäugern*. Vienna and Leipzig, 1784.

Taylor, John. *African Rifles and Cartridges*. 1948; reprint, Highland Park, N.J.: Gun Room Press, 1977.

Temme, J. D. H. *Die Volkssagen von Pommern und Rügen*. Berlin, 1840; reprint, Hildesheim: Georg Olms Verlag, 1976.

Tettau, W. J. A., and J. D. H. Temme, eds. *Die Volkssagen Ostpreussens, Litthauens und Westpreussens*. Berlin, 1837.

Tetzner, Franz. *Die Slawen in Deutschland*. Braunschweig, 1902.

Thomas, Thomas M. *Eleven Years in Central South Africa*. 1872.

Thompson, Stith. *Motif-Index of Folk-Literature*. 5 vols. Helsinki: Suomalainen tiedeakatemia, 1932–35.

Tillhagen, C. H. "Funeral and Death Customs of the Swedish Gypsies." *Journal of the Gypsy Lore Society* 31 (1952): 29–54.

Tilney, Philip V. R. "Supernatural Prophylaxes in a Bulgarian Peasant Funeral." *Journal of Popular Culture* 4:1 (1970): 213–29.

Timm, Klaus. "Blut und rote Farbe im Totenkult." *Ethnographische-Archäologische Zeitschrift* 5 (1964): 39–55.

Toeppen, M. *Aberglauben aus Masuren*. Danzig, 1867.

Tournefort, M. Pitton de. *Relation d'un voyage du Levant*. Vol. 1. Paris, 1717.

Toynbee, J. M. C. *Death and Burial in the Roman World*. Ithaca: Cornell University Press, 1971.

Tozer, Henry Fanshawe. *Researches in the Highlands of Turkey*. London, 1869.

Trigg, Elwood B. *Gypsy Demons and Divinities: The Magic and Religion of the Gypsies*. Secaucus, N.J.: Citadel Press, 1973.

Turi, Johan. *Turi's Book of Lappland*. London: Harper & Brothers [ca. 1910].

Tylor, Edward B. *Primitive Culture*. Vol. 2. London, 1871.

Uhlik, Rade. "Serbo-Bosnian Gypsy Folktales, N. 4." *Journal of the Gypsy Lore Society* 19 (1940): 42–49.

Vaillant, Pierre. "La danse macabre de 1485 et les fresques du charnier des Innocents." In *La mort au moyen âge: Colloque de l'Association des Historiens médiévistes français réunis à Strasbourg en juin 1975 au Palais universitaire.* Strasbourg: Librairie Istra, 1977.

Vakarelski, Christo. *Bulgarische Volkskunde.* Berlin: de Gruyter Verlag, 1969.

Valvasor, Johann Weichard, Freiherr von. *Die Ehre des Herzogthums Krain.* Vols. 2 and 3. 1689; reprint, Laibach-Nürnberg, 1877.

Van Gennep, Arnold. *The Rites of Passage.* Trans. by Monika B. Vizedom and Gabrielle L. Caffee. 1908; reprint, Chicago: University of Chicago Press, 1960.

Veckenstedt, Edmund. *Die Mythen, Sagen und Legenden der Zamaiten.* Vols. 1 and 2. Heidelberg, 1883.

————. *Wendische Sagen, Märchen und abergläubische Geschichten.* Graz, 1880.

Vermeule, Emily. *Aspects of Death in Early Greek Art and Poetry.* Berkeley and Los Angeles: University of California Press, 1979.

Vildomec, Veroboj. *Polnische Sagen.* Intro. and notes by Will-Erich Peuckert. Berlin: Erich Schmidt Verlag, 1979.

Virgil. *Aeneid.* Cambridge, Mass., and London: Loeb Classical Library, 1974.

Vukanovic, T. P. "The Vampire." *Journal of the Gypsy Lore Society* 36 (1957): 125–33; 37 (1958): 21–31; 38 (1959): 111–18; 39 (1960): 44–55.

Wainwright, G. A. "The Ritual of Dismemberment." In W. M. Flinders Petrie et al. *The Labyrinth Gerzeh and Mazghuneh.* London, 1912.

Weicker, Georg. *Der Seelenvogel in der alten Litteratur und Kunst.* Leipzig, 1902.

Weigand, Gustav. *Volksliteratur der Aromunen.* Leipzig, 1894.

Weitershagen, Paul. *Zwischen Dom und Münster.* Cologne: Greven Verlag, 1959.

Weslowski, Elias. "Die Vampirsage im rumänischen Volksglauben." *Zeitschrift für österreichische Volkskunde* 16 (1910): 209–16.

Westermarck, Edward. *Ritual and Belief in Morocco.* Vol. 2. London, 1926.

Wiedemann, A. *Die Toten und ihre Reiche im Glauben der alten Ägypter.* Leipzig, 1900.

————. "Der 'Lebende Leichnam' im Glauben der alten Ägypter." *Zeitschrift für rheinische und westfälische Volkskunde* 14 (1917): 3–36.

Wiegelmann, Günter. "Der 'lebende Leichnam' im Volksbrauch." *Zeitschrift für Volkskunde* 62:2 (1966): 161–83.

Willoughby-Meade, G. *Chinese Ghouls and Goblins.* New York, 1928.

Wlislocki, Heinrich. *Volksglaube und religiöser Brauch der Magyaren.* Münster, 1893.

————. *Volksglaube und Volkbrauch der Siebenbürger Sachsen.* Berlin, 1893.

Wright, Thomas. *Essays on Archaeological Subjects, and on Various Questions Connected with the History of Art, Science, and Literature in the Middle Ages.* 2 vols. Vol. 1: *On Saints' Lives and Miracles.* London, 1861.

Wuttke, Adolf. *Der deutsche Volksaberglaube der Gegenwart.* Hamburg, 1860.

Yovanovitch, Voyslav M. *'La Guzla' de Prosper Mérimée.* Paris, 1911.

Yudin, S. S. "Transfusion of Stored Cadaver Blood." *Lancet* 2 (1937): 361–66.

Zandee, Jan. *Death as an Enemy, According to Ancient Egyptian Conceptions.* New York: Arno Press, 1977.

Zedler, Johann Heinrich. *Grosses vollständiges Universal-Lexikon.* Graz: Akademische Druck- u. Verlagsanstalt, 1962. Vol. 46: "Vampyren; vol. 44: "Toden (Schmatzen der)." [Reprint of 1745 ed.]

Zelenin, Dmitrij. *Russische (Ostslavische) Volkskunde*. Berlin and Leipzig, 1927.
Zender, Mathias. *Atlas der deutschen Volkskunde*. Marburg: N. G. Elwert, 1958-.
————. *Sagen und Geschichten aus der Westeifel*. Bonn: Ludwig Röhrscheid Verlag, 1966.
Zingerle, Ignaz. *Sitten, Bräuche und Meinungen des Tiroler Volkes*. 2d ed. Innsbruck, 1871.
Zopf, Johann Heinrich. *Dissertatio de vampyris serviensibus*. Duisburg, 1733.

Index